Pocket
Guide
to
Legal
Ethics

DELMAR CENGAGE Learning

Options.
Over 300 products in every area of the law: textbooks, online courses, CD-ROMs, reference books, companion websites, and more – helping you succeed in the classroom and on the job.

Support.
We offer unparalleled, practical support: robust instructor and student supplements to ensure the best learning experience, custom publishing to meet your unique needs, and other benefits such as Delmar Cengage Learning's Student Achievement Award. And our sales representatives are always ready to provide you with dependable service.

Feedback.
As always, we want to hear from you! Your feedback is our best resource for improving the quality of our products. Contact your sales representative or write us at the address below if you have any comments about our materials or if you have a product proposal.

Accounting and Financials for the Law Office • Administrative Law • Alternative Dispute Resolution • Bankruptcy Business Organizations/Corporations • Careers and Employment Civil Litigation and Procedure • CLA Exam Preparation • Computer Applications in the Law Office • Constitutional Law • Contract Law • Court Reporting • Criminal Law and Procedure • Document Preparation • Elder Law • Employment Law • Environmental Law • Ethics Evidence Law • Family Law • Health Care Law • Immigration Law • Intellectual Property • Internships • Interviewing and Investigation • Introduction to Law • Introduction to Paralegalism • Juvenile Law • Law Office Management • Law Office Procedures • Legal Nurse Consulting • Legal Research, Writing, and Analysis • Legal Terminology • Legal Transcription • Media and Entertainment Law • Medical Malpractice Law • Product Liability Real Estate Law • Reference Materials • Social Security • Sports Law • Torts and Personal Injury Law • Wills, Trusts, and Estate Administration • Workers' Compensation Law

---

DELMAR CENGAGE Learning
5 Maxwell Drive
Clifton Park, New York 12065-2919

For additional information, find us online at:
www.delmar.cengage.com

Pocket Guide

Guide

to

Legal

Ethics

ANGELA SCHNEEMAN

DELMAR
CENGAGE Learning™

Australia • Canada • Mexico • Singapore • Spain • United Kingdom • United States

DELMAR
CENGAGE Learning™

Pocket Guide to Legal Ethics
Angela Schneeman

Vice President, Career and
Professional Editorial:
Dave Garza

Director of Learning Solutions:
Sandy Clark

Acquisitions Editor:
Shelley Esposito

Managing Editor:
Larry Main

Editorial Assistant:
Melissa Zaza

Vice President, Career and
Professional Marketing:
Jennifer McAvey

Marketing Director:
Deborah S. Yarnell

Marketing Coordinator:
Jonathan Sheehan

Production Director:
Wendy Troeger

Production Manager:
Mark Bernard

Content Project Manager:
Betty Dickson

Art Director:
Joy Kocsis

For product information and technology assistance,
contact us at **Professional & Career Group Customer
Support, 1-800-648-7450**

For permission to use material from this text or product,
submit all requests online at **cengage.com/permissions.**
Further permissions questions can be e-mailed to
permissionrequest@cengage.com

Library of Congress Control Number: 2007941007

ISBN-13: 978-14180-5378-9
ISBN-10: 1-4180-5378-3

Delmar
5 Maxwell Drive
Clifton Park, NY 12065-2919
USA

Cengage Learning products are represented in Canada by
Nelson Education, Ltd.

For your lifelong learning solutions, visit **delmar.cengage.com**
Visit our corporate website at **cengage.com**

Notice to the Reader

Publisher does not warrant or guarantee any of the products described herein or perform any independent analysis in connection with any of the product information contained herein. Publisher does not assume, and expressly disclaims, any obligation to obtain and include information other than that provided to it by the manufacturer. The reader is expressly warned to consider and adopt all safety precautions that might be indicated by the activities herein and to avoid all potential hazards. By following the instructions contained herein, the reader willingly assumes all risks in connection with such instructions. The reader is notified that this text is an educational tool, not a practice book. Since the law is in constant change, no rule or statement of law in this book should be relied upon for any service to any client. The reader should always refer to standard legal sources for the current rule or law. If legal advice or other expert assistance is required, the services of the appropriate professional should be sought. The Publisher makes no representation or warranties of any kind, including but not limited to, the warranties of fitness for particular purpose or merchantability, nor are any such representations implied with respect to the material set forth herein, and the publisher takes no responsibility with respect to such material. The Publisher shall not be liable for any special, consequential, or exemplary damages resulting in whole or part, from the readers' use of, or reliance upon, this material.

Printed in Canada
1 2 3 4 5 XX 10 09 08

Contents

Chapter 2 30
Competent, Diligent Representation of the Client

xii Contents

Preface

The *Pocket Guide to Legal Ethics* is a guide to the rules of ethics for paralegal students and working paralegals. The brevity and focus of this book make it the perfect supplemental text for any paralegal course. The easy-to-use format makes it a useful tool for the working paralegal.

This text focuses on the rules of ethics that apply to attorneys—the rules that every paralegal must be familiar with. In addition, each chapter includes information specifically for paralegals, including practical advice and the ethical guidance provided by the paralegal associations.

This book is best read from cover to cover to gain a full understanding of the rules of legal ethics. However, the checklists, charts, tables, and FAQs in each chapter make it a quick and easy reference to answer your questions concerning legal ethics.

This book includes several resources for additional research, including URLs to the Rules of Professional Conduct for each state.

The first chapter is an introduction to legal ethics, including information on the sources of our rules of ethics and the consequences of unethical behavior by both attorneys and paralegals.

The remaining chapters of the text explore the rules of ethics by focusing on the rules applicable to attorneys as well as to paralegals and practical tips for ethical behavior within those rules. The specific topics covered include

- ▶ providing competent diligent representation of the client.
- ▶ maintaining integrity and public respect for the legal profession.
- ▶ avoiding the unauthorized practice of law.
- ▶ confidentiality.
- ▶ conflicts of interest.
- ▶ fees and financial matters.
- ▶ advertising and solicitation.

This is a book that effectively transitions from the classroom to the law office.

Chapter 1

An Introduction to Legal Ethics

"The needs of society determine its ethics."
— Maya Angelou

INTRODUCTION

Ethics deals with what is good and what is bad as well as with moral duty and obligation. This branch of philosophy deals with values relating to human conduct and with respect to the right and wrong of certain actions as well as the good and bad of motives. **Legal ethics** refers to the moral and professional duties attorneys owe to their clients, to other attorneys, to the courts, and to the public. The role of legal ethics is to identify and remove inappropriate conduct from the legal profession and to protect the client. Rules and guidelines for legal ethics are established in the codes of ethics and professional responsibility adopted in each state.

Paralegals must become familiar with the rules and guidelines for legal ethics to avoid unethical behavior that may result in **sanctions** against them or their supervising attorneys and to protect the rights and interests of clients. Although you may be a moral and ethical person, you will need to study the rules of professional conduct because in many instances the rules go beyond common sense. Some of the rules of legal ethics that apply to paralegals may even seem counterintuitive. It may take some study and consideration before you understand the reasoning behind some of the most important rules of ethics.

This chapter introduces you to legal ethics by first exploring the several sources of rules for legal ethics, the consequences of unethical behavior by attorneys, and attorney responsibility for paralegal ethics. Our focus in this chapter then changes to legal ethics from the paralegal's perspective. In that section, we will explore the paralegal associations and the ethical guidance they provide, the consequences of unethical paralegal behavior, and the regulation of paralegals.

This chapter concludes with a quick look at some resources available to assist you with questions of ethics you may have throughout your career.

> "A man is truly ethical only when he obeys the compulsion to help all life which he is able to assist, and shrinks from injuring anything that lives."

—*Albert Schweitzer*

SOURCES OF LEGAL ETHICS REGULATION

Legal ethics and professional responsibility standards are established by each state and set forth in a **Code of Ethics** (also known as a Code of Professional Responsibility or a Code of Professional Conduct). The code of ethics adopted by each state or jurisdiction is binding on every attorney licensed to practice law in that state. It is essential that paralegals are familiar with the code of ethics that dictates the ethical behavior for attorneys in any state in which they work.

The state judiciary, state **bar associations**, and state legislatures all play a role in adopting the codes of ethics for attorneys and for overseeing the ethical behavior of attorneys licensed to practice law in each state. Exactly what roles the judiciary, bar associations, and state legislature play vary from state to state.

State Judicial System

Each state's highest court has the ultimate authority over attorney conduct. The judicial system works closely with the state bar associations to oversee the ethical behavior of the state's attorneys, and the state's code of ethics may be adopted by either the state's highest court or its bar association. State courts often delegate much of their responsibility for overseeing the ethical behavior of attorneys to their state bar associations.

State Bar Associations

State bar associations are responsible for regulating attorneys, proposing new legislation, and overseeing the continuing education of attorneys. Courts or legislatures often empower state bar associations to adopt and enforce codes of ethics. To ensure compliance with the codes of ethics, states that delegate authority to the bar association to adopt and enforce the code of ethics *require* membership in the bar association as a condition of the privilege to practice law in that state. State bar associations with mandatory membership for all attorneys licensed in that state are **integrated bars.** In states where the judiciary maintains the authority to adopt and enforce the code of ethics, state bar membership is voluntary. Those states have **nonintegrated bars.** Whether it is the bar association or the judicial branch that adopts the code of ethics in your state, the courts may interpret, modify, and even override the provisions of the state's code of ethics. Either the state bar association or the state judiciary is responsible for admitting new attorneys to practice law and for disciplining the unethical behavior of attorneys.

State Statutes

State **statutes** also have an effect on the ethical behavior of attorneys. Again, the exact role played by the state legislature varies by state. However, in every instance, the state legislature passes legislation concerning the ethical practice of law that attorneys must abide by. State laws may be passed regarding the requirements for licensing attorneys and admitting attorneys to the state bar. In addition, state legislatures may pass laws regarding the unauthorized practice of law, handling trust account funds, and other matters that directly affect attorneys. The unethical conduct of an attorney may also be a violation of state law in some instances.

State Ethics Committees

In some states, the courts and state bar associations have appointed committees to answer questions on ethics and to render opinions when requested. These ethics committees provide advice and guidance in the form of advisory opinions that are often published for the benefit of all attorneys within the jurisdiction. Because these opinions are not court opinions but rather the opinions of an ethics committee, they are not considered binding authority. However, they are considered very helpful in interpreting the code of ethics in the jurisdiction to which they apply.

American Bar Association

The **American Bar Association (ABA)** is the country's largest voluntary professional association of attorneys. More than half of the attorneys in the United States belong to the ABA and its specialty sections. Paralegals may join the ABA as associate members. The ABA's influence in lawmaking and the practice of law, particularly through the development of model rules and guidelines, is substantial.

OF INTEREST

The American Bar Association's mission is to be the national representative of the legal profession, serving the public and the profession by promoting justice, professional excellence, and respect for the law.

Membership in the ABA is voluntary, and the ABA has no actual authority to enforce its model codes and rules. However, by adopting model rules and codes, the ABA offers guidance to its members as to appropriate ethical behavior and to state judicial systems and state bar associations in adopting their own, enforceable codes of ethics.

The first model code of ethics adopted by the ABA was the Canons of Professional Ethics, which was adopted in 1908 and amended several times thereafter. The Canons of Professional Ethics was replaced with the **Model Code of Professional Responsibility** in 1969 and with the **Model Rules of Professional Conduct** (Model Rules) in 1983.

Model Rules of Professional Conduct

The Model Rules of Professional Conduct have been amended several times since 1983, and revisions occur on an ongoing basis. The Model Rules are intended to serve as a national framework for implementation of standards of professional conduct.[1]

Nearly every state has adopted rules of professional conduct based on the ABA's Model Rules of Professional Conduct.[2] For that reason, we will use the Model Rules as the basis for much of our discussion. However, remember that the ABA's Model Rules are not binding on the attorneys in your state, but the rules adopted by your state's court, bar association, or legislature are. Your state's code may vary from the Model Rules in several different respects. For the name and URL of the code of ethics adopted by your state, see Exhibit 1-1.

Exhibit 1-1

State Rules of Professional Conduct

State	Rules of Professional Conduct
Alabama Rules of Professional Conduct	http://www.alabar.org/ogc/ropc.cfm
Alaska Rules of Professional Conduct	http://www.state.ak.us/courts/prof.htm
Arizona Rules of Professional Conduct	http://www.myazbar.org/Ethics/rules.cfm
Arkansas Rules of Professional Conduct	http://courts.state.ar.us/opinions/2005a/20050303/arpc2005.html
California Rules of Professional Conduct	http://www.calbar.ca.gov/state/calbar/calbar_extend.jsp?cid=10158
Colorado Rules of Professional Conduct	http://www.cobar.org/group/index.cfm?category=384&EntityID=CETH
Connecticut Rules of Professional Conduct	http://www.jud.ct.gov/pb.htm
Delaware Rules of Professional Conduct	http://courts.delaware.gov/Rules/?FinalDLRPCclean.pdf
District of Columbia Rules of Professional Conduct	http://www.dcbar.org/new_rules/index.cfm

Florida Rules of Professional Conduct	http://www.law.cornell.edu/ethics/fl/code/
Georgia Rules of Professional Conduct	http://www.gabar.org/handbook/part_iv_after_january_1_2001_-_georgia_rules_of_professional_conduct/
Hawaii Rules of Professional Conduct	http://www.state.hi.us/jud/ctrules/hrpcond.htm
Idaho Rules of Professional Conduct	http://www.isc.idaho.gov/irpc0304_cov.htm
Illinois Rules of Professional Conduct	http://www.state.il.us/court/SupremeCourt/Rules/Art_VIII/
Indiana Rules of Professional Conduct	http://www.state.in.us/judiciary/rules/prof_conduct/index.html
Iowa Rules of Professional Conduct	http://www.judicial.state.ia.us/Professional_Regulation/Rules_of_Professional_Conduct/
Kansas Revised Rules of Professional Conduct	http://www.kscourts.org/rules/Rule-List.asp?r1=Rules+Relating+to+Discipline+of+Attorneys
Kentucky Rules of Professional Conduct	http://www.kybar.org/Default.aspx?tabid=237
Louisiana Rules of Professional Conduct	http://www.ladb.org/Publications/ropc2006-04-01.pdf
Maine Code of Professional Responsibility	http://www.mebaroverseers.org/Home/Code%20of%20Professional%20Responsibility.html
Maryland Lawyers Rules of Professional Conduct	http://www.law.cornell.edu/ethics/md/code/
Massachusetts Rules of Professional Conduct	http://www.mass.gov/obcbbo/rpcnet.htm
Michigan Rules of Professional Conduct	http://www.michbar.org/generalinfo/pdfs/mrpc.pdf
Minnesota Rules of Professional Conduct	http://www.courts.state.mn.us/lprb/conduct.html
Mississippi Rules of Professional Conduct	http://www.mslegalforms.com/mrpccontents.html
Missouri Rules of Professional Conduct	http://www.law.cornell.edu/ethics/mo/code/MO_CODE.HTM
Montana Rules of Professional Conduct	http://www.montanaodc.org/Portals/ODC/docs/rules_of_professional_conduct.pdf
Nebraska Rules of Professional Conduct	http://www.supremecourt.ne.gov/rules/pdf/rulesprofconduct-34.pdf
Nevada Rules of Professional Conduct	http://www.leg.state.nv.us/CourtRules/RPC.html
New Hampshire Rules of Professional Conduct	http://www.courts.state.nh.us/rules/pcon/index.htm
New Jersey Rules of Professional Conduct	http://www.judiciary.state.nj.us/rules/apprpc.htm

Exhibit 1-1 (*Continued*)

State Rules of Professional Conduct

State	Rules of Professional Conduct
New Mexico Rules of Professional Conduct	http://www.law.cornell.edu/ethics/nm/code/NM_CODE.htm
New York Lawyers Code of Professional Responsibility	http://www.nysba.org/Content/NavigationMenu/ForAttorneys/ProfessionalStandardsforAttorneys/lawyerscodeupdatedNov07.pdf
North Carolina Rules of Professional Conduct	http://www.ncbar.com/rules/rpcsearch.asp
North Dakota Rules of Professional Conduct	http://www.court.state.nd.us/rules/conduct/contents.htm
Ohio Rules of Professional Conduct	http://www.sconet.state.oh.us/Atty-Svcs/ProfConduct/default.asp
Oklahoma Rules of Professional Conduct	http://www.okbar.org/ethics/ORPC.htm
Oregon Rules of Professional Conduct	http://www.osbar.org/_docs/rulesregs/orpc.pdf
Pennsylvania Rules of Professional Conduct	http://www.padisciplinaryboard.org/documents/Pa%20RPC.pdf
Rhode Island Rules of Professional Conduct	http://www.courts.state.ri.us/supreme/disciplinary/rulesofprofessionalconduct.htm
South Carolina Rules of Professional Conduct	http://www.judicial.state.sc.us/courtReg/newrules/NewRules.cfm
South Dakota Rules of Professional Conduct	http://www.sdbar.org/Rules/Rules/PC_Rules.htm
Tennessee Rules of Professional Conduct	http://www.tba.org/ethics2002.html
Texas Disciplinary Rules of Professional Conduct	http://www.txethics.org/reference_rules.asp?view=conduct
Utah Rules of Professional Conduct	http://www.utahbar.org/rules_ops_pols/
Vermont Rules of Professional Conduct	http://www.vermontjudiciary.org/PRB1.htm
Virginia Rules of Professional Conduct	http://www.vsb.org/site/regulation/guidelines/
Washington Rules of Professional Conduct	http://www.law.cornell.edu/ethics/wa/code/WA_CODE.HTM
West Virginia Rules of Professional Conduct	http://www.wvbar.org/BARINFO/rulesprofconduct/index.htm
Wisconsin Rules of Professional Conduct	http://www.wisbar.org/AM/Template.cfm?Section=Lawyer_Regulation_and_Discipline&template=/CM/ContentDisplay.cfm&contentid=62724
Wyoming Rules of Professional Conduct	http://courts.state.wy.us/CourtRules_Entities.aspx?RulesPage=AttorneysConduct.xml

Ethics Opinions

The ABA also provides ethical guidance to attorneys in the form of ethics opinions issued by its **Standing Committee on Ethics and Professional Responsibility**. The opinions issued by the ABA have no binding authority, but they do interpret the standards of ethics established by the ABA's Model Rules. The ABA's ethics opinions are often relied on by attorneys to answer questions they have concerning ethics, and they are an often-cited authority.

In addition to all the sources of legal ethics, attorneys must also look inward. As set forth in the Preamble to the Model Rules, ". . . a lawyer is also guided by personal conscience and the approbation of professional peers. A lawyer should strive to attain the highest level of skill, to improve the law and the legal profession, and to exemplify the legal profession's ideals of public service."[3]

Exhibit 1-2 is a summary of the various sources of the rules of legal ethics.

Exhibit 1-2

Sources of Legal Ethics Regulation

State Judicial System	State Bar Associations	State Legislature	American Bar Association
• The highest court in the state has the ultimate authority for regulating the ethical behavior of attorneys licensed within the state. • May adopt the code of ethics governing attorneys under its jurisdiction. • The courts have the authority to interpret, modify, and override provisions of the code of ethics. • May be responsible for overseeing admission of new attorneys to practice law in that state. • May be responsible for disciplining unethical attorneys or may delegate disciplinary authority to the bar association and be required to approve serious disciplinary actions, especially disbarment.	• May adopt the code of ethics governing attorney members. • Often responsible for enforcing the state's code of ethics. • May be responsible for overseeing admission of new attorneys to practice law in that state. • May be responsible for disciplining unethical attorneys. • May have appointed committee to answer questions on ethics and to issue ethics opinions.	• May pass laws establishing the ethical behavior of attorneys. • May pass laws regarding requirements for licensing attorneys and admitting attorneys to the state bar association.	• Adopted Model Rules of Professional Conduct as guidance to the states in establishing their own codes of ethics. • Issues Ethics Opinions to answer questions and interpret the standards of ethics established by the Model Rules.

◼ CONSEQUENCES OF UNETHICAL ATTORNEY BEHAVIOR

Possible consequences to unethical behavior by attorneys include disciplinary action by the court or a court-appointed disciplinary agency, civil lawsuits for malpractice, and even criminal prosecution.

Discipline by the Court or Court-Appointed Disciplinary Agency

Each state has its own manner for treating complaints against attorneys. The exact method of handling attorney complaints and the names of the agencies involved in attorney discipline vary among the states. However, in every state, at least one agency exists to handle attorney complaints and disciplinary matters. The discussion in this section is based on terms and procedures commonly used in the states and by the Model Rules for Lawyer Disciplinary Enforcement approved by the ABA.

The highest court in each state or other jurisdiction usually has the authority for attorney disciplinary matters. The court typically appoints a **disciplinary board** of about nine individuals and a **disciplinary counsel,** to which it delegates much of that authority.

The disciplinary board is the agency that receives complaints against attorneys from the public. Either the disciplinary board or some similar agency must be easily accessible to the public to protect clients and the public. When the disciplinary board receives a complaint, it may refer the matter to mediation or arbitration (as is often the case with fee disputes) or it may refer the matter to the disciplinary counsel and staff for investigation and possible formal charges against the attorney. The disciplinary counsel and staff will investigate the matter to determine if there is evidence of wrongdoing that warrants a hearing. If so, the disciplinary counsel may turn the matter over to a **hearing committee** with a recommendation for its disposition.

OF INTEREST

Most states allow public access to disciplinary proceedings after the board finds probable cause to believe misconduct occurred.

—*Journal of the National Association of Administrative Law Judges, Fall 2001*

The hearing committee hears formal charges brought by the disciplinary counsel and may consent to or modify the disciplinary counsel's recommended disposition. If the hearing committee finds an attorney guilty of misconduct, it has several different options for sanctions against the attorney, including disbarment by the court, suspension of license to practice by the court, probation, or reprimand. **Admonition** by the disciplinary counsel is an option if formal charges have not been brought. That is the only sanction that is typically not made a public record.

A **reprimand** is somewhat more severe because of the implications to an attorney when the reprimand is made public. Public censure, or a public reprimand, is generally appropriate when an attorney acts negligently without reasonable diligence in representing a client and causes injury or potential injury to the client.[4]

Probation is often the sanction imposed when the disciplinary counsel and hearing committee feel that the attorney should be allowed to continue practicing law with supervision.

Suspension of an attorney's license is not permanent, and the suspension typically provides for a certain date by which the attorney's license will be reinstated.

Disbarment revokes the attorney's license to practice law. Disciplinary proceedings for the disbarment or suspension of attorneys are judicial proceedings that may be warranted for a continuing pattern of gross incompetence, neglect of client matters, negligence concerning supervision of office staff, maintaining adequate records, and for conversion of funds.[5] In certain situations, disbarred attorneys may apply for a new license to practice law after a certain time period has lapsed.

OF INTEREST

According to a survey by the ABA Center for Professional Responsibility, approximately 940 attorneys were disbarred in the United States in 2004.

—*http://www.abanet.org/cpr/discipline/sold/04-ch2.xls*

Attorneys accused of an offense by the disciplinary board have the right to **due process**, which includes the right to respond to those charges. The accused attorney has the right to receive written notice of any charges filed against him or her and the right to respond to those charges and defend him or herself in a trial-type proceeding.

Attorneys also have the right to appeal the decision of the disciplinary board to the highest court in the state. When the court issues an opinion on the appeal of a disciplinary matter, the opinion becomes binding and a precedence in similar disciplinary actions brought in that state.

Civil Lawsuits

Unethical behavior that results in harm to a client or a third party may result in a civil action being brought against the attorney for monetary damages in a **legal malpractice** suit. Legal malpractice suits are usually filed on the basis of professional negligence or breach of fiduciary obligations.

As with the medical profession, a legal malpractice suit against an attorney can have devastating effects. A legal malpractice suit can result in damages being awarded against the attorney's law firm and against the specific attorney. Attorneys, therefore, carry legal malpractice insurance to protect themselves against potential malpractice suits.

A violation of the rules of ethics, in itself, does not establish a malpractice claim in a civil lawsuit.[6] Most courts, however, allow the rules of ethics as evidence in legal malpractice cases. A breach of the code of ethics may show that the conduct of the attorney has fallen short of professional standards, which can be considered legal malpractice.

Because attorneys are responsible for their employees' actions, legal malpractice suits may also arise from the unethical actions of a paralegal under their supervision. If a paralegal acts unethically in a manner that harms the client, such as breaching the client's confidence, the attorney and law firm may be found liable in a legal malpractice suit.

CASE ON POINT

One 2001 disciplinary proceeding in New York resulted in the disbarment of an attorney when it was found that he failed to adequately supervise the finalizing of an estate, a task he delegated to his paralegal. The attorney's failure to adequately supervise the paralegal resulted in a loss of more than $80,000 to the estate.

—Disciplinary Board v. Carrigan, 383 A.D.2d 63 (NY 2001)

Criminal Prosecution

Some types of unethical behavior are specifically prohibited by law and are considered crimes. Unethical acts considered to be a serious crime, such as **fraud,** may result in **felony** charges. An attorney who commits a crime may be subject to both criminal prosecution and disciplinary action. An attorney found guilty of a crime in a court of law will have to pay the penalty prescribed by the court. Often, the attorney will also face sanctions from the disciplinary board.

ATTORNEY RESPONSIBILITY FOR PARALEGAL ETHICS

Attorneys may be held directly responsible for the unethical actions of the paralegals and other nonlawyer personnel they employ. For that reason, a paralegal's knowledge of legal ethics is essential to the attorneys to whom the paralegal reports.

Most states have followed the guidance of the ABA's Model Rule 5.3 concerning an attorney's responsibility for nonlawyer assistants, although there are several differences in the details. Most states provide that attorneys are responsible for paralegals and other nonlawyer employees in three ways.

First, a partner or shareholder of a law firm has a duty to ensure that the firm's employees are reasonably familiar with the rules of ethics that apply to attorneys and that they know their conduct should be compatible with the rules of ethics applicable to the attorneys. For example, law firms may hold seminars on ethics for all employees and have a written policy stating the basic rules of ethics that employees are expected to comply with.

Second, any attorney responsible for the supervision of paralegals or other nonlawyer employees is expected to make reasonable efforts to ensure that those employees are performing their duties in an ethical manner. A supervising attorney may not turn his or her back on the unethical behavior of a subordinate. The level of supervision required will depend on the paralegal's level of experience and knowledge.

CASE ON POINT

In a 1998 disciplinary action in Kentucky, an attorney was suspended from practice for 60 days for violation of Rule 5.3(a) when one of the firm's employees used a blank trust account check to purchase a dog.

—Curtis v. Kentucky Bar Association, 959 S.W. 2d 94 (KY. 1998)

Finally, attorneys are responsible for actions of paralegals or other nonlawyer personnel if they instruct the paralegal to act in an unethical manner or if the attorney is aware of unethical conduct and does nothing to prevent it. Attorneys may not avoid the rules of ethics by requesting their nonlawyer personnel to perform an unethical task.

Several states have followed Model Rule 5.3 when adopting their own rules concerning nonlawyer supervision. One example is found in Exhibit 1-3 from Minnesota. Remember, it is always important to consult the rules of ethics in the state in which you work.

Exhibit 1-3

From the Minnesota Rules of Professional Conduct

Rule 5.3 Responsibilities Regarding Nonlawyer Assistants

With respect to a nonlawyer employed or retained by or associated with a lawyer:

(a) A partner in a law firm shall make reasonable efforts to ensure that the firm has in effect measures giving reasonable assurance that the person's conduct is compatible with the professional obligations of the lawyer;

(b) A lawyer having direct supervisory authority over the nonlawyer shall make reasonable efforts to ensure that the person's conduct is compatible with the professional obligations of the lawyer; and

(c) A lawyer shall be responsible for conduct of such a person that would be a violation of the Rules of Professional Conduct if engaged in by a lawyer if:

(1) the lawyer orders or, with the knowledge of the specific conduct, ratifies the conduct involved; or

(2) the lawyer is a partner in the law firm in which the person is employed, or has direct supervisory authority over the person, and knows of the conduct at a time when its consequences can be avoided or mitigated but fails to take reasonable remedial action.

The rules of Minnesota, as with the rules of most states, make it clear that attorneys have the duty to educate paralegals on proper ethical conduct and to supervise paralegals to ensure their ethical behavior. Again, as with most states, these rules also make it clear that attorneys can be held responsible for the unethical behavior of their paralegals.

Model Guidelines for the Utilization of Paralegal Services

The Model Guidelines for the Utilization of Legal Assistant Services were drafted by the American Bar Association Standing Committee on Legal Assistants and adopted by the American Bar Association's House of Delegates in 1991. These guidelines were revised in 2003 to reflect modern legal and policy developments concerning the utilization of paralegals and renamed the **Model Guidelines for the Utilization of Paralegal Services.** The guidelines—which have been adopted, at least to a degree, by most states—are intended to "provide lawyers with useful and authoritative guidance in working with paralegals."[7] Model Guidelines emphasize that attorneys are responsible for the ethical conduct of paralegals under their supervision. Guideline 1 of the Model Guidelines states that:

> *A lawyer is responsible for all of the professional actions of a paralegal performing services at the lawyer's direction and should take reasonable measures to ensure that the paralegal's conduct is consistent with the lawyer's obligations under the rules of professional conduct of the jurisdiction in which the lawyer practices.*

The full text of the Model Guidelines may be found on the ABA's Web site at http://www.abanet.org/legalservices/paralegals/downloads/modelguidelines.pdf.

FROM THE PARALEGAL'S PERSPECTIVE

For all the reasons just discussed, a paralegal's knowledge and adherence to the rules of ethics is critical to a paralegal's employers—and even more significant to the paralegal. In the next section, we will discuss the ethical guidance provided by the paralegal associations, the consequences of unethical paralegal behavior, and regulation of the paralegal profession. This chapter will conclude with a look at the resources available for more information on legal ethics.

PARALEGAL ASSOCIATIONS AND PARALEGAL ETHICS

Paralegals must know and abide by the code of ethics that is binding on the attorneys they work for. That code of ethics will be binding on the paralegal as an employee and agent of the attorney. There are several sources of guidance for ethical conduct that apply specifically to paralegals. National, state, and local paralegal associations adopt codes of ethics for their paralegal members.

Two main national paralegal associations exist in the United States: the **National Association of Legal Assistants (NALA)** and the **National Federation of Paralegal Associations (NFPA)**. In addition, most states have at least one state paralegal association and may have numerous local paralegal associations. Although membership in a paralegal association is not mandatory for paralegals, membership provides many benefits. Paralegal associations promote professionalism, offer continuing legal education to paralegals, set ethical guidelines for paralegals to follow, and offer assistance in many forms to paralegals.

The National Association of Legal Assistants

The NALA was formed in 1975 and currently has approximately 18,000 paralegal members through individual memberships and through its 90 state and local affiliated associations. Student membership is available to individuals who are pursuing a course of study to become **legal assistants.** The NALA monitors events affecting paralegals and represents paralegals on some of the more important national issues, including education and certification. The NALA publishes *Facts & Findings,* a quarterly journal for paralegals.

The NALA's Code of Ethics and Professional Responsibility

The NALA's Code of Ethics and Professional Responsibility was initially adopted in 1975 and has been revised several times since. Members of the NALA are bound by the Code of Ethics and Professional Responsibility, and any violation of the code is cause for a loss of membership. The NALA affiliated associations must adopt the NALA Code of Ethics and Professional Responsibility as their standard of conduct. **Canon** 9 of the NALA's code specifically states that legal assistants are governed by the bar association's code of professional responsibility and rules of professional conduct. The full text of the NALA's Code of Ethics and Professional Responsibility is on the NALA's Web site at http://www.nala.org/code.htm. Exhibit 1-4 introduces the NALA's Code of Ethics and Professional Responsibility.

Exhibit 1-4
From the NALA's Code of Ethics and Professional Responsibility

Each NALA member agrees to follow the canons of the NALA Code of Ethics and Professional Responsibility. Violations of the Code may result in cancellation of membership. First adopted by the NALA membership in May of 1975, the Code of Ethics and Professional Responsibility is the foundation of ethical practices of paralegals in the legal community.

The NALA's Model Standards and Guidelines for Utilization of Legal Assistants

To assist attorneys and others in the legal profession with regard to the best means to utilize paralegals, the NALA has prepared Model Standards and Guidelines for

Utilization of Legal Assistants. This document offers recommendations for minimum qualifications for paralegals and standards of performance and professional responsibility guidelines to aid attorneys and paralegals. The full text of the NALA's Model Standards and Guidelines is available on the NALA's Web site at www.nala.org.

The National Federation of Paralegal Associations

The NFPA was formed in 1974 and is a federation of 55 member associations representing over 17,000 individual members nationwide. Student memberships are also available. Membership in some state associations automatically constitutes membership in the NFPA.

The NFPA monitors and reports on developments in courts, bar associations, and legislation that may affect paralegals and represents paralegals in a national forum on the issues of paralegal education and paralegal licensing. The NFPA publishes the *National Reporter*, a quarterly journal for paralegals. The NFPA has also adopted a code of ethics for paralegals' guidance. See Exhibit 1-5 for a summary of the features of the national paralegal associations.

Exhibit 1-5

The National Paralegal Associations

The National Association of Legal Assistants (NALA):	The National Federation of Paralegal Associations (NFPA):
• Recognizes the terms *legal assistant* and *paralegal* as identical terms.	• Prefers the title *paralegal*.
• Has adopted the ABA's definition of legal assistant/paralegal.	• Defines *paralegal* as follows: A person, qualified through education, training or work experience to perform substantive legal work that requires knowledge of legal concepts and is customarily, but not exclusively, performed by a lawyer. This person may be retained or employed by a lawyer, law office, governmental agency or other entity or may be authorized by administrative, statutory or court authority to perform this work. Substantive shall mean work requiring recognition, evaluation, organization, analysis, and communication of relevant facts and legal concepts.
• A legal assistant or paralegal is a person qualified by education, training or work experience who is employed or retained by a lawyer, law office, corporation, governmental agency or other entity who performs specifically delegated substantive legal work for which a lawyer is responsible.	
• Has over 18,000 paralegal members through individual memberships and through approximately 90 state and local affiliated associations.	• Is a federation of 55 member associations representing over 17,000 individual members nationwide.
• Is headquartered at 1516 S. Boston, #200, Tulsa, OK 74119, phone: 918-587-6828; fax: 918-582-6772, e-mail: nalanet@nala.org, Web site: http://www.nala.org.	• Is headquartered in Edmonds, Washington. Mailing address: P.O. Box 2016, Edmonds, WA 98020; phone: 425-967-0045;

- NALA believes it is the responsibility and duty of a profession to regulate itself rather than being subject to statewide governmentally imposed regulations.

- Offers the Certified Legal Assistant (CLA), Certified Legal Assistant Specialist (CLAS), and Certified Paralegal (CP) credentials to those who meet certain education and testing requirements.

- Considers continuing education for paralegals to be one of its primary functions.

- Has adopted Model Standards and Guidelines for Utilization for Legal Assistants.

- Has adopted a Code of Ethics and Professional Responsibility that is binding on its members.

fax: 425-771-9588; e-mail: info@paralegals. org, Web site: http://paralegals.org.

- Supports the regulation of paralegals by licensure at the state level. The NFPA has drafted a Model Act for Paralegal Licensure to assist state legislatures in adopting their own licensing statutes, recommending that each jurisdiction should modify the Model Act to its particular needs and requirements.

- Offers the **Paralegal Advanced Competency Exam (PACE)** as a means for experienced paralegals to validate their knowledge to themselves and their employers. PACE is intended to be part of a regulatory scheme, not replace it.

- Has adopted a Model Code of Ethics and Professional Responsibility and Guidelines for Enforcement.

- Has appointed the Ethics and Professional Responsibility Committee that responds to questions and renders opinions regarding ethical conduct, obligations, utilization and/or discipline of paralegals.

The NFPA's Model Code of Ethics and Professional Responsibility

The NFPA's Model Code of Ethics and Professional Responsibility was adopted in 1993 to "delineate the principles for ethics and conduct to which every paralegal should aspire."[8] As with other Model Codes, the NFPA's Model Code of Ethics and Professional Responsibility has no binding authority on paralegals. Many state paralegal associations have, however, adopted the Model Code as their own code of ethics. The NFPA's Model Code consists of eight canons supplemented by ethical considerations. The full text of the NFPA Model Code with Ethical Considerations may be found on the NFPA's Web site at www.paralegals.org. Exhibit 1-6 offers the eight canons from the NFPA's Model Code of Ethics and Professional Responsibility and Guidelines for Enforcement.

Exhibit 1-6
From the NFPA's Model Code of Ethics and Professional Responsibility and Guidelines for Enforcement

The eight canons of the NFPA's Model Code of Ethics and Professional Responsibility:

1.1 A Paralegal Shall Achieve and Maintain a High Level of Competence.

1.2 A Paralegal Shall Maintain a High Level of Personal and Professional Integrity.

Exhibit 1-6 (*Continued*)

From the NFPA's Model Code of Ethics and Professional Responsibility and Guidelines for Enforcement

1.3 A Paralegal Shall Maintain a High Standard of Professional Conduct.

1.4 A Paralegal Shall Serve the Public Interest by Contributing to the Improvement of the Legal System and Delivery of Quality Legal Services, Including Pro Bono Publico Services.

1.5 A Paralegal Shall Preserve All Confidential Information Provided by the Client or Acquired From Other Sources Before, During, and After the Course of the Professional Relationship.

1.6 A Paralegal Shall Avoid Conflicts of Interest and Shall Disclose any Possible Conflict to the Employer or Client, as Well as to the Prospective Employers or Clients.

1.7 A Paralegal's Title Shall Be Fully Disclosed.

1.8 A Paralegal Shall Not Engage in the Unauthorized Practice of Law.

The NFPA has appointed an Ethics and Professional Responsibility Committee, which is formed for the purposes of accepting and responding to inquiries concerning ethical conduct, obligations, utilization, and/or discipline of paralegals.[9] This committee responds to inquiries from any paralegal, attorney, corporation, or government agency employing a paralegal; court; legislature; or bar association. The committee issues opinions based, in large part, on the following:

▶ The NFPA Model Code of Ethics and Professional Responsibility
▶ Other policy statements and/or positions by the NFPA
▶ The ABA Model Guidelines for Utilization of Paralegal Services
▶ The ABA Model Rules of Professional Conduct and as said rules may be adopted and/or amended by the state from which the inquiry arose
▶ The ABA Model Code of Professional Responsibility and as said code may be adopted and/or amended by the state from which the inquiry arose
▶ Any published decision concerning paralegal and/or attorney ethics or discipline

The opinions issued by the NFPA Ethics and Professional Responsibility Committee are not binding. However, they may be used for guidance and as a persuasive argument in favor of the findings of the NFPA.

■ CONSEQUENCES OF UNETHICAL PARALEGAL BEHAVIOR

A paralegal who acts unethically is not in any danger of being disbarred. However, this does not mean that unethical paralegal behavior does not have serious consequences. A paralegal's unethical behavior can result in a loss of respect for the paralegal, the loss of a client to the firm, and disciplinary action against the responsible attorney. In addition, paralegals may lose their employment and may even be subject to criminal prosecution or a civil lawsuit. In some jurisdictions, paralegals who belong to certain paralegal associations may be subject to disciplinary action by committees appointed by those associations.

Loss of Respect

At a minimum, unethical behavior by a paralegal can lead to the loss of respect by the paralegal's superiors, coworkers, and local legal community and to a poor reputation with the paralegal's peers. The legal community is often the target of negative stereotyping, and unethical behavior by one of its members reflects poorly on everyone. No one wants to be associated with an unethical paralegal.

Loss of Clients

In addition to losing coworkers' respect, unethical behavior can cause the law firm employing the paralegal to lose clients. Unethical behavior that jeopardizes a client's case will not be well thought of. Clients will hold their attorneys responsible for the behavior of their employees. If a paralegal breaks a client's trust with unethical behavior, the attorney may very well lose the client.

Disciplinary Action against a Responsible Attorney

As discussed earlier, unethical behavior by a paralegal can lead to disciplinary action against the responsible attorney. Attorneys can be disciplined or even disbarred for violations of the code of ethics by the paralegals they are responsible for supervising.

Loss of Employment

Behavior by a paralegal that is clearly unethical and damaging to a client, supervising attorney, or the law firm often leads to loss of employment. Not only does the paralegal become unemployed, but the paralegal will probably not receive a favorable recommendation from the discharging employer.

Criminal Prosecution

Some rules of ethics are also rules of law. Depending on the exact nature of the unethical behavior, these same acts may also be criminal. Paralegals may find themselves facing criminal charges when their unethical behavior is also illegal behavior.

CASE ON POINT

In 2005, a paralegal from Schenectady, New York, who pled guilty to grand larceny after she was caught stealing more than $86,000 from her employer, was sentenced to prison for one to three years if she pays back the entire sum stolen, but two to seven years if she does not.

—Legal Assistant Today, November/December 2005

Civil Lawsuits

When the unethical behavior of a paralegal causes a client or another party to be injured, the injured party may sue the firm that employs the paralegal. Paralegals are rarely the target of legal malpractice suits, although they are often covered under the law firm's malpractice insurance. It is more likely that the attorneys who supervise the paralegal will be the targets of a civil action, with the paralegal also being named as a defendant in the suit.

Discipline by Paralegal Association

Paralegals who are members of their local or state paralegal associations may find that they are subject to discipline by those associations if they behave in a manner contrary to the association's code of ethics. For example, members of associations that are affiliated with the NFPA are subject to the NFPA Guidelines for the Enforcement of the Model Code of Ethics and Professional Responsibility. The NFPA adopted these guidelines in response to its determination that the "NFPA Model Code of Ethics and Professional Responsibility should be recognized as setting forth the enforceable obligations of all paralegals."[10] These guidelines are discussed further in Chapter 3.

■ PARALEGAL REGULATION

Attorneys must be licensed and admitted to the bar in any state in which they practice—but there is little regulation of paralegals. Currently, no national requirements for paralegal education, certification or licensing exist.

In recent years, a few states have begun to regulate paralegals—usually just those paralegals who provide their services directly to the public. Paralegal regulation in the form of registration, certification, and licensing has been proposed in a few other states. Appendix A is a chart depicting paralegal regulation by state, as of early 2008. It is always important to make sure you are aware of any regulation requirements in any jurisdiction in which you may be working.

OF INTEREST

According to a recent survey, nearly 80% of the responding paralegals indicated that they believe the term "paralegal" denotes a higher professional status than "legal assistant."

—*Legal Assistant Today,* "*15th Annual Salary Survey,*" *March/April 2007*

Regulation by Definition

Some states have passed laws defining the term "paralegal." These definitions include minimum requirements for anyone who uses the title "paralegal." See Exhibit 1-7 for a list of state statutes and court rulings defining the terms "paralegal" and "legal assistant,"as of early 2007. When a state adopts statutes defining the term "parale-gal," attorneys and the public can have a reasonable expectation of the qualifications and responsibilities of individuals who refer to themselves as paralegals.

Exhibit 1-7

Paralegal Definitions

Arizona 17A A.R.S. Sup.Ct.Rules, Rule 31	C. "Legal assistant/ paralegal" means a person qualified by education and training who performs substantive legal work requiring a sufficient knowledge of and expertise in legal concepts and procedures, who is supervised by an active member of the State Bar of Arizona, and for whom an active member of the state bar is responsible, unless otherwise authorized by supreme court rule.
California West's Ann.Cal.Bus. & Prof.Code § 6450	6450. Paralegal defined; prohibited activities; qualifications; continuing legal education (a) "Paralegal" means a person who holds himself or herself out to be a paralegal, who is qualified by education, training, or work experience, who either contracts with or is employed by an attorney, law firm, corporation, governmental agency, or other entity, and who performs substantial legal work under the direction and supervision of an active member of the State Bar of California, as defined in Section 6060, or an attorney practicing law in the federal courts of this state, that has been specifically delegated by the attorney to him or her. Tasks performed by a paralegal include, but are not limited to, case planning, development, and management; legal research; interviewing clients; fact gathering and retrieving information; drafting and analyzing legal documents; collecting, compiling, and utilizing technical information to make an independent decision and recommendation to the supervising attorney; and representing clients before a state or federal administrative agency if that representation is permitted by statute, court rule, or administrative rule or regulation.
Florida Fl Stat. Ann Bar Rule 20-1.	A paralegal is a person with education, training, or work experience, who works under the direction and supervision of a member of The Florida Bar and who performs specifically delegated substantive legal work for which a member of The Florida Bar is responsible.
Illinois Ill Stat. 70/1.35	§ 1.35. Paralegal. "Paralegal"means a person who is qualified through education, training, or work experience and is employed by a lawyer, law office, governmental agency, or other entity to work under the direction of an attorney in a capacity that involves the performance of substantive legal work that usually requires a sufficient knowledge of legal concepts and would be performed by the attorney in the absence of the paralegal. A reference in an Act to attorney fees includes paralegal fees, recoverable at market rates.

Exhibit 1-7 (*Continued*)

Paralegal Definitions

Indiana West's Annotated Indiana Code 1-1-4-6	1-1-4-6 Attorney's fees as including paralegal's fees Sec. 6. (a) As used in this section, "paralegal" means a person who is: (1) qualified through education, training, or work experience; and (2) employed by a lawyer, law office, governmental agency, or other entity; to work under the direction of an attorney in a capacity that involves the performance of substantive legal work that usually requires a sufficient knowledge of legal concepts and would be performed by the attorney in the absence of the paralegal. (b) A reference in the Indiana Code to attorney's fees includes paralegal's fees.
Kentucky SCR, Rule 3.700, Baldwin's Kentucky Rev. Stat. Ann, SCR 3.700	SCR 3.700 Provisions relating to paralegals For purposes of this rule, a paralegal is a person under the supervision and direction of a licensed lawyer, who may apply knowledge of law and legal procedures in rendering direct assistance to lawyers engaged in legal research; design, develop or plan modifications or new procedures, techniques, services, processes or applications; prepare or interpret legal documents and write detailed procedures for practicing in certain fields of law; select, compile and use technical information from such references as digests, encyclopedias or practice manuals; and analyze and follow procedural problems that involve independent decisions.
Maine 4 M.R.S.A. §§ 921, 922	Paralegals and Legal Assistants § 921. Definitions As used in this chapter, unless the context otherwise indicates, the following terms have the following meanings. 1. Paralegal and legal assistant. "Paralegal" and "legal assistant" mean a person, qualified by education, training or work experience, who is employed or retained by an attorney, law office, corporation, governmental agency or other entity and who performs specifically delegated substantive legal work for which an attorney is responsible. § 922. Restriction on use of titles Prohibition. A person may not use the title "paralegal" or "legal assistant" unless the person meets the definition in section 921, subsection 1. Penalty. A person who violates subsection 1 commits a civil violation for which a forfeiture of not more than $1000 may be adjusted.

Montana MCA 37-60-101	37-60-101. Definitions . . . (12) "Paralegal" or "legal assistant" means a person qualified through education, training, or work experience to perform substantive legal work that requires knowledge of legal concepts and that is customarily but not exclusively performed by a lawyer and who may be retained or employed by one or more lawyers, law offices, governmental agencies, or other entities or who may be authorized by administrative, statutory, or court authority to perform this work.
New Hampshire Sup.Ct.Rules, Rule 35	RULE 35. GUIDELINES FOR THE UTILIZATION BY LAWYERS OF THE SERVICES OF LEGAL ASSISTANTS UNDER THE NEW HAMPSHIRE RULES OF PROFESSIONAL CONDUCT . . . C. Definition of "Legal Assistant." As used in these Guidelines, the term "legal assistant" shall mean a person not admitted to the practice of law in New Hampshire who is an employee of or an assistant to an active member of the New Hampshire Bar, a partnership comprised of active members of the New Hampshire Bar or a Professional Association within the meaning of RSA chapter 294-A, and who, under the control and supervision of an active member of the New Hampshire Bar, renders services related to but not constituting the practice of law.
New Mexico NMRA, Rule 20-102	RULE 20-102. DEFINITIONS As used in these rules: A. a "paralegal" is a person who: (1) contracts with or is employed by an attorney, law firm, corporation, governmental agency or other entity; (2) performs substantive legal work under the supervision of a licensed attorney who assumes professional responsibility for the final work product; and (3) meets one or more of the education, training or work experience qualifications set forth in Rule 20-115 NMRA of these rules; and B. "substantive legal work" is work that requires knowledge of legal concepts and is customarily, but not exclusively, performed by a lawyer. Examples of substantive legal work performed by a paralegal include: case planning, development and management; legal research and analysis; interviewing clients; fact gathering and retrieving information; drafting legal documents; collecting, compiling, and utilizing technical information to make an independent decision and recommendation to the supervising attorney; and representing clients before a state or federal administrative agency if that representation is authorized by law. Substantive legal work performed by a paralegal for a licensed attorney shall not constitute the unauthorized practice of law.

Exhibit 1-7 (*Continued*)

Paralegal Definitions

North Dakota N.D.R. Prof. Conduct, Rule 1.0	"Legal Assistant" (or paralegal) means a person who assists lawyers in the delivery of legal services, and who through formal education, training, or experience, has knowledge and expertise regarding the legal system and substantive and procedural law which qualifies the person to do work of a legal nature under the direct supervision of a licensed lawyer.
Rhode Island Sup.Ct.Rules, Art. V, Rules of Prof. Conduct, Rule 5.5	PROVISIONAL ORDER NO. 18–USE OF LEGAL ASSISTANTS These guidelines shall apply to the use of legal assistants by members of the Rhode Island Bar Association. A legal assistant is one who under the supervision of a lawyer, shall apply knowledge of law and legal procedures in rendering direct assistance to lawyers, clients and courts; design, develop and modify procedures, techniques, services and processes; prepare and interpret legal documents; detail procedures for practicing in certain fields of law; research, select, assess, compile and use information from the law library and other references; and analyze and handle procedural problems that involve independent decisions. More specifically, a legal assistant is one who engages in the functions set forth in Guideline 2. Nothing contained in these guidelines shall be construed as a determination of the competence of any person performing the functions of a legal assistant, or as conferring status upon any such person serving as a legal assistant.
South Dakota SDCL § 16-18-34	16-18-34. Definition of legal assistant Legal assistants (also known as paralegals) are a distinguishable group of persons who assist licensed attorneys in the delivery of legal services. Through formal education, training, and experience, legal assistants have knowledge and expertise regarding the legal system, substantive and procedural law, the ethical considerations of the legal profession, and the Rules of Professional Conduct as stated in chapter 16-18, which qualify them to do work of a legal nature under the employment and direct supervision of a licensed attorney. This rule shall apply to all unlicensed persons employed by a licensed attorney who are represented to the public or clients as possessing training or education which qualifies them to assist in the handling of legal matters or document preparation for the client.
Utah UT Bar Rules for Integr. & Mgmt. Rule I4-113	(a) Paralegal defined. A paralegal is a person qualified through education, training, or work experience, who is employed or retained by a lawyer, law office, governmental agency, or the entity in the capacity of function which involves the performance, under the ultimate direction and supervision of an attorney, of specifically delegated substantive legal work, which work, for the most part, requires a sufficient knowledge of legal concepts that absent such assistance, the attorney would perform. A paralegal includes a paralegal on a contract or free-lance basis who works under the supervision of a lawyer or who produces work directly for a lawyer for which a lawyer is accountable.

Paralegal Registration

Some jurisdictions have started to provide for the regulation of certain paralegals through registration. If paralegal registration is required in a particular jurisdiction, paralegals who fall under certain categories (most likely those offering their services directly to the public) must register with the county clerk, or some similar officer, of that jurisdiction. In order to properly register, a paralegal is likely required to meet certain education, bonding, and character requirements. For example, California has recently passed legislation requiring the registration of legal document assistants. Legal document assistants are paralegals who provide certain self-help services to individuals who represent themselves in legal matters. The registration requirements do not apply to paralegals who work under an attorney's supervision.

As of late 2007, few jurisdictions require the registration of paralegals who work under the supervision of licensed attorneys.

Paralegal Certification

Certification is usually a voluntary process that may be done by a court or a paralegal association. The paralegal is certified to possess certain qualifications with regard to education and expertise. Certain groups, including the NALA, endorse the voluntary certification of paralegals by their organization. Individuals who meet predetermined qualifications—usually in the areas of education, experience, and passing a test established by the certifying group—will receive certification. Other groups have proposed voluntary certification by state bar associations.

Paralegal Licensing

A license is a privilege conferred on a person by the government to do something that he or she otherwise would not have the right to do. No form of licensing for paralegals is currently required in any state in this country. However, two types of licensing have been proposed, and either or both may be adopted in some states in the near future.

The first type of proposed licensing requires that all paralegals must meet certain requirements and be licensed in the state in which they work. The second type of licensing requires that only paralegals who offer their services to the public without the supervision of an attorney must meet certain requirements and be licensed by the state.

Limited licensure refers to a process currently utilized in a few jurisdictions that authorizes nonlawyers, who are often paralegals, the authority to perform certain, specific functions that are customarily performed by attorneys. For example, laws have been passed to allow licensed nonattorneys to oversee real estate closings or represent clients in noncontested family court matters. This type of licensure expands the work that paralegals can lawfully do without *practicing law.*

OF INTEREST

In Washington, nonattorneys who meet certain conditions are authorized to perform specific functions incident to the closing of real estate and personal property transactions, including preparation of legal documents and other tasks traditionally considered to be the practice of law.

—*Washington Local Rules of Court and West's Washington Court Rules, Part I, Rule 12 (1997)*

Most paralegal associations and other associations concerned with the qualifications and ethical standards of paralegals have taken a formal stand on the issue of paralegal regulation.

The ABA's Position

The ABA has taken the position that paralegal regulation is a matter best handled at the state level. It has not proposed a formal plan or model for paralegal regulation. The ABA has approved the following definition of legal assistant/paralegal:

> *A legal assistant or paralegal is a person qualified by education, training or work experience who is employed or retained by a lawyer, law office, corporation, governmental agency or other entity who performs specifically delegated substantive legal work for which a lawyer is responsible.*

Under this definition, the supervising lawyer is clearly responsible for the paralegal's work.

The ABA also approves select paralegal education programs throughout the country that meet ABA guidelines to foster high-quality paralegal education. The Standing Committee on Paralegals and Approval Commission conducts intensive reviews and onsite evaluations of paralegal education programs applying for approval.

The NALA's Position

The NALA does not support paralegal licensing or mandatory regulation of any type. Instead, the NALA prefers voluntary certification. Paralegals who meet certain requirements earn the designations of **Certified Legal Assistant (CLA)**, Certified Legal Assistant Specialist (CLAS), and Certified Paralegal (CP). See Chapter 2 for more information on the NALA's Certified Legal Assistant designation.

The NFPA's Position

The NFPA endorses a two-tiered regulatory scheme consisting of licensing and specialty licensing at the state level as the preferred form of regulation. The NFPA resolution outlines standards for the profession, including a minimum level of education, continuing legal education and experience requirements, and standards of ethics and character. The NFPA supports regulation as long as the role of the paralegal is expanded. For more information on the NFPA's position on regulation of the paralegal profession, see the NFPA's Position Statement on Non-Lawyer Practice at the NFPA Web site at www.paralegals.org.

The **Paralegal Advanced Competency Exam (PACE)** was developed for the NFPA in 1996 as a means for paralegals to validate their knowledge to themselves and their employers. Also, the members of the NFPA feel that with the increasing numbers of states considering regulation of paralegals, the PACE exam may be one means for establishing competency for future regulation and licensing requirements. Unlike the NALA's CLA test, which promotes voluntary certification, the PACE exam is not intended to be used in place of regulation but rather as a part of a regulation scheme. See Chapter 2 for more information on the NFPA's PACE.

Arguments abound both for and against each type of regulation. Proponents of paralegal regulation feel that it will allow paralegals to expand their role without engaging in the unauthorized practice of law and will promote the profession while protecting the public. Many feel that certain legal services can be well performed by nonattorneys, making needed legal services more affordable and more available to the public, thus providing a very valuable service to society.

Opposition to regulation comes from a diverse group of members of the legal community, including some attorneys, judges, and paralegals who argue that regulation is unnecessary, that it would increase legal fees, and would negatively impact the paralegal profession. They feel that the provision of legal services should be restricted to licensed attorneys and that the provision of any legal services by paralegals without attorney supervision should be considered the unauthorized practice of law.

PARALEGAL SPECIALTIES

The work of paralegals throughout the United States is incredibly diverse. The work of a paralegal employed by a sole practitioner specializing in family law will be very different from the work of a paralegal employed by a Fortune 100 company and specializing in intellectual property law. The majority of paralegals work in private law firms, although an increasing number, roughly 15% to 20%, work for corporation legal departments. In addition, federal, state, and local governments employ a number of paralegals who work in their court systems and administrative agencies. Although the same rules of ethics generally apply to all paralegals, the ethical concerns they have will vary greatly. In several subsequent chapters, we will take a look at how the rules of ethics may apply to some of the more common paralegal specialties. Being aware of how the rules apply to your position is vital to your ability to properly do your job.

RESOURCES

As illustrated throughout this chapter, numerous resources exist where you can find answers to your questions concerning legal ethics. These resources include your supervising attorney and your employer, your state's code of ethics, and your paralegal association. Various legal research Web sites also offer a wealth of information about legal ethics.

Supervising Attorney or Employer's Resources

Perhaps one of the best places to turn initially for answers to questions concerning ethical conduct is your supervising attorney or an ethics committee within the law firm or legal department where you work. Your primary resource will depend on who your employer is. If you work for a private law firm, your supervising attorney will probably be your best resource. In addition, you may have a paralegal manager or a law firm manager who can answer your questions. If you work for a larger law firm, your firm probably has an established code of ethics to give you guidance or possibly even an ethics committee to answer your questions.

Paralegals who work for in corporate legal departments may find that their question is addressed in the corporation's code of ethics or in guidelines specifically for the corporation's legal department.

Paralegals who work in the public sector for a government agency may find answers to their questions in additional rules of ethics prescribed for their particular administrative agency.

State Codes of Ethics

The primary source for further research and information is the code of ethics that is binding on the attorneys you work for. See Exhibit 1-1 for a list of state codes of ethics and their URLs.

Paralegal Associations

Ethical advice and guidelines specific to paralegal concerns can be obtained through your local, state, or national paralegal association. The codes of ethics and ethical guidelines published by the national paralegal associations can be accessed from their sites.

National Association of Legal Assistants (NALA):
www.nala.org

National Federation of Paralegal Associations:
www.paralegals.org

■ ONLINE RESOURCES

Information about legal ethics, including general information and links to state codes of ethics, can be found on the following Web sites:

AllLaw
www.alllaw.com

American Legal Ethics Library
www.law.cornell.edu/ethics

FindLaw
www.findlaw.com

Hieros Gamos
www.hg.org

Katsuey's Legal Gateway
www.katsuey.com

Law.com
www.law.com

The 'Lectric Law Library
www.lectlaw.com

Legalethics.com
www.legalethics.com

Legal Information Institute
www.law.cornell.edu

■ CHAPTER SUMMARY

> ▶ Legal ethics is the code of conduct among members of the legal profession that governs their moral and professional duties toward one another, toward their clients, and toward the courts.
> ▶ The role of legal ethics is to identify and remove inappropriate conduct from the legal profession and to protect the public.
> ▶ Attorneys are subject to the code of ethics adopted by the state in which they are licensed to practice. The state judicial system, the state bar association, or the state legislature may adopt that code.
> ▶ The code of ethics adopted by most states follows the American Bar Association's Model Rules of Professional Conduct.
> ▶ Attorneys can be held responsible for the unethical behavior of their nonlawyer employees, including paralegals.
> ▶ The NALA and the NFPA are both national paralegal associations that have adopted rules and guidelines for ethical behavior by paralegals.
> ▶ Currently, no state or national legislation requires a supervised paralegal to have a license or certificate.

▶ Unethical behavior by an attorney may result in disciplinary action by the state disciplinary board, a civil suit against the attorney for legal malpractice, or even criminal prosecution.

▶ Unethical behavior by a paralegal may result in the loss of respect of coworkers and others, the loss of the firm's client, disciplinary action against the attorney to whom the paralegal reports, loss of employment, being named in a civil lawsuit, or criminal prosecution.

■ FREQUENTLY ASKED QUESTIONS

Are paralegals subject to the state rules of ethics that are applicable to attorneys?

The rules of ethics are written for attorneys, and paralegals are not *directly* subject to those rules. However, as a paralegal, you must abide by these rules for several reasons.

1. The attorneys you work for are responsible for your ethical behavior. As an employee/agent of the attorneys you work for, you must abide by their rules of ethics. Your breach of the rules of ethics could leave your supervising attorneys subject to discipline.

2. The rules of ethics of any paralegal association you may belong to probably indicate that you are subject to the rules of ethics written for the attorneys in your state.

3. The rules of ethics are written to ensure ethical behavior. To behave in an ethical manner, you must follow those rules and guidelines too.

Where can I find answers to questions about ethics in my state?

If you are new to a job, you may want to explore the options available through your employer. If you work for a large law firm, your firm may have several resources, including an ethics committee and a code of ethics drafted just for your firm. Your state's code of ethics should be available online (see Exhibit 1-1). Also, local, state, and national paralegal associations are great resources for information on ethics for paralegals.

Do I need a license to work as a paralegal?

No. Although some states set forth minimum qualifications for individuals who use the title *paralegal*, no state currently requires a license to work as a paralegal.

If I am not an attorney, I cannot be disbarred. What are the negative consequences to unethical paralegal behavior?

Several negative consequences can result from unethical paralegal behavior. Depending upon its nature and severity, paralegal misconduct can lead to the following:

■ loss of respect among colleagues
■ loss of employment

- supervising attorneys may be subject to discipline by the state bar and the court that has licensed them
- possible discipline by a paralegal association
- civil lawsuits
- criminal prosecution

Where can I find a copy of the paralegal Code of Ethics that applies to me?

If you are a member of either national paralegal association, you can find a copy of their codes of ethics at their Web sites at www.paralegals.org (NFPA) or www.nala.org (NALA). Several state paralegal associations have adopted their own codes of ethics that are available online.

■ ENDNOTES

1. Chair's Introduction to Model Rules of Professional Conduct, by Robert W. Meserve, then chairman of the American Bar Association Commission on Evaluation of Professional Standards (1983).
2. As of May 2007, all states but California, Maine, and New York had adopted their own version of the ABA's Model Rules of Professional Conduct.
3. Preamble to the Model Rules of Professional Conduct, as amended through 1996.
4. *People v. Fry*, 875 P.2d 222 (Colo. 1994).
5. *Disciplinary Board v. Nassif*, 547 N.W.2d. 541 (N.D. 1996).
6. *Nagy v. Beckley*, 578 N.E. 2d 1134 (Ill. App. 1991).
7. Preamble to the ABA Model Guidelines for the Utilization of Paralegal Services, American Bar Association (2003).
8. National Federation of Paralegal Associations, Inc. Model Code of Ethics and Professional Responsibility Preamble (1993).
9. National Federation of Paralegal Associations Guidelines for Rendering Ethics and Disciplinary Opinions (1995).
10. National Federation of Paralegal Associations, Inc. Model Code of Ethics and Professional Responsibility and Guidelines for Enforcement Preamble (1997).

Chapter 2

Competent, Diligent Representation of the Client

"The leading rule for the lawyer, as for the man of every other calling, is diligence. Leave nothing for to-morrow which can be done to-day."

— Abraham Lincoln

■ PART I: COMPETENT DILIGENT REPRESENTATION

Attorneys must provide their clients with **competent,** diligent representation and with **diligence.** Competent representation requires attorneys to have the legal knowledge, skill, thoroughness, and preparation reasonably necessary for the representation.

Diligent representation requires attorneys to pursue matters on behalf of their clients with commitment and dedication. Attorneys must pursue each client's matter, despite any personal inconvenience to the attorney, with zeal through whatever legal and ethical means appropriate and without procrastination.

Attorneys who do not provide their clients with competent and diligent representation are in violation of the codes of ethics that apply to them and may be subject to disciplinary action. In addition, the attorney may be liable for legal malpractice if a disgruntled client brings a civil lawsuit.

All paralegals have an ethical duty to perform their work competently and to assist attorneys in providing competent and diligent representation to their clients. As part of the legal representation team, you must be aware of the standards for competence and diligence applied to attorneys and paralegals. You must have an understanding of what zealous representation means and the legal and ethical limits of zealous representation.

This chapter begins by defining the terms "competent" and "diligent" as well as discussing the standards that must be met by attorneys. Part I concludes with a look at zealous client representation within the law. Part II looks at competence and diligence from the paralegal's perspective and the knowledge and skills a paralegal must possess to be considered competent. This chapter concludes with a look at standards for measuring paralegal competence.

COMPETENT REPRESENTATION DEFINED

Rule 1.1 of the ABA Model Rules states that competent representation requires the following at a level reasonably necessary for representation:

1. legal knowledge
2. skill
3. thoroughness
4. preparation

The standard of competence that must be provided by attorneys is the skill and knowledge normally possessed by other attorneys in good standing undertaking similar matters. In most instances, attorneys are held to the proficiency of a general practitioner. However, under certain circumstances, expertise in a particular field of law may be required.

Legal Knowledge

Attorneys must have the requisite knowledge and skill in any matter in which they represent a client. That knowledge must include an understanding of legal principles applicable to each matter in which the attorney undertakes representation. "A lawyer is expected to be familiar with well-settled principles of law applicable to a client's needs."[1]

In addition to possessing knowledge of basic legal principles, competent attorneys must have an understanding of the court rules and court procedures that apply to every matter that they undertake as well as the knowledge required to conduct the research necessary to provide clients with competent representation. Courts have found that attorneys must "discover those additional rules of law which, although not commonly known, may be readily found by standard research techniques."[2]

OF INTEREST

According to LawPro, a leading provider of legal malpractice insurance, only 6% of legal malpractice claims are due to the attorney's failure to know or apply the law.

—LawPro, www.lawpro.ca, accessed January 28, 2007

Skills

A unique set of skills is required of attorneys in their representation of clients. Some of the specific skills attorneys must possess to competently represent clients include document-drafting skills, the ability to analyze precedent and evaluate evidence, and the management and supervisory skills necessary to manage their practice of law and supervise employees.

Exhibit 2-1 is a checklist of skills required of competent attorneys.

Exhibit 2-1

Skills Required of Competent Attorneys

- Legal document drafting
- Legal research skills
- Analytical skills
- Office and time management skills
- Supervisory skills

Drafting

Competent attorneys must be skilled in drafting pleadings and other legal documents. An attorney's ability to draft legal documents is so critical that a deficiency in this area can lead to ineffective representation. In one Minnesota case, an attorney was publicly reprimanded and ordered to complete continuing education courses as specified by the court when the court found his lack of writing skills amounted to incompetent representation. The reprimanded attorney had filed documents with the bankruptcy court that were rendered unintelligible due to "numerous spelling, grammatical, and typographical errors."[3]

Office Management

Attorneys must possess the office management skills needed to serve their clients in a competent manner. Office management skills include accurate calendaring, billing, filing, recordkeeping, and supervision of office staff.

One of the most common sources of complaints against attorneys involves lapsed **statutes of limitations**. Statutes of limitations are the state and federal laws that set a limit on the maximum time period during which a lawsuit may be filed. The time period begins when the cause of action begins. For example, suppose that a new client comes into your office to discuss a possible personal injury lawsuit involving an automobile accident. The accident occurred five years ago, but the client was severely injured and is still receiving treatment. The lawsuit must be served before the statute of limitations period lapses for this type of matter (usually no more than six years from the date of the accident) or your client will lose his or her right to bring any type of legal action against the responsible party. Maintaining a calendar system that alerts the responsible attorney to upcoming deadlines for filing court documents is of the utmost importance. An improperly kept calendar can result in missed court dates and missed filing dates that may result in the total dismissal of a client's claim.

Thoroughness and Preparation

For an attorney to provide competent representation to a client, the attorney must be thorough and prepared. The attorney must undertake necessary investigation of the facts of each case, and the attorney must research the law pertaining to each case as necessary. Failure to handle a client matter with the proper preparation can lead to serious consequences for both the client and the attorney.

In a disciplinary proceeding in Colorado, an attorney was disbarred for several infractions, including attending a hearing in a marriage dissolution case with her only preparation being in the car on the way to the courthouse. The attorney in this case was found to be handling a legal matter without adequate preparation, which violates Model Rule 1.1.[4]

Investigation and Research

Being adequately prepared and thorough includes an attorney's responsibilities to investigate the facts of each matter and research the applicable law. "An attorney owes his client the duty of diligent investigation and research."[5]

Attorneys have a duty to thoroughly investigate the applicable facts and circumstances surrounding each particular matter to the degree necessary for preparing the case or otherwise advising the client. The amount of preparation required depends on the complexity of the matter and what is at stake. "Competent handling of a particular matter includes inquiry into and analysis of the factual and legal elements of the problem and use of methods and procedures meeting the standards of competent practitioners."[6]

Attorneys cannot know every aspect of the law, even in those areas in which they specialize. Attorneys must research the pertinent law in each case as necessary to provide competent representation. Although attorneys are not expected to be infallible, they must conduct the measure of research sufficient to allow their clients to make informed decisions.[7]

ACCEPTING OR DECLINING REPRESENTATION

When attorneys are presented with cases that require legal knowledge or skill they do not possess, they have a few options. The attorney may associate with, or consult, an attorney with known competence in that area; make a commitment to self-education; or turn down the representation. For example, a personal injury attorney who is offered a case involving copyright or trademark issues would probably seek the assistance of an intellectual property attorney, unless the personal injury attorney is willing to commit several hours to self-education with regard to intellectual property law. If the attorney is not associated with an intellectual property attorney and does not want to commit to the time it would take to gain the required knowledge, the attorney must turn down the case.

Whichever route an attorney decides to take in compensating for a lack of knowledge in a certain area of law, the action must be clearly communicated to the client. If an attorney determines that he or she cannot represent a potential client, the attorney must notify the potential client in writing as soon as possible. If an attorney decides to consult with an outside specialist in the relevant area of law concerning a client's case, the client should be notified and consulted concerning the details of the professional relationship.

Specialization

With the complexity of modern law, most attorneys specialize in one or more areas of law. Because it is difficult for attorneys to be knowledgeable and competent in areas outside of their specialty, they often refer such business to specialists. For example, it is not uncommon for attorneys who specialize in family law to refer divorcing clients who have complicated income tax questions to tax attorneys.

While specialists have always existed in the practice of law in the United States, only in recent years have these specialists been recognized by certification. To obtain the Certified Specialist designation, attorneys must meet requirements set by the certifying board, which usually include a specific amount of experience in the area and passing a written examination. Attorneys may be certified as specialists by state-sponsored certification plans or by private organizations that offer certification programs that are accredited by the ABA. Currently, Arizona, California, Florida, Louisiana, Minnesota, New Jersey, New Mexico, North Carolina, South Carolina, and Texas offer state-sponsored certification plans. The ABA Accredited Certification Programs include certification in business and consumer bankruptcy, accounting, legal and medical professional liability, elder law, estate planning, and civil and criminal trial advocacy.

Attorneys may even be *required* to refer certain types of business to specialists when they lack the necessary competency. In a 1979 California case, where an attorney who set up a defective **irrevocable trust** for a client's three sons and was subsequently sued for legal malpractice, the court held that a general practitioner has a duty to refer a client to a specialist under certain circumstances or to meet the standard of care of a specialist.[8] Exhibit 2-2 is a list of accredited ABA certification programs.

Exhibit 2-2

ABA Accredited Private Certification Programs

- Accounting Professional Liability
- Business Bankruptcy
- Civil Trial Advocacy

- Consumer Bankruptcy
- Creditor's Rights
- Criminal Trial Advocacy
- DUI Defense Law
- Elder Law
- Estate Planning
- Family Law
- Juvenile Law (Child Welfare)
- Legal Professional Liability
- Medical Professional Liability
- Social Security Disability Law
- Trial Advocacy

MAINTAINING COMPETENCE

To ensure their continued competence, attorneys are required to educate themselves to keep abreast of new developments. "To maintain the requisite knowledge and skill, a lawyer should engage in continuing study and education."[9] Continuing Legal Education (CLE) courses are offered throughout the country to help attorneys maintain their competence and expertise in almost every area of law. A majority of the state bar associations now requires that attorneys complete a certain number of hours of education through approved CLE courses.

BASIC RULES CONCERNING DILIGENT REPRESENTATION OF CLIENT

Attorneys must represent their clients with reasonable diligence. An attorney who has the required legal knowledge and skill does not offer adequate representation of a client if the attorney demonstrates a lack of diligence or promptness. "A lawyer should pursue a matter on behalf of a client despite opposition, obstruction, or personal inconvenience to the lawyer, and may take whatever lawful and ethical measures are required to vindicate a client's cause or endeavor."[10] Attorneys must avoid procrastination when acting on a client's behalf, and they must keep current in their communications with their clients.

The obligation to act diligently encompasses providing services within a reasonable time, attending promptly to legal matters with which one is entrusted and committing to achieve clients' lawful objectives. Procrastination, neglect, forgetfulness, or lack of reasonable efficiency can each result in discipline and liability for malpractice.

The attorney's duty regarding diligence does not mean that the attorney should forego professionalism and courtesy. "The lawyer's duty to act with reasonable diligence does not require the use of offensive tactics or preclude the treating of all persons involved in the legal process with courtesy and respect."[11]

Procrastination and Failure to Act in a Timely Manner

Although almost all of us are guilty of procrastinating in our personal lives, such a trait in the practice of law can have serious consequences. Failure to act on behalf of a client in a timely manner is one of the most frequent causes of legal malpractice suits. An attorney's procrastination, in addition to being a source of irritation to the client, can lead to missed deadlines, resulting in the termination of legal rights and remedies of the client.

Communication with Clients

Attorneys must communicate effectively with their clients as to the status of the matters they are handling for them. Failure on the part of an attorney to communicate with a client and respond to a client's inquiries can result in discipline for lack of diligence.

Attorneys must share with clients all pertinent facts required to enable the client to make the best decision possible regarding negotiations. Attorneys must communicate to clients:

1. all serious proposals by the opposing counsel.
2. a review of all important provisions of the proposed offer or settlement.
3. a description of communications regarding the proposal received from the opposing counsel.
4. the details of any offers for a plea bargain.
5. any other information that may be needed by the client to make the best decision possible.

Competence and diligence are closely related, and a lack of competence can often lead to a lack of diligence.

CASE ON POINT

In 1989, a Colorado attorney was suspended for 90 days for his incompetence and lack of diligence when he agreed to represent a client in a medical malpractice case. The attorney lacked the requisite competence to represent such a suit, and he failed to consult with a medical malpractice specialist. To make matters worse, the attorney's lack of diligence led to poor communication with the client and a lapse of the statute of limitations on the client's potential claim before anything was done.

—*People v. Pooley, 774 P.2d 239 (Colo. 1989)*

ZEALOUS REPRESENTATION

A lawyer must act with commitment and dedication to the interests of the client and with zeal in advocacy upon the client's behalf.[12] The word zeal means "eager and ardent interest in the pursuit of something."[13] **Zealous** representation is characterized by enthusiasm and fervent dedication on the part of the attorney. It requires attorneys to do everything legally and ethically possible to gain an acquittal for a defendant.[14]

To provide zealous representation to clients, attorneys shall:

1. seek the lawful objectives of clients through reasonably available means permitted by law and the rules of professional conduct.

2. carry out employment contracts to provide legal services without withdrawing pursuant to the pertinent rules of professional conduct.

3. not prejudice or damage clients during the course of the professional relationship, except as required by the pertinent rules of professional conduct.[15]

Remaining within the Bounds of the Law

Zealous representation of a client must remain within the bounds of the law. The attorney's ethical duty is to do everything *legally* and *ethically* permitted to pursue a client's interest. Attorneys must always be careful not to cross the line to illegal or unethical behavior in pursuing their clients' interests.

There are numerous rules concerning actions considered to be unethical or outside the bounds of the law in the representation of clients. These rules are set forth in the codes of ethics adopted by each state. Here are some of the more important rules for keeping zealous representation within the bounds of the law.

1. Attorneys must not file unwarranted, frivolous suits or claims or take other actions merely to harass or maliciously injure others.

2. Attorneys have a duty of candor toward the court.

3. Attorneys must not communicate directly with jurors or with an adverse party who is represented by an attorney.

4. Attorneys must never threaten criminal prosecution charges solely to gain advantage in a civil matter.

5. Attorneys must abide by all legal and ethical rules concerning trial conduct and publicity.

6. Attorneys must be aware of and comply with the rules of ethics and court rules concerning contact with witnesses or potential witnesses to a legal matter.

PART II: FROM THE PARALEGAL'S PERSPECTIVE

Much like attorneys, paralegals have an ethical responsibility to perform their jobs with competence and diligence. As a paralegal, you must have the requisite knowledge and skill to complete your assignments, and they must be completed promptly to the best of your ability.

■ PARALEGAL COMPETENCE AND DILIGENCE

As part of the legal services team, paralegals must provide competent and diligent services to the attorneys they work for and, ultimately, to the client. You must be certain you have the requisite knowledge and skill to perform the tasks that have been assigned to you.

The attorneys you work for may not always be aware of your knowledge and abilities—and your limits. It is vital that you do not misrepresent the level of your knowledge and skill. To do so can have serious consequences to you, the attorneys you work for, and to the clients they represent. If you are given an assignment that you feel is beyond your abilities, you must educate yourself to the extent necessary to accomplish the task. If time does not permit, you must ask for help from an experienced paralegal or an attorney.

Paralegals must be diligent in the completion of their assignments. Attorneys will rely on your ability, skills, and your diligence to get work done thoroughly and on time. Do not get put in a position where a heavy workload tempts you to set aside difficult tasks that you do not feel competent to complete. Procrastination on the part of a paralegal can be just as destructive as procrastination on the part of an attorney.

A competent paralegal has a basic knowledge of the American legal system and possesses skill in the following areas:

- ▶ organization and management
- ▶ communication
- ▶ critical thinking
- ▶ computer
- ▶ legal research and investigation
- ▶ interpersonal

Organization and Management Skills

Both attorneys and paralegals must have excellent organizational skills to provide clients with competent, diligent representation. Calendaring deadlines and case management are two of the tasks most commonly assigned to paralegals.[16] By tracking important court dates and other deadlines and assisting with accurate timekeeping and recordkeeping, you will help to ensure that the attorneys you report to comply with the rules of ethics regarding competent, diligent representation of clients.

Communication Skills

As a paralegal, you must use excellent communication skills when communicating with attorneys, clients, and other individuals. You must have basic communications skills, including good grammar and a good vocabulary, and you must be able to communicate effectively in person and in writing.

Your in-person communication will include meeting with and speaking to attorneys, your coworkers, and clients. Clients should receive personal attention and have their questions answered within a reasonable time period. Attorneys do not always have time to answer phone calls and correspondence and meet with clients when those clients desire. As a paralegal, you may serve as the communication link between the attorney and the clients.

Paralegals often attend client meetings—either with the attorneys they work for or on their own. It is imperative that you have effective communication skills. You must have the ability to communicate clearly, concisely, and politely. Your nonverbal communication must match your spoken words.

OF INTEREST

According to a recent survey, 80% of the responding paralegals participate in attorney/client meetings at least occasionally.

—*NALA 2004 National Utilization and Compensation Survey Report (2004)*

Paralegals must also be able to communicate effectively in writing. Most paralegals find themselves drafting correspondence on a daily basis.[17] Exhibit 2-3 is a list of some resources that may help you with your writing.

Exhibit 2-3

Legal Writing Assistance

General Writing Assistance

1. The Chicago Manual of Style: The Essential Guide for Writers, Editors, and Publishers, 15th Edition (2003).

2. Elements of Style, 4th Edition, William Strunk Jr. (1999).

3. Grammatically Correct, Ann Stillman (1997).

4. The Merriam-Webster Collegiate Dictionary, 11th Edition (2003).

5. The Gregg Reference Manual, 10th Edition (2004).

Legal Writing Assistance

6. Black's Law Dictionary, 8th Edition, Bryan Garner (2006).

7. A Dictionary of Modern Legal Usage, 2nd Edition, Bryan Garner (2001).

8. The Elements of Legal Style, 2nd Edition, Bryan A. Garner (2002).

9. The Elements of Legal Writing, Martha Faulk (1996).

10. Legal Writing in Plain English, Bryan Garner (2001).

11. Pocket Guide to Legal Writing, William Putman (2006).

Exhibit 2-3 (*Continued*)

Legal Writing Assistance

Online Writing Assistance

12. *The Elements of Style*, William Strunk Jr., http://www.bartleby.com/141/

13. *Merriam-Webster Online*, http://www.m-w.com/

14. Legal Writing: Legal Information Institute,
    http://www.law.cornell.edu/wex/index.php/Legal_writing

15. Guide to Grammar and Writing, http://grammar.ccc.commnet.edu/grammar/

16. Ask Oxford (Oxford Dictionaries), http://www.askoxford.com/?view=uk

Attorneys have an ethical duty to keep clients informed about the status of their legal matters, to promptly reply to requests for information, and to explain legal matters to clients to the extent necessary to permit them to make informed decisions. As a paralegal, your assistance to the attorneys you work for and your communication with clients can ensure that clients receive competent, diligent legal services.

Critical Thinking Skills

Competent paralegals must have the critical thinking skills necessary to analyze and summarize legal documents. As a paralegal, you will often be responsible for analyzing a given set of facts and summarizing them for the attorneys you work for or for clients. Your critical-thinking skills are also important for legal analysis—applying the law to a given set of facts.

Computer Skills

Competent paralegals are computer literate and skilled in several computer applications frequently used in the practice of law. As a paralegal, you may need to use several computer applications daily. Some of the more frequently used computer applications include word processing, legal research, billing, and timekeeping. See Exhibit 2-4.

Legal Research and Investigation Skills

Attorneys have an ethical duty to be diligent in their research and investigation on each legal matter that they represent. As a paralegal, you will probably be given research and investigation assignments on a regular basis. Your assignments will provide the attorneys you work for with information that may be critical to the competent representation of their clients. The legal research you conduct may include research done by computer and by telephone. It may also

Exhibit 2-4

Computer Applications Commonly Used by Paralegals

1. E-Mail Communication
2. Word Processing
3. Calendar/Docket
4. Timekeeping and Billing
5. Legal Research

include checking a simple procedure in a handbook or manual. Understanding the basics of what is required to perform adequate legal research is of the utmost importance to every paralegal.

To offer clients competent and diligent services, the legal team must thoroughly investigate the facts of a legal matter as well as the law. The term "investigate" means to inquire; to look into; to make an investigation. When the term is taken literally, much of any paralegal work involves investigating. Whether you are searching for witnesses and evidence for a trial or trying to locate the registered office of a corporation, you must have excellent investigative skills.

Interpersonal Skills

As a competent paralegal, you must possess the interpersonal skills required to successfully interact with those you come into contact with. As part of the legal team, you must have effective team-building skills and be able to communicate, empathize, and interact with individuals with diverse backgrounds and education. Your interpersonal skills must also include the interviewing skills necessary to conduct thorough investigations in **litigation** matters.

STANDARDS FOR PARALEGAL COMPETENCE

Paralegal competence is a sensitive issue with many paralegals because there are no universally accepted standards. Both national paralegal associations have been working to combat this problem—by requiring a certain level of competence in their codes of ethics and by providing tests to identify competent paralegals and give them credibility.

The NFPA's Recognition of Competence

The NFPA's Model Code of Ethics and Professional Responsibility sets forth its standards for paralegal competency (See Exhibit 2-5).

Exhibit 2-5

From the NFPA's Model Code of Ethics and Professional Responsibility and Guidelines for Enforcement

1.1 A PARALEGAL SHALL ACHIEVE AND MAINTAIN A HIGH LEVEL OF COMPETENCE

EC-1.1(a)   A paralegal shall achieve competency through education, training, and work experience.

EC-1.1(b)   A paralegal shall aspire to participate in a minimum of twelve (12) hours of continuing legal education, to include at least one. (1) hour of ethics education, every two (2) years in order to remain current on developments in the law.

EC-1.1(c)   A paralegal shall perform all assignments promptly and efficiently.

The NFPA also recommends that paralegals prove their competence by passing the PACE.

PACE

PACE is not currently required by the NFPA or any state-regulating agency. PACE is a two-tiered exam that may be taken by experienced paralegals who meet certain education requirements to "validate experience and job skills, establish credentials and confirm their value to the legal industry."[18] Tier One of the exam tests critical-thinking skills and problem-solving abilities, including general legal and ethical questions. Tier Two tests the knowledge of the paralegal in specific legal practice areas. The PACE may only be taken by paralegals who meet with certain education and experience requirements, including:

▶ An associate degree in paralegal studies obtained from an institutionally accredited school and/or an ABA-approved paralegal education program and six years of substantive paralegal experience; or

▶ A bachelor's degree in any course of study obtained from an institutionally accredited school and three years of substantive paralegal experience; or

▶ A bachelor's degree and completion of a paralegal program with an institutionally accredited school (said paralegal program may be embodied in a bachelor's degree) and two years of substantive paralegal experience; or

▶ Four years of substantive paralegal experience by December 31, 2000.

The NFPA has also prepared a Model Act for Paralegal Licensure that it recommends for adoption at the state level.

The NALA's Recognition of Competence

Canon 6 of the National Association of Legal Assistants' Code of Ethics and Professional Responsibility addresses paralegal competence for NALA members (See Exhibit 2-6).

Exhibit 2-6

From the NALA's Code of Ethics and Professional Responsibility

CANON 6

A paralegal must strive to maintain integrity and a high degree of competency through education and training with respect to professional responsibility, local rules and practice, and through continuing education in substantive areas of law to better assist the legal profession in fulfilling its duty to provide legal service.

NALA also promotes standards for paralegal competence in its NALA Model Standards and Guidelines for Utilization of Legal Assistants. The Model Standards included in that document are as follows:

Standards

A legal assistant should meet certain minimum qualifications. The following standards may be used to determine an individual's qualifications as a legal assistant:

1. Successful completion of the Certified Legal Assistant certifying (CLA) examination of the National Association of Legal Assistants;
2. Graduation from an ABA approved program of study for legal assistants;
3. Graduation from a course of study for legal assistants which is institutionally accredited but not ABA approved, and which requires not less than the equivalent of 60 semester hours of classroom study;
4. Graduation from a course of study for legal assistants, other than those set forth in (2) and (3) above, plus not less than six months of in-house training as a legal assistant;
5. A baccalaureate degree in any field, plus not less than six months in-house training as a legal assistant;
6. A minimum of three years of law-related experience under the supervision of an attorney, including at least six months of in-house training as a legal assistant; or
7. Two years of in-house training as a legal assistant.

NALA encourages paralegals to take the CLA examination to obtain a CLA designation as evidence of their competence.

CLA

As of February 1, 2006, there were 13,325 CLAs. In 2004, NALA registered the mark CP (Certified Paralegal) for those who meet the CLA requirements but prefer to use the term "paralegal."[19] Requirements for the CLA designation include minimum education and experience requirements and the successful completion of a two-day comprehensive examination based on federal law and procedure covering communications, ethics, human relations and interviewing techniques, judgment and analytical ability, legal research, and legal terminology. In addition, the test covers substantive areas of law, including the American legal system, administrative law, bankruptcy law, business organizations/corporate law, contracts, family law, criminal law and procedure, litigation, probate and estate planning, and real estate. An Advanced Paralegal Certification is also offered to paralegals who already have the CLA credential and wish to complete additional training in a specialty area pertinent to their work.

The CLA credential is awarded for five years, provided the CLA submits proof of participation in the required 50 hours of continuing legal education. Becoming a CLA is not a requirement in any jurisdiction in the United States. However, according to the NALA, surveys of legal assistants consistently show that paralegals with the CLA designation are better paid and better utilized in a field where attorneys are looking for a credible, dependable way to measure ability. The CLA credential is recognized by the ABA and by over 47 legal assistant organizations. Over 1,000 applicants per year take the NALA's CLA exam.

OF INTEREST

According to a recent survey, 79% of the responding paralegals who had passed a voluntary certification exam felt that it had helped their careers in terms of increased salary and opportunities.

—*Legal Assistant Today, May/June 2007*

Exhibit 2-7 is a chart depicting average salaries earned by paralegals with various certifications from 2006–2007.

At this time, no jurisdiction requires paralegals to pass either the CLA exam or the PACE, and few paralegal employers require passing either exam as a prerequisite to employment. Exhibit 2-8 is a summary of the CLA and PACE requirements.

Exhibit 2-7

Paralegal Certification–Average Salary

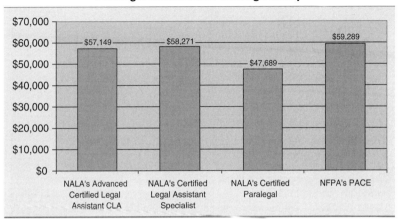

National Average Salary from the Legal Assistant Today 15th Annual Salary Survey, Legal Assistant Today, March/April 2007.

Exhibit 2-8

CLA Certification vs. PACE

CLA	PACE
• Is offered by the National Association of Legal Assistants (NALA).	• Is offered by the National Federation of Paralegal Associations (NFPA).
• Was developed by the NALA as a self-regulatory program that offers nationwide credentials for legal assistants.	• Was developed for the NFPA as a means for paralegals to validate their knowledge to themselves and their employers.
• Is not required by the NALA or any state regulating agency at this time.	• Is not required by the NFPA or any state regulating agency at this time.
• Is a two-day comprehensive exam covering communications, ethics, research, human relations and interviewing, judgment and analytical ability, and legal terminology as well as five mini-examinations covering the American legal system and four selected areas of substantive law.	• Is a two-tiered exam testing the critical-thinking skills and problem-solving abilities of paralegals (Tier One) and the paralegal's knowledge in specific legal practice areas (Tier Two).
	• May be taken by paralegals who have an associate's degree in paralegal studies from an accredited school plus six years paralegal experience; or who have a bachelor's degree and an accredited paralegal program and who have

Exhibit 2-8 (*Continued*)

CLA Certification vs. PACE

CLA	PACE
• May be taken by legal assistants who have graduated from an approved legal assistant program; who have a bachelor's degree in any field plus one year's work experience; or who have a high school diploma and seven year's work experience.	three years of experience; or who have completed a bachelor's degree in any course of study and who have at least two years of work experience.

The American Association for Paralegal Education Core Competencies

The American Association for Paralegal Education (AAfPE) is a national organization of paralegal educators. The AAfPE's primary purposes are to develop higher quality education for paralegal students and to be the main source of authority in paralegal academics. As that source of authority, the AAfPE has developed Paralegal Core Competencies that paralegals should possess.[20] The AAfPE recommends that all paralegal education programs should design their core courses to develop the following core competencies:

1. critical-thinking skills

2. organizational skills

3. general communication skills

4. legal research skills

5. legal writing skills

6. computer skills

7. interviewing and investigation skills

8. knowledge of the paralegal profession and ethical obligations

9. law office management skills

The full text of the AAfPE's recommended Core Competencies can be found at their Web site at www.aafpe.org.

Exhibit 2-9 is a summary of how each of the paralegal associations addresses paralegal competence within their definition of the term "paralegal."

Exhibit 2-9

Paralegal Competence as Addressed in the Definitions of the Terms "Paralegal" and "Legal Assistant"

THE ABA DEFINITION:

A legal assistant or paralegal is a person, qualified by education, training or work experience . . . who performs specifically delegated substantive legal work for which a lawyer is responsible.

THE NALA DEFINITON:

. . . Through formal education, training and experience, legal assistants have knowledge and expertise regarding the legal system and substantive and procedural law which qualify them to do work of a legal nature under the supervision of an attorney.

THE NFPA DEFINITION:

. . . A person qualified through education, training or work experience to perform substantive legal work that requires knowledge of legal concepts and is customarily but not exclusively performed by a lawyer. . . .

THE AAfPE DEFINITION:

Paralegals perform substantive and procedural legal work as authorized by law, which work, in the absence of the paralegal, would be performed by an attorney. Paralegals have knowledge of the law gained through education, or education and work experience, which qualifies them to perform legal work. Paralegals adhere to recognized ethical standards and rules of professional responsibility.

MAINTAINING COMPETENCE

Changes in the law and in the legal environment require paralegals to work to maintain their competence—usually through continuing legal education. Although there are no mandatory requirements for continuing legal education at this time, both national paralegal associations strongly recommend continuing education. A minimum number of hours of continuing legal education are required to maintain the registered paralegal status (for paralegals who pass the PACE) and the CLA credential (for paralegals who pass the CLA exam).

It has never been easier for paralegals to maintain competence in their profession. Although new laws are being adopted at a rapid rate and the legal environment is constantly changing, there are numerous CLE options available—even to busy paralegals. National, state, and local paralegal associations as well as private organizations offer continuing education courses. Paralegals are also often invited to attend many CLE opportunities that are designed for attorneys. CLE courses can be taken by attending seminars, by watching seminars on videos, by listening to audio tapes, and more and more over the Internet.

PARALEGAL SPECIALTIES AND SPECIAL CONCERNS

With the complexities of modern law, it would be nearly impossible for a single paralegal to be competent in every area of law. Each specialty for paralegals has it own subset of competencies. In the following section, we will discuss some of the unique knowledge and skills competent paralegals possess in the areas of litigation, probate and estate planning, corporate law, real estate law, family law, and criminal law.

Litigation Paralegal Competencies

Paralegals who specialize in litigation will need to be particularly familiar with the state statutes that are most pertinent to their practice, including the statute of limitations and court rules and procedures. Attorneys are often much more familiar with what needs to be done than the procedures for accomplishing the task within the court systems. Litigation paralegals need to be familiar with the procedures for obtaining service of process, scheduling depositions, filing suits with the courts, and accomplishing the many procedural tasks required to see a lawsuit to its successful completion.

Litigation paralegals must be especially familiar with the rules of ethics for remaining within the bounds of the law while providing zealous representation of clients. For example, it would be considered unethical for a paralegal to directly contact an adverse party in a lawsuit when that party is represented by counsel. A paralegal cannot coerce or persuade a client to commit perjury or provide false information to a court.

Some of the tasks that litigation paralegals must be competent to perform include:

- ▶ Research state and federal statutes, case law, and court rules.
- ▶ Draft motions, discovery documents, pleadings, and correspondence.
- ▶ Schedule depositions and prepare deposition summaries.
- ▶ Maintain litigation calendar and diary system with deadlines for responding to pleadings, court dates, statutes of limitations, etc.
- ▶ Interview clients and witnesses.
- ▶ Arrange for service of process.
- ▶ Retain investigators and assist with investigations.
- ▶ Retain outside investigator if necessary.
- ▶ Draft interrogatories, requests for admissions, requests for production of documents, and requests for examination or inspection.
- ▶ Assemble documents for trial.
- ▶ Arrange for expert witnesses.
- ▶ Analyze and summarize facts and evidence.
- ▶ Prepare chronologies from deposition transcripts, documents, and other factual records.
- ▶ Communicate with the client to keep the client informed on the status of the case.
- ▶ Assist the attorney and the client at trial.

Probate Paralegal Competencies

Probate paralegals must be familiar with the probate procedures of the local probate courts. Paralegals who work in the probate area must know which forms need to be completed and filed to probate an estate and how to complete those forms. Probate paralegals must be very detail oriented and able to work well with clients who may be under a certain amount of stress.

Some of the tasks that probate paralegals must be competent to perform include:

▶ Inventory safe deposit box.
▶ Order certified copies of documents from the probate court.
▶ Review wills.
▶ Draft and file documents to commence probate proceedings.
▶ Collect information about assets and arrange for appraisals when necessary.
▶ File life insurance claims and other claims for death benefits.
▶ Prepare income tax and gift tax returns for deceased and estate.
▶ Maintain bank accounts and trust accounts.
▶ Prepare documents to transfer real estate, securities, bank accounts, etc.
▶ Draft the final settlement of the estate and order for distribution.

Corporate Paralegal Competencies

Competent corporate paralegals must be familiar with the corporate laws in any state in which their corporate clients are incorporated. In addition, if the paralegal's employer is a publicly held corporation (or represents publicly held corporations), the corporate paralegal must have an understanding of state and federal securities laws.

Some of the tasks that corporate paralegals must be competent to perform include:

▶ Check name availability and reserve or register the corporate name with appropriate state authority.
▶ Draft and file articles or certificate of incorporation.
▶ Draft corporate bylaws.
▶ Draft notices of meetings of shareholders and directors.
▶ Prepare resolutions of shareholders and directors.
▶ Assemble and maintain corporate minute books.
▶ Apply for tax identification numbers.
▶ Prepare Sub S Election forms.
▶ Prepare and file certificates of assumed or fictitious names.
▶ Draft employment, confidentiality, and buy-sell agreements.
▶ Draft amendments to articles of incorporations and bylaws.
▶ Prepare stock certificates and documents required for stock transfers.
▶ Prepare disclosure documents for publicly held corporations as required by the securities regulations.
▶ Prepare agendas and attend and assist at corporate meetings.

Real Estate Paralegal Competencies

Real estate paralegals must be familiar with the laws concerning clear title and transfer of real estate in the jurisdictions in which they work. Their work often involves assisting with the transfer of real estate and helping to resolve title problems. Increasingly, real estate paralegals work to help clients comply with environmental regulations.

Some of the tasks that real estate paralegals must be competent to perform include:

▶ Draft the purchase agreement.
▶ Draft deeds.
▶ Arrange for title searches.
▶ Prepare drafts of title opinions.
▶ Prepare satisfaction of liens on property.
▶ Arrange for title policies.
▶ Draft loan documents, including agreement, promissory note, mortgage documents, etc.
▶ Prepare closing checklists and attend real estate closings.

Family Law Paralegal Competencies

Family law paralegals must have the interpersonal skills needed to deal with clients who may find themselves in stressful situations. Typically, clients who are in the midst of a divorce or other family trauma are not at their best. Family law paralegals must be familiar with the laws concerning divorce, adoptions, and guardianships.

Some of the tasks that family law paralegals must be competent to perform include:

▶ Meet with clients to obtain background information, including information on marriages, number and ages of children, sources of support, income, assets, liabilities, living arrangements, etc.
▶ Discuss options with clients including counseling, legal separation, reconciliation, and mediation.
▶ Prepare monthly income and expense sheet for client.
▶ Determine requirements for spousal and child support.
▶ Analyze the value of retirement benefits.
▶ Draft petition for dissolution of marriage or response to petition for dissolution.
▶ Draft discovery documents.
▶ Track important dates for filing responses to pleadings and for court dates.
▶ Draft the application for temporary relief and restraining order as needed.
▶ Draft stipulation and property settlement agreements.
▶ Draft the proposed judgment and decree.

Criminal Law Paralegal Competencies

Criminal law paralegals must be familiar with the rules of criminal procedure in the jurisdiction in which they work. They must be very familiar with criminal law procedures prior to, during, and after trial.

Some of the tasks that criminal law paralegals must be competent to perform include:

▶ Prepare the motion for bond reduction and file with the court.
▶ Arrange for bail for the client.
▶ Assist with the case investigation.
▶ Obtain police reports, witness interviews, and other discovery documents.
▶ Draft motions and other court documents.
▶ Draft trial memorandum.
▶ Assist at the trial.

■ CHAPTER SUMMARY

▶ Attorneys have an ethical duty to provide their clients with competent, diligent, and zealous representation.
▶ Competent representation requires the attorney to have legal knowledge, skill, thoroughness, and preparation at a level reasonably necessary for representation.
▶ Attorneys lacking the requisite level of knowledge can seek assistance from an expert or a more experienced attorney, educate him or herself as necessary, or decline the representation.
▶ Attorneys must undertake the necessary level of investigation and legal research to competently represent their clients.
▶ Attorneys maintain their competence through CLE courses.
▶ Attorneys must provide their clients with diligent representation by providing services within a reasonable time, attending promptly to legal matters, and making a commitment to achieve the client's legal objectives.
▶ Attorneys have an ethical duty to communicate to clients all pertinent facts required to enable the client to make the best possible decisions.
▶ Zealous representation requires attorneys to do everything legally and ethically possible to gain an acquittal for a defendant or otherwise promote their client's claims.
▶ A competent paralegal has a basic knowledge of the American legal system and possesses organization and management, communication, analytical, computer, legal research and investigation, and interpersonal skills.
▶ Mandatory requirements or standards for paralegal competence have not yet been established.
▶ Both of the national paralegal associations have set standards and guidelines for paralegal competence.
▶ The NFPA recommends that paralegals prove their competence by passing the PACE.
▶ The NALA recommends that paralegals show their competence by passing the CLA exam.

■ FREQUENTLY ASKED QUESTIONS

Do I need to pass a test to prove I am competent to work as a paralegal?

Probably not. Although most employers do not require their paralegals to be certified by a paralegal association, a growing number of employers do require their paralegals to be graduates of ABA-approved paralegal programs or to have four-year college degrees. Some surveys have shown that paralegals who have passed one of the NALA's CLA tests or the NFPA's PACE earn more on the average than paralegals who do not have such credentials.

What skills do I need to be a competent paralegal?

The skills you will need will depend on the specific requirements of your position but will probably include:

- The ability to organize and manage your workload, which may include several different ongoing matters. You will need the ability to set priorities, manage your time, and manage accurate calendaring, timekeeping and recordkeeping systems.

- The ability to communicate clearly and concisely both verbally and in writing with your coworkers, the attorneys you work for, and the clients you work with.

- Legal research and investigation skills are important to most paralegals. You cannot know all the answers, but you need to know how to find them.

- You will need the ability to work well with others—possibly a very diverse group of people: clients, attorneys, and other professionals. You will need the ability to put people at ease and earn their respect.

The attorney I just started working is not very organized. How can I help this disorganized attorney to provide clients with competent and diligent representation?

Attorneys often rely on their paralegals to keep them organized at the office and to ensure that they meet crucial deadlines and never miss a court date. You will want to diligently maintain a diary/calendar system. Never file away a piece of correspondence or a client file without first considering what followup must be done and making sure that the appropriate dates are noted on your calendar system. You must be aware of what the statute of limitations is for each case your attorney is working on and be sure that the proper action is taken before the statutory time period lapses. A missed date can be very costly to clients and attorneys if the statute of limitations period lapses before an action is filed.

Recently, I've been asked to help fill in for a real estate paralegal in our firm who has gone on maternity leave. I have my own work to do in the corporate department, and I am not that familiar with real estate procedures. The work is starting to pile up because I do not know what to do. I am afraid to ask the real estate attorneys for help because I do not know them well. What can I do?

Ask for help immediately. It's easy to procrastinate when you are unsure of what to do. However, your work as a paralegal makes it extremely important that you not do that. If you are uncomfortable talking with the real estate attorneys, talk with your immediate supervising attorney or office manager immediately. It is much better to admit you are unfamiliar with the work and ask for help than to have to explain when costly mistakes are made because you were not acting diligently.

As a paralegal, will I have to pay for my own continuing education classes?

It depends on who you work for. According to a recent survey, nearly 80% of the responding paralegals reported that their employers paid the full cost, or at least shared the cost, of continuing legal education classes. Less than 20% of the responding paralegals indicated that they had to pay the entire cost of their continuing education.[21]

■ ENDNOTES

1. *Spangler v. Sellers*, 5 F. 882 (C.C.S.D. Ohio 1881).
2. *Baird v. Pace*, 752 P2d 507 (Ariz. 1987).
3. In *Hawkins*, 502 N.W.2d 770 (Minn. 1993).
4. *People v. Felker*, 770 P.2d 402 (Colo. 1989).
5. Muse v. St. Paul Fire and Marine Insurance Company, 328 So. 2d 698 (La. App. 1st Cir. 1976) (2004).
6. Comment [5] to Rule 1.1 of the Model Rules of Professional Conduct.
7. *Collas v. Garnick*, 624 a.2D 120 (Pa).
8. *Horne v. Peckham*, 97 Cal.App.3d 404 (1979).
9. Comment [6] to Rule 1.1 of Model Rules of Professional Conduct (2004).
10. Comment [1] to Rule 1.3 of Model Rules of Professional Conduct (2004).
11. Comment [1] to Rule 1.3 of Model Rules of Professional Conduct (2004).
12. Comment [1] to Rule 1.3 of the Model Rules of Professional Conduct (2004).
13. The *Merriam-Webster Dictionary*, Merriam-Webster, Incorporated (1995).
14. Comment [1] to Rule 1.3 of the Model Rules of Professional Conduct (2004); DR 7-101(a) of the ABA Model Code of Professional Responsibility (1983).
15. Canon 7 of the Code of Professional Responsibility.
16. National Association of Legal Assistants 2004 National Utilization and Compensation Survey Report (2004).
17. National Association of Legal Assistants, 2004 National Utilization and Compensation Survey Report (2004).
18. *The Paralegal's Partner in Progress*, from the NFPA's Web site at www.paralegals.org (March 1998).
19. Professional Certification, www.nala.org, accessed July 30, 2006.
20. Web site of the American Association for Paralegal Education, www.aafpe.org, accessed September 17, 2006.
21. *Legal Assistant Today*, "15th Annual Salary Survey," March/April 2007.

Chapter 3

Maintaining Integrity and Public Respect for the Legal Profession

"No man can ever be a truly great lawyer, who is not in every sense of the word a good man. . . ."

— G. Sharswood, *Professional Ethics* (1844)

■ PART I: INTEGRITY AND RESPECT FOR THE LEGAL PROFESSION

Judges, attorneys, paralegals, and other legal professionals all have a duty to maintain the integrity and public respect for the legal profession. This includes following the applicable rules of ethics, remaining honest and always staying within the law, and reporting any serious incidents of **misconduct** by attorneys or other legal professionals. Legal professionals must also strive to improve the legal system and offer assistance wherever possible, especially in offering their services **pro bono.**

The rules of ethics discussed here in Part I are designed to maintain the integrity of the legal profession. These rules concern bar admissions and disciplinary matters, misconduct, reporting professional misconduct, and pro bono work.

Part II examines many of the same issues from the paralegal's perspective, beginning with a look at recommendations by the paralegal associations for maintaining integrity and public respect for the paralegal profession and the legal profession in general. Next, the focus will be on misconduct within the profession and a paralegal's ethical duty to report the misconduct of attorneys and other paralegals. Part II concludes with a look at pro bono opportunities for paralegals.

BAR ADMISSION

Attorneys must be licensed and admitted to the bar of any jurisdiction in which they practice. The state bar associations and legislatures work to ensure the integrity of the legal profession by setting competence and moral character standards for bar applicants.

The Bar Application

Each applicant to the bar must file a written request for admission to the bar with the appropriate authority. The applicant must respond completely and truthfully to each question asked on the application and in any subsequent hearings or other proceedings held in connection with the application process. Falsifying an application for bar admission may result in failure to be admitted to the bar or later disbarment. In *People v. Culpepper*, the attorney-respondent was disbarred after it was determined that he had falsified his college records to obtain admission into law school and then again lied in his application to the bar. The Supreme Court of Colorado found that the respondent's conduct was "contrary to the high standards of honesty, justice and morality required for lawyers. . . ."[1]

Good Moral Character Prerequisite

Certification of the applicant's good moral character is required as a prerequisite for admission to the bar in every state. The burden is on the applicant to furnish the committee with evidence of his or her good moral character and general fitness to practice law.[2] Good moral character is a requirement to protect the public and to protect the bar's image as well as the image of the profession. It is believed better to prevent future problems caused by an immoral applicant by denying admission rather than to remedy a problem after it occurs and a client has been victimized.

Determining whether an applicant has *good moral character* can be problematic. A series of questions, determined to give guidance to the admission review board, is included in the application. Some of the *red flags* on applications that may be considered an indication of a lack of good moral character include:

- ▶ misconduct in employment.
- ▶ acts involving dishonesty, fraud, deceit, or misrepresentation.
- ▶ abuse of legal process.
- ▶ neglect of financial responsibilities.
- ▶ neglect of professional obligations.
- ▶ violation of an order of a court, including child support orders.
- ▶ evidence of serious mental or emotional instability.
- ▶ evidence of drug or alcohol dependence or abuse.
- ▶ denial of admission to the bar in another jurisdiction on character and fitness grounds.
- ▶ disciplinary action by a lawyer disciplinary agency or other professional disciplinary agency of any jurisdiction.

Chapter 3

Any character traits considered in denying admission to a bar applicant must have a rational connection to the applicant's present fitness to practice law and must relate to the state's legitimate interest in protecting prospective clients and the system of justice. In Minnesota, the Board of Law Examiners rejected the application of an individual who filed bankruptcy shortly after his graduation from law school—a decision that was supported by the Supreme Court of Minnesota. It was the board's opinion that the applicant did not make every effort possible to pay his creditors but rather that he filed bankruptcy merely to avoid his obligation to repay his student loans.

One of the more infamous cases concerning a rejected bar applicant involved Matthew Hale. Hale graduated from law school and passed the Illinois Bar Exam. In 1999, when he applied for admission to the Illinois Bar, Hale was an admitted racist and the Supreme Leader of the World Church of the Creator. The church's followers admired Adolf Hitler and believed that "the most deadly enemies of the White Race are first of all the Jews, and secondarily, all the other mud races who are competing for food and living space on this limited planet." Hale's bar application was rejected because of his overt racist opinions and beliefs. The Illinois Supreme Court's Committee on Character and Fitness found that Hale did not possess the character and fitness required for admission. Hale appealed the decision, claiming that he could support the U.S. Constitution, the Constitution of Illinois, and the Illinois Rules of Professional Conduct. He also claimed that he had committed no felony and that he did not condone violence. For a time, Hale drew support from a few defenders of his First Amendment rights who felt that he should not be rejected for expressing his personal views, no matter how repugnant they may be. The majority of Hale's supporters abandoned his quest to become an attorney when Benjamin Nathanial Smith, a friend, supporter, and former church member, went on a three-day shooting rampage aimed at African Americans, Jews, and Asians during the Fourth of July weekend in 1999, killing two people and wounding nine others. Hale was not admitted to the bar and is currently serving a 40-year prison term for soliciting an undercover FBI informant to murder a federal judge in an unrelated matter.

OF INTEREST

"The purpose of lawyer disciplinary proceedings is not primarily to punish the lawyer but rather to maintain appropriate standards of professional conduct to safeguard the public, to preserve the integrity of the legal profession, and to deter other lawyers from engaging in violations of the standards of the profession."

—Louisiana State Bar Association v. Guidry, 571 So.2d 161 (La. 1990)

DISCIPLINARY MATTERS

The legal disciplinary system is designed to safeguard the public and maintain the integrity of the legal profession.[3] Attorneys have an ethical duty of candor to any disciplinary board with jurisdiction as well as the duty to cooperate fully with any disciplinary proceeding. The failure to respond truthfully and fully in connection with a disciplinary proceeding constitutes a violation of the rules of ethics. An attorney's false and misleading information to bar authorities constitutes a separate basis for discipline.[4]

When a serious charge has been brought by a disciplinary agency against an attorney, the attorney must respond, cooperate, and answer any questions put forth by the board in their investigation. Under certain circumstances, an attorney can claim the Fifth Amendment privilege and refuse to answer certain questions that may incriminate him or her. However, when this is done, the disciplinary agency may impose appropriate sanctions based on the evidence presented.

■ MISCONDUCT

The legal profession is largely self-governing. This means that it is attorneys who are responsible for establishing ethical guidelines for members of their profession to follow. They are also responsible for policing their profession and handling misconduct among its members. The rules of professional conduct of each state determine exactly what is considered to be misconduct. In states that follow the Model Rules of Professional Conduct, the following actions are considered to be misconduct:

1. violating any of the rules of professional conduct.

2. the commission of certain criminal acts.

3. dishonesty, fraud, deceit, or misrepresentation.

4. conduct that is prejudicial to the administration of justice.

5. stating or implying the ability to improperly influence a government agency or official.

6. assisting a judge or judicial officer in the violation of the rules of judicial conduct.

Violation of the Rules of Professional Conduct

An attorney's first professional obligation is to obey the rules of professional ethics of the jurisdictions in which the attorney is licensed to practice. Any violation of the rules, or assisting another in violating the rules, is considered misconduct.

Criminal Acts

Attorneys may be disciplined for criminal conduct, even if it is unrelated to their practice of law. The reasoning behind this rule is that to allow attorneys to break the law without discipline from the bar association leads to loss of respect for the legal profession itself.

The commission of crimes, especially those dealing with dishonesty, fraud, deceit, misrepresentation, or others that adversely affect the attorney's fitness to practice law, may be punished by both the criminal courts and by the bar association or another disciplinary agency.

CASE ON POINT

In the disciplinary proceeding In re *Brown, 674 So.2d 243 (La. 1996)*, it was found that the attorney being disciplined had violated the Rules of Professional Conduct, and she was disbarred after being convicted of negligent homicide for shooting her roommate during an apparent argument.

Dishonesty, Fraud, Deceit, or Misrepresentation

"Dishonest conduct by an attorney with his own client goes to the very core of a lawyer's fitness to practice law."[5] Dishonesty, fraud, deceit, and misrepresentation are prohibited by Section 8.4 of the Model Rules as well as several other sections of the Model Rules. Rule 8.4 provides that lawyers shall not knowingly (a) make a false statement of material fact or law to a third person or (b) fail to disclose a material fact when disclosure is necessary to avoid assisting a criminal or fraudulent act by a client, unless disclosure is prohibited by Rule 1.6 regarding client confidentiality.

Because public confidence is so vital to the legal profession, and public confidence is easily shaken by the dishonest action of attorneys, the state disciplinary boards tend to come down hard on attorneys who have been dishonest with their clients or with the courts. As stated by the Mississippi Supreme Court, "This Court will not hesitate to impose substantial sanctions upon an attorney for any act which evinces want of personal honesty and integrity or renders such attorney unworthy of public confidence."[6]

CASE ON POINT

In a 2002 case in Louisiana, an attorney was disbarred for assisting his paralegal in the unauthorized practice of law and deceiving his clients into thinking his paralegal was an attorney.

—*In re Brown, NO. 01-B-2863, 2002 WL 449793 (LA. March 22, 2002)*

Conduct Prejudicial to the Administration of Justice

Attorneys must not engage in any conduct that could be considered prejudicial to the administration of justice. Violation of this broad rule often involves litigation and court proceedings, although it may be applied in a wide variety of contexts. Some examples of violations of this rule include obstructing the discovery process, lying to the court to cover error, appearing in court while intoxicated, and filing false and fraudulent pleadings.

Sexual misconduct also falls under this rule. According to the ABA Committee on Ethics and Professional Responsibility, "A sexual relationship between lawyer and client may involve unfair exploitation of the lawyer's fiduciary position, and/or significantly impair a lawyer's ability to represent the client competently, and therefore may violate both the Model Rules of Professional Conduct and the Model Code of Professional Responsibility."[7] Pursuant to the Model Rules of Professional Conduct, a lawyer shall not have sexual relations with a client unless a consensual sexual relationship existed between them when the client-lawyer relationship commenced. As of 2003, ten states had adopted rules that explicitly prohibit sexual relationships between lawyers and clients.[8]

OF INTEREST

In a 1993 nationwide survey, 32% of the attorneys who responded indicated that they knew of at least one attorney who had engaged in sexual relations with a client.

—*Dan S. Murrell et al., Loose Canons: A National Survey of Attorney-Client Sexual Involvement, 23 Memphis St. U.L. Rev. 48 (1993)*

Stated or Implied Ability to Improperly Influence a Government Agency or Official

Even the suggestion that one may be able to improperly influence, or bribe, a government or judicial official is a violation of the rules of ethics. An attorney may not suggest that he or she can obtain results through improper government influence or political power. In one case in Indiana, an attorney was disbarred for several violations, including telling his client that he was a close friend of the chief justice of the U.S. Supreme Court and that his friendship would influence a successful outcome of the client's case.[9]

Assisting Judge or Judicial Officer in Violation of Rules of Judicial Conduct

Any action taken by an attorney to assist a judge or judicial officer to violate any of the rules of judicial conduct that apply to judges and judicial officers is considered unethical and in violation of Model Rule 8.4.

There are differences in how the states define "misconduct." Exhibit 3-1 shows examples of how the rules of New York and Ohio treat misconduct.

Exhibit 3-1

From the New York Lawyer's Code of Professional Responsibility

DR 1-102 [1200.3] Misconduct.

A. A lawyer or law firm shall not:

1. Violate a Disciplinary Rule.
2. Circumvent a Disciplinary Rule through actions of another.
3. Engage in illegal conduct that adversely reflects on the lawyer's honesty, trustworthiness, or fitness as a lawyer.
4. Engage in conduct involving dishonesty, fraud, deceit, or misrepresentation.
5. Engage in conduct that is prejudicial to the administration of justice.
6. Unlawfully discriminate in the practice of law, including in hiring, promoting, or otherwise determining conditions of employment, on the basis of age, race, creed, color, national origin, sex, disability, marital status, or sexual orientation. Where there is a tribunal with jurisdiction to hear a complaint, if timely brought, other than a Departmental Disciplinary Committee, a complaint based on unlawful discrimination shall be brought before such tribunal in the first instance. A certified copy of a determination by such a tribunal, which has become final and enforceable, and as to which the right to judicial or appellate review has been exhausted, finding that the lawyer has engaged in an unlawful discriminatory practice shall constitute *prima facie* evidence of professional misconduct in a disciplinary proceeding.
7. Engage in any other conduct that adversely reflects on the lawyer's fitness as a lawyer.

From the Ohio Rules of Professional Conduct

Rule 8.4: Misconduct

It is professional misconduct for a lawyer to do any of the following:

(a) violate or attempt to violate the Ohio Rules of Professional Conduct, *knowingly* assist or induce another to do so, or do so through the acts of another;

(b) commit an *illegal* act that reflects adversely on the lawyer's honesty or trustworthiness;

(c) engage in conduct involving dishonesty, *fraud*, deceit, or misrepresentation;

(d) engage in conduct that is prejudicial to the administration of justice;

(e) state or imply an ability to influence improperly a government agency or official or to achieve results by means that violate the Ohio Rules of Professional Conduct or other law;

(f) *knowingly* assist a judge or judicial officer in conduct that is a violation of the Ohio Rules of Professional Conduct, the applicable rules of judicial conduct, or other law;

(g) engage, in a professional capacity, in conduct involving discrimination prohibited by law because of race, color, religion, age, gender, sexual orientation, national origin, marital status, or disability;

(h) engage in any other conduct that adversely reflects on the lawyer's fitness to practice law.

REPORTING MISCONDUCT

Because law is a self-governing profession responsible for policing itself, it is mandatory that attorneys report misconduct by their fellow attorneys to the state bar disciplinary agency, a peer review agency, or another proper authority as designated by the pertinent rules of ethics. Rule 8.3(a) of the Model Rules specifically states that an attorney who has knowledge of another attorney's violation of the Rules of Professional Conduct shall inform the appropriate professional authority.

Conduct that Must Be Reported

Attorneys are not required to report all types of misconduct they witness, but they are required to report a violation:

1. that the attorney has knowledge of;
2. that raises a substantial question as to the other attorney's honesty, trustworthiness, or fitness as a lawyer in other respects and
3. that is not protected by the rules of confidentiality.

The knowledge that the attorney has must be real. While it does not require the attorney to have all knowledge necessary to prosecute the matter, it does require that the attorney's knowledge of the misconduct amount to more than simple rumor or suspicion. To report all rumors or suspicion would mean unfair harassment to attorneys who may be victims of gossip.

Attorneys are only required to report misconduct of a serious nature. The attorney's duty to report misconduct is limited to actions that "a self-regulating profession must vigorously endeavor to prevent."[10] Exhibit 3-2 is a checklist indicating when attorneys must report misconduct.

Exhibit 3-2

When an Attorney Must Report Misconduct

Attorneys have an obligation to report misconduct when:

- The attorney has knowledge of the misconduct.
- The attorney's knowledge is not protected as a confidence or secret.
- The conduct violated a disciplinary rule.
- The violation raises a substantial question as to honesty, trustworthiness, or fitness to practice law.

Preserving Client Confidences

So important is preserving client confidences that an attorney is prohibited from reporting misconduct if doing so would breach a duty of client confidentiality.

The information protected under client confidentiality is very broad, and at times, the attorney may be required to get permission from any client involved in the misconduct before reporting it.

Failure to Report Misconduct

Although rarely pursued, an attorney's failure to report misconduct is in itself misconduct. In one case before the Illinois Supreme Court, an attorney was suspended from practice for one year for failing to report the serious misconduct of another attorney of which he had knowledge.[11]

At times, it may be appropriate to take measures short of filing a disciplinary complaint against another attorney. For lawyers who are struggling with alcohol or drug abuse who have not stepped over the line to serious misconduct, an intervention with a bar-related lawyer assistance program may be an option. Lawyer assistance programs may intervene at the request of an attorney's family, friends, or colleagues.

Of Interest

The ABA estimates that 15% to 20% of lawyers suffer from alcoholism or substance abuse—nearly twice the rates of the general population.

—*Janet Piper Voss, Lawyers' Assistance Program Celebrates 25 Years, CBA Record,* October 2005

Reporting Judicial Misconduct

Judges also have the ethical duty to report attorney misconduct to the proper disciplinary board, and attorneys are responsible for reporting judicial misconduct to the proper authority. The type of judicial misconduct that must be reported is limited to violations that raise a substantial question as to the judge's fitness for office.

PRO BONO SERVICE

Access to the legal system for all Americans is something members of the legal community aspire to. Attorneys contribute to this ideal by providing **pro bono** services. The term "pro bono" means "for the good; used to describe work or services (e.g., legal services) done or performed free of charge."[12] Attorneys have an ethical duty to volunteer their time to provide legal services to the poor and to charitable organizations. The codes of ethics in most jurisdictions state that attorneys should aspire to render pro bono services by rendering a certain number of hours of pro bono services per year to:

1. persons of limited means or

2. charitable, religious, civic, community, governmental, and educational organizations that address the needs of persons of limited means.

Rules concerning pro bono activities are aspirational. That means that attorneys should strive to achieve these goals, but the rules are not enforceable. The Model Rules of Professional Conduct clearly state that attorneys should contribute at least 50 hours of service each year to pro bono activities, but this rule is not enforceable by disciplinary action.

Chapter 3

PART II: FROM THE PARALEGAL'S PERSPECTIVE

Although attorneys are typically responsible for the ethical conduct of the paralegals they supervise, paralegals must follow their own set of ethical guidelines and rules and do their part to maintain the integrity of the legal profession in general and the paralegal profession in particular. As a paralegal, you must be certain your actions maintain and build on the integrity and public perception of the paralegal profession. You must avoid any form of misconduct and report serious misconduct you witness to the appropriate authorities. You must also do your part to make our legal system accessible to everyone, including those who cannot afford to pay for legal services.

A QUESTION OF ETHICS

Suppose you are a paralegal in the corporate department of a law firm in your hometown. You have just finished working on a huge merger deal. You and your coworker, Diane, another paralegal, have made a significant contribution to the successful closing of the deal, and you are working on the final documentation and billing.

You are filing away copies of the final bill when you notice Diane has considerably more billable time on the file than you do. You know that this is not correct. You have worked side by side with Diane and, in fact, you are sure you put in more time on the file than she did. When you ask Diane about it, she just shrugs and says something about needing more billable hours to reach her quota for the year. "With a bill this size, no one will notice if I add a few hours." Her padding the bill has actually amounted to more than $4,000. Your supervising attorney has already signed off on the bill with barely a glance, and the bill will leave the office by the end of the week. What, if anything, should you do?

Answer and Discussion

As a paralegal, you have an ethical duty to report certain serious misconduct of both attorneys and paralegals. Diane's padding of the bill is misconduct. It is dishonest, unethical, and an attempt to cheat your client out of $4,000. If you have a good working relationship with Diane, you may want to talk with her and urge her to resubmit her hours fairly and honestly. If you do not want to talk with Diane or if Diane refuses to change her hours, you should report her behavior to your supervising attorney on the merger. The supervising attorney is responsible for any misconduct by Diane, and both Diane and your supervising attorney could face serious consequences if the dishonest billing ever came to light.

MAINTAINING THE INTEGRITY OF THE PARALEGAL PROFESSION

Every working paralegal has a responsibility to all members of the paralegal profession. You are responsible for conducting yourself in a professional and ethical manner. Every paralegal represents the entire paralegal profession through his or her behavior.

You can help to maintain the integrity of the profession by always acting in a professional manner and by following the code of ethics of any paralegal association to which you belong. Because your supervising attorneys are responsible for your ethical behavior, you must conduct yourself in a manner that will never cause your supervising attorneys to violate their codes of ethics. Exhibit 3-3 is an excerpt from the NFPA Model Code of Ethics that sets forth the NFPA's rules for maintaining a high level of personal and professional integrity.

Exhibit 3-3

From the NFPA Model Code of Ethics and Professional Responsibility and Guidelines for Enforcement

1.2 A PARALEGAL SHALL MAINTAIN A HIGH LEVEL OF PERSONAL AND PROFESSIONAL INTEGRITY.

ETHICAL CONSIDERATIONS

EC-1.2(a)   A paralegal shall not engage in any ex parte communications involving the courts or any other adjudicatory body in an attempt to exert undue influence or to obtain advantage or the benefit of only one party.

EC-1.2(b)	A paralegal shall not communicate, or cause another to communicate, with a party the paralegal knows to be represented by a lawyer in a pending matter without the prior consent of the lawyer representing such other party.
EC-1.2(c)	A paralegal shall ensure that all timekeeping and billing records prepared by the paralegal are thorough, accurate, honest, and complete.
EC-1.2(d)	A paralegal shall not knowingly engage in fraudulent billing practices. Such practices may include, but are not limited to: inflation of hours billed to a client or employer; misrepresentation of the nature of tasks performed; and/or submission of fraudulent expense and disbursement documentation.
EC-1.2(e)	A paralegal shall be scrupulous, thorough and honest in the identification and maintenance of all funds, securities, and other assets of a client and shall provide accurate accounting as appropriate.
EC-1.2(f)	A paralegal shall advise the proper authority of non-confidential knowledge of any dishonest or fraudulent acts by any person pertaining to the handling of the funds, securities or other assets of a client. The authority to whom the report is made shall depend on the nature and circumstances of the possible misconduct (e.g., ethics committees of law firms, corporations and/or paralegal associations, local or state bar associations, local prosecutors, administrative agencies, etc.). Failure to report such knowledge is in itself misconduct and shall be treated as such under these rules.

Chapter 3

Disbarred Attorneys as Paralegals

While most paralegals strive to uphold the integrity of their profession, they are presented with a unique dilemma—disbarred attorneys who are hired as paralegals. In some instances, attorneys who have been disbarred or suspended are hired by law firms to work as paralegals. They might work under the close supervision of attorneys who are willing to give the disbarred attorney a chance to maintain their livelihood and keep their legal knowledge current until their licenses are reinstated. However, in some instances—in the worst case scenarios—attorneys who have been disbarred for a breach of ethics continue practicing without their licenses by calling themselves paralegals. They work with little or no supervision and often continue the same unethical behavior that got them suspended or disbarred in the first place. Basically, they give paralegals a bad name.

Recognizing the problems associated with hiring disbarred attorneys as paralegals, the NFPA has taken a stand. During its 2001 spring convention, the NFPA adopted a resolution submitted by the Georgia Association of Paralegals. The NFPA resolution states, in part, that "It is in the best interest of the entire paralegal profession that no suspended or disbarred attorney work in the capacity and/or hold the title of a paralegal or engage in and/or perform any substantive legal work."[13]

Attorneys also recognize there is a problem with disbarred attorneys working as paralegals. Several states have either placed total bans on hiring disbarred attorneys as paralegals or they have placed restrictions on the practice.

PARALEGAL MISCONDUCT

Paralegal misconduct occurs whenever a paralegal violates any applicable code of ethics. Paralegal misconduct is defined as "the knowing or unknowing commission of an act that is in direct violation of those Canons and Ethical Considerations of any and all applicable codes and/or rules of conduct."[14] This definition includes any violation of the applicable paralegal codes of ethics (the code of ethics adopted by any paralegal association to which the paralegal belongs) as well as the pertinent sections of the code of ethics binding on the attorneys in the jurisdiction in which the paralegal works.

Although the NALA does not specifically address misconduct in its Code of Ethics and Professional Responsibility or Model Standards and Guidelines, Canon 9 of the NALA Code of Ethics does state that "A paralegal must do all other things incidental, necessary, or expedient to the attainment of the ethics and responsibilities as defined by statute or rule of court."[15] Furthermore, Canon 10 of the code states that "A paralegal's conduct is guided by bar associations' codes of professional responsibility and rules of professional conduct."[16] Canons 9 and 10 are set forth in Exhibit 3-4.

Exhibit 3-4

CANON 9.

A paralegal must do all other things incidental, necessary, or expedient for the attainment of the ethics and responsibilities as defined by statute or rule of court.

CANON 10.

A paralegal's conduct is guided by bar associations' codes of professional responsibility and rules of professional conduct.

■ THE PARALEGAL'S DUTY TO REPORT MISCONDUCT

To maintain the integrity of the legal profession in general and the paralegal profession in particular, you have an ethical duty to report certain serious misconduct, by paralegals or attorneys, to the proper authorities.

Reporting Paralegal Misconduct

As members of the legal service team, paralegals should police themselves in order to continue to grow and gain respectability. As a paralegal, you have an ethical duty to report the misconduct of other paralegals under certain circumstances. This concept is supported in the code of ethics of both national associations as well as the codes of local associations.

Exactly what type of paralegal misconduct must be reported to authorities often remains a judgment call on behalf of the paralegal. It is clearly your ethical duty to report the misconduct of other paralegals when that misconduct may be harmful to clients, employers, or the paralegal profession as a whole, especially when that misconduct is habitual. Some types of behavior that may require reporting include the unauthorized practice of law by a paralegal, improper contact with an opposing party or witnesses in litigation by a paralegal, unfair timekeeping, theft or misappropriation of a client's funds, or other fraudulent or dishonest acts in violation of the code of ethics of paralegals or attorneys.

The NFPA Model Code of Ethics and Professional Responsibility requires reporting of the following types of paralegal misconduct:

(a) any action of another legal professional that clearly demonstrates fraud, deceit, dishonesty, or misrepresentation

(b) dishonest or fraudulent acts by any person pertaining to the handling of the funds, securities, or other assets of a client

If you have witnessed unethical behavior of another paralegal, you may be *required* to report that behavior under the code of ethics of the paralegal association you belong to. The Model Code of Ethics and Professional Responsibility of the NFPA describes several different types of unethical paralegal behavior that must be reported and further states that "Failure to report such knowledge is in itself misconduct and shall be treated as such under these rules."[17]

If you are ever required to report misconduct of an attorney or paralegal outside of your law firm or legal department, you must remember client confidences and be sure you never break any rules of client confidentiality.

If you are unsure if the behavior you have witnessed must be reported, it is best to research the matter to find out. You can usually consult with your supervising attorney or your local or national paralegal association.

If you have witnessed unethical behavior by a paralegal, and you have determined that you are required to report the behavior, you must next decide to whom that behavior should be reported. Unlike attorneys, paralegals have several options in this area. At times, it may be most appropriate to report the behavior to your supervising attorney. If your supervising attorney is also responsible for supervising the paralegal you suspect of misconduct, you must remember that he or she could be held responsible for that paralegal's misconduct. The circumstances may also warrant reporting the misconduct to your paralegal manager or to an ethics committee within your law firm or corporate legal department. At other times, the behavior and circumstances may require you to go to the paralegal association, local or state bar association, or even to the local law enforcement.

Who you report misconduct to will depend on the type of misconduct and the circumstances surrounding it. For example, if you witness a paralegal coworker stealing funds from a client trust account and falsifying documents to cover it up, you definitely must report this behavior. The conduct should be reported to your supervising attorney or an ethics committee within your law firm or corporate legal department, depending on your employer's policy. If you are in need of guidance, contact your local paralegal association or its affiliated national association.

If you witness misconduct by a paralegal from another law firm, your actions will be different. For example, if you are working on a civil litigation matter and you have knowledge that a paralegal for the opposition has destroyed documents that your law firm has requested in discovery, you will need to take action. First, talk to your supervising attorney. Your supervising attorney may decide the paralegal's supervising attorney should be reported for disciplinary action—either for conspiring with the paralegal to destroy the documents or for lack of supervision. You then may want to contact your local paralegal association to see if there is any further action you should take. If the other paralegal is a member of that association, he or she may be subject to discipline from that association. Exhibit 3-5 is a list of suggested actions you can take if you witness misconduct.

Exhibit 3-5

What You Can Do If You Witness Misconduct

- Talk to the paralegal or attorney you suspect of misconduct–perhaps you have misunderstood what you witnessed.
- Consult your office policy–does your office have a policy for reporting unethical behavior?
- Talk to your supervising attorney about it.
- Talk to your paralegal manager or office manager about it.
- Report the misconduct to your office ethics committee.
- Report the misconduct to your paralegal association (if the suspected individual is a paralegal).
- Report the misconduct to the bar association disciplinary agency (if the suspected individual is an attorney).
- Report serious, criminal misconduct to the appropriate law enforcement authority.

As discussed previously, enforcing ethical paralegal behavior is somewhat more problematic than enforcing the codes of ethics for attorneys. Attorneys must be licensed to practice law and they must be members of the bar. In becoming a member of the bar, they agree to abide by the applicable code of ethics. If an attorney does not abide by the pertinent rules of ethics, he or she can be disbarred and lose the privilege to practice law. Bar associations and the judiciary have authority over the ethical behavior of attorneys.

Paralegals, on the other hand, are not licensed. Although you may subscribe to a code of ethics of the paralegal association you belong to, there is no paralegal association that has authority over you and no court of law that has jurisdiction over the ethics of paralegals, unless there is criminal activity involved.

The NFPA recognizes this dilemma and also recognizes the necessity for enforcement of its Code of Ethics and Professional Responsibility. In 1997, the NFPA drafted Model Guidelines for the Enforcement of the Model Code of Ethics and Professional Responsibility. These guidelines, which may be adopted by paralegal associations, provide for the creation of a Disciplinary Committee and set forth procedures for reporting alleged violations of the Model Code and Disciplinary Rules. Under the Model Guidelines for Enforcement, paralegals who witness misconduct can report that misconduct confidentially to a Disciplinary Committee. The Disciplinary Committee then investigates the complaint and takes such further action as may be required. The report of misconduct can be made to the committee anonymously under certain circumstances. The Guidelines for Enforcement provide for the following possible sanctions that may be imposed on a paralegal upon a finding of misconduct:

1. letter of reprimand to the Responding Party; counseling;
2. attendance at an ethics course approved by the Tribunal; probation;
3. suspension of license/authority to practice; revocation of license/authority to practice;
4. imposition of a fine; assessment of costs; or
5. in the instance of criminal activity, referral to the appropriate authority.

Obviously, a paralegal cannot be disciplined by an association to which he or she does not belong, and paralegals are not required to belong to the NFPA or to any paralegal association. However, in the event that paralegals are regulated in the future, either by licensing, certification, or registration, the Model Disciplinary Rules may serve as a model that will be adopted by any paralegal regulation board or agency for enforcing the adopted code of ethics for paralegals. The NFPA Guidelines for the Enforcement of the Model Code of Ethics and Professional Responsibility can be found on the NPFA's Web site at www.paralegals.org.

Reporting Attorney Misconduct

One of the most difficult ethical dilemmas paralegals may encounter is discovering unethical behavior by one of the attorneys they work for. Suppose you witness one of the attorneys you work for shredding documents that have been requested by the opposing counsel in a civil lawsuit or that you discover him or her borrowing money from a client trust account. Is it unethical to remain silent? Yes. Paralegals have an ethical duty to report misconduct of attorneys. The code of ethics for attorneys in nearly every jurisdiction requires attorneys to report misconduct by other attorneys. This duty then extends to paralegals. A paralegal who reports the misconduct of her employers may be protected from employer retaliation under state or federal **whistle-blower acts.**

There are measures short of reporting an attorney to the state's professional authority that you can take if you witness unethical behavior by your attorney employer. Depending on your relationship, you may want to discuss the behavior with the attorney who appears to be acting unethically. Are there circumstances you are unaware of? Possibly the action is not, in fact, unethical. If it becomes clear after addressing the attorney that the actions are unethical and/or illegal, perhaps the matter can be handled by others within the firm. You may feel it is more appropriate to bring the matter to the attention of the appropriate individual or committee within the law firm. If this still does not produce positive results, the attorney should be reported to the ethics committee of the state bar association.

To date, there have been no cases involving a paralegal's duty to report unethical or illegal behavior. However, it remains clear that if questioned by a court or an ethics committee of the state bar, you have a duty to report the full truth concerning any actions you have knowledge about. Any time you are involved in testifying or reporting unethical attorney behavior, you must use extreme caution not to divulge confidential client information.

If you find yourself in a serious ethical dilemma that may require reporting an attorney, you may want to seek independent legal advice on the proper steps to take. Your paralegal association may also be able to help.

▪ PRO BONO FOR PARALEGALS

Pro bono work is not only an ethical duty for paralegals, but it is also an opportunity. Many paralegals report that the pro bono work they have done has been the most rewarding work of their careers.

The ABA as well as both national paralegal associations and most local associations promote pro bono work for paralegals. The ABA's Model Guidelines for Utilization of Paralegal Services includes the following guideline:

> *GUIDELINE 10: A lawyer who employs a paralegal should*
> *facilitate the paralegal's participation in appropriate continuing*
> *education and pro bono publico activities.*

The NFPA provides for pro bono work in its Model Code as follows in Exhibit 3-6:

Exhibit 3-6

From the NFPA Model Code of Ethics and Professional Responsibility

1.4 A PARALEGAL SHALL SERVE THE PUBLIC INTEREST BY CONTRIBUTING TO THE IMPROVEMENT OF THE LEGAL SYSTEM AND DELIVERY OF QUALITY LEGAL SERVICES, INCLUDING PRO BONO PUBLICO SERVICES.

ETHICAL CONSIDERATIONS

EC-1.4(a) A paralegal shall be sensitive to the legal needs of the public and shall promote the development and implementation of programs that address those needs.

EC-1.4(b) A paralegal shall support efforts to improve the legal system and access thereto and shall assist in making changes.

EC-1.4(c) A paralegal shall support and participate in the delivery of Pro Bono Publico services directed toward implementing and improving access to justice, the law, the legal system or the paralegal and legal professions.

EC-1.4(d) A paralegal should aspire annually to contribute twenty-four (24) hours of Pro Bono Publico services under the supervision of an attorney or as authorized by administrative, statutory or court authority to:

1. persons of limited means; or

2. charitable, religious, civic, community, governmental and educational organizations in matters that are designed primarily to address the legal needs of persons with limited means; or

3. individuals, groups or organizations seeking to secure or protect civil rights, civil liberties or public rights.

The twenty-four (24) hours of Pro Bono Publico services contributed annually by a paralegal may consist of such services as detailed in this EC-1.4(d), and/or administrative matters designed to develop and implement the attainment of this aspiration as detailed above in EC-1.4(a) B (c), or any combination of the two.

As a paralegal, you can independently volunteer your services for tasks that do not constitute the practice of law. You can also work with attorneys as part of a legal team to provide pro bono services.

Many law firms and corporate legal departments have pro bono committees that set the standards for pro bono participation by attorneys and paralegals of their firms, and they encourage a certain amount of pro bono work on firm time. They recognize that active pro bono programs in the law firm provide unique experience and training to the attorneys and paralegals in the firm and that pro bono work can enhance the reputation of the firm in the community.

Although paralegals must not partake in activities that can be considered the practice of law, there are numerous ways in which paralegals are uniquely qualified to assist those in need. Some of the ways paralegals can offer their pro bono services include:

▶ working as advocates for victims of abuse and domestic violence.

▶ acting as an advocate for children within the court system or administrative agencies (i.e., working with children who are limited by medically determined physical or mental conditions to see that the families of these children receive the SSI benefits they are due from the Social Security Administration).

▶ assisting at legal aid clinics that strive to meet the legal needs of the poor, including assistance with divorces, bankruptcies, and landlord-tenant disputes.

▶ working in homeless shelters and homeless legal clinics.

▶ assisting with the drafting of wills and other estate planning documents for indigent, sick, and elderly people.

▶ assisting with the legal work performed for nonprofit organizations.

▶ educating children regarding law-related careers.

▶ mentoring children and young adults in their communities.

While you are helping others, you will also be helping yourself. Many pro bono programs offer free training to paralegals—training that may be valuable throughout your career.

If you want to volunteer your time for a good cause, there is no shortage of opportunities or resources. Most state and local paralegal associations have pro bono committees that work to match paralegal volunteers with pro bono opportunities. Your school, employer, and state bar association may also assist in finding the right opportunity for you.

■ CHAPTER SUMMARY

▶ Bar applicants have a duty of candor when applying for admission to the bar, and attorneys have a duty of candor when involved in any disciplinary proceeding.

▶ An applicant's good moral character is required as a prerequisite to admission to the bar.

▶ Any violation of the pertinent rules of ethics by an attorney is considered misconduct.

► Commission of certain crimes, even crimes unrelated to an attorney's profession, is considered misconduct and grounds for disbarment or other discipline if the crime reflects adversely on the attorney's honesty, trustworthiness, or fitness as an attorney.

► Attorneys have a duty to report unethical conduct of other attorneys if they have knowledge of that conduct, if that conduct raises a substantial question as to the attorney's fitness as an attorney, and if that information is not protected by rules concerning client confidentiality.

► Rule 6.1 of the Model Rules of Professional Conduct provides that attorneys should aspire to render at least 50 hours of pro bono service per year.

► Paralegal misconduct occurs when a paralegal violates rules of the applicable codes of ethics.

► Paralegals have a duty to report certain types of misconduct of other paralegals and attorneys.

► There are many opportunities for paralegals to offer pro bono services.

Chapter 3

■ FREQUENTLY ASKED QUESTIONS

One of our firm's clients has asked me out on a date. Is it okay for me to accept?

While attorneys and law firm personnel often have social outings with their clients, a date between a paralegal and a client can be improper for several reasons. First, does your law firm have a written policy against dating clients? If the answer is yes, you definitely must decline. Second, how would the responsible attorney feel about it? If you start dating the client and things do not go well, it could be uncomfortable for all of you. Also, several states have rules prohibiting sexual relations between a client and attorney. These rules may apply to you as well—even the appearance of a possible sexual relationship with a client could be viewed as questionable ethical behavior.

I think the attorney I work for has a substance abuse problem. She has been coming in late in the morning, sneaking out of the office for several hours at a time, and missing client appointments. I have covered for her several times, but I am concerned that things are getting worse. Do I need to report her to the bar association?

This is a tough situation. If you have a close personal relationship with the attorney you work for, you may be able to encourage her to get help or work with an attorney assistance program through your local or state bar association. If you find this does not work, and the attorney is not providing adequate representation to clients, you will probably need to talk with a managing attorney at your firm to see that the attorney gets the help she needs.

One of the attorneys I work for has been writing checks out of a client's trust account to cover personal expenses. I think he always pays it back. Do I need to report this?

First, you must make sure that you have your facts straight. Is the attorney reimbursing himself for expenditures on behalf of the client's trust account? Such a practice would not be recommended but probably would not rise to the level embezzlement. If you have a good working relationship with the attorney, you may want to ask him about it. Possibly just asking can clear up the situation. If not, you should talk with someone at your firm—either your supervisor, the attorney's supervisor, or a managing partner of the firm.

During a recent meeting, a new client told me about her previous attorney. She had threatened a witness in our new client's case, which led to a favorable outcome for our new client. Our client ended her story with "Please don't tell anyone." Do we have an obligation to report this behavior?

Under most circumstances, you would have an obligation to report the unethical behavior of your client's former attorney. However, in this case, your obligation to keep your client's information confidential would prohibit you from reporting the behavior.

I just realized that the new paralegal in our firm is a disbarred attorney who is a friend of one of the partners here. Is that legal?

Probably, although a few states do prohibit disbarred attorneys from working as paralegals. You can find out by checking the rules of court in the state in which you work.

■ ENDNOTES

1 *People v. Culpepper,* 645 P.2d 5 (Colo. 1982).
2 *In re Martin-Trigona,* 302 N.E. 2d 68 (Ill. 1973).
3 *In re Russell Vernon Guilford,* 505 N.E. 2d 342 (Ill. 1987).
4 *The Florida Bar v. Vaughn,* 608 So. 2d 18 (Fla. 1992).
5 *Reid v. Mississippi State Bar,* 586 So. 2d 786 (Miss. 1991).
6 *Foote v. Mississippi State Bar Association,* 517 So. 2d 561 (Miss. 1987).
7 The ABA Committee on Ethics and Professional Responsibility, Formal Opinion 92-364 (1992).
8 California, Florida, Iowa, Minnesota, New York, North Carolina, Oregon, Utah, West Virginia, and Wisconsin.
9 *In re Dahlberg,* 611 N.E. 2d 641 (Ind. 1993).
10 Comment [3] to Rule 8.3 of the Model Rules of Professional Conduct (2004), *Annotated Model Rules of Professional Conduct,* American Bar Association (1999).
11 *In re Himmel,* 533 N.E. 2d 790 (Ill. 1988).
12 *Black's Law Dictionary,* Abridged Sixth Edition (1991).
13 NFPA Resolution 01S-11, Approved at NFPA Policy Meeting April 21 and April 22, 2001.
14 The *NFPA Model Guidelines for the Enforcement of the Model Code of Ethics and Professional Responsibility* (1997).
15 Canon 9, NALA Code of Ethics and Professional Responsibility.
16 Canon 10, NALA Code of Ethics and Professional Responsibility.
17 EC-1.2(f) NFPA Model Code of Ethics and Professional Responsibility and Guidelines for Enforcement.

Chapter 4

Unauthorized Practice of Law

"Stripped of ethical rationalizations and philosophical pretensions,
a crime is anything that a group in power chooses to prohibit."
— Freda Adler

INTRODUCTION

Anyone who practices law without the proper **license** is considered to be guilty of the **unauthorized practice of law**. Unauthorized individuals are prohibited from practicing law because it is assumed that they do not have the necessary knowledge and skill to adequately represent others in matters of a legal nature. Unauthorized practice of law rules are designed to protect the public from "rendition of legal services by unqualified persons."[1] Unauthorized practice of law rules are also designed to protect the integrity of the judicial system and the legal profession. Whereas attorneys are subject to a code of ethics, laypersons cannot be held to such codes.

The need to protect the public by prohibiting the unauthorized practice of law must be weighed against the need to provide affordable legal services to everyone—including the poor and the indigent. According to some estimates, as many as 80% of low-income persons are unable to obtain legal assistance when they need and want it.[2]

OF INTEREST

According to some estimates, for every 9,000 financially eligible poor persons, there is only one lawyer providing legal services.

—Tremblay, Paul. Acting "A Very Moral Type of God": Triage Among Poor Clients, Fordham Law Review (April 1999)

This chapter starts with a look at the basic rules of ethics and laws concerning the unauthorized practice of law and then examines what is generally considered to be the unauthorized practice of law. Next, this chapter focuses on some of the professions at risk of engaging in the unauthorized practice of law, the effect of the Internet on the unauthorized practice of law, the individual's right to self-representation, and the consequences to attorneys who engage in, or aid others in, the commission of the unauthorized practice of law. Part I concludes with a look at the guidelines available to assist attorneys with the proper utilization of paralegals. Part II of this chapter explores the issue of the unauthorized practice of law from the paralegal's perspective, including traditional, **freelance**, and independent paralegals. This chapter concludes with a look at the guidance available from the paralegal associations and how you, as a paralegal, can avoid the unauthorized practice of law.

PART I: BASIC RULES CONCERNING THE UNAUTHORIZED PRACTICE OF LAW

Rules prohibiting attorneys from practicing law in any state in which they are unauthorized or assisting others who are unauthorized with the practice of law are established by the code of ethics adopted by each state for attorneys, by case law, by court rules, and by general statutes.

Attorneys Must Not Engage in the Unauthorized Practice of Law

Admission to the bar is done on a state-by-state basis, and attorneys who are admitted in one state are not authorized to practice law in any other state without special permission. Attorneys may be admitted to the bar in more than one state, allowing them to practice law in neighboring states or in states where it may be beneficial to their practice for other reasons. Attorneys may, on occasion, receive special permission from a court for handling a specific matter in a state where they are not licensed. Most states extend **reciprocity** to attorneys from neighboring states who have practiced for a minimum number of years. Attorneys who practice law in any state where they are not licensed or do not otherwise have permission are engaging in the unauthorized practice of law.

Attorneys whose practice brings them before federal courts must be admitted to practice before those courts. Federal courts usually admit all attorneys who are licensed in the state where the court is located.

Attorneys Must Not Assist Others in the Unauthorized Practice of Law

Attorneys must not assist unauthorized individuals in practicing law. If an attorney is associated with a disbarred or suspended attorney, the licensed attorney must not in any way aid his or her unauthorized associate in any action that would constitute the unauthorized practice of law.

Attorney Supervision of Their Employees

As set forth in Rule 5.3 of the Model Rules of Professional Conduct and similar rules in each state, attorneys are responsible for the conduct of their nonattorney employees, and they may be held accountable for the unethical actions of their employees. Licensed attorneys must responsibly supervise their paralegals and other nonattorney staff to ensure they are not engaging in the unauthorized practice of law. Attorneys who do not properly supervise their paralegals and other nonattorney staff may be guilty of aiding and abetting the unauthorized practice of law.

> **CASE ON POINT**
>
> In a recent case in Louisiana, an attorney was disbarred for several acts of misconduct, including aiding in the unauthorized practice of law, when he admitted to allowing his nonattorney assistants to run his practice with only marginal supervision.

—*In re Goff, 837 So.2d 1201 (La. 2003)*

Just how close must the attorney supervision be? This question has been addressed in several venues, with varying results. Generally, the attorney must have direct contact with his or her employees. It would not be acceptable for paralegals to run one or more offices for an attorney who would not be located onsite. The ABA Commission on Professional Ethics, Opinion 316 (1967), states that lawyers can employ any number of lay employees to perform a wide variety of tasks "except counsel clients about law matters, engage directly in the practice of law, appear in court or appear in formal proceedings as part of the judicial process, so long as it is he who takes the work and vouches for it to the client and becomes responsible to the client." Attorneys cannot delegate their role of appearing in court on behalf of a client or of giving legal advice to a client. An attorney "must not under any circumstances delegate to such person the exercise of the lawyer's professional judgment in behalf of the client or even allow it to be influenced by the non-lawyer's assistance."[3]

◼ WHAT CONSTITUTES THE UNAUTHORIZED PRACTICE OF LAW?

The unauthorized practice of law is simply the practice of law by someone who is unauthorized. Anyone who is not a properly licensed attorney is *unauthorized*. The difficulty with the term unauthorized practice of law lies with the definition of "practice of law." While it is clear that representing others before a court of law constitutes the practice of law, the practice of law extends beyond litigation and includes giving legal advice and counsel, rendering a service that requires the use of legal knowledge or skill, and preparing instruments and contracts by which legal rights are secured, whether or not the matter is pending in a court.[4] In determining whether the unauthorized practice of law has been engaged in, courts often consider the following:

1. Was the service rendered a service typically performed by attorneys or commonly understood to involve the practice of law?
2. Did the service rendered require legal skills and knowledge beyond that of the average layperson?[5]
3. Was there harm done to the consumer as a result of the services rendered?

The practice of law generally includes the following activities:

▶ setting fees for legal work
▶ giving legal advice
▶ preparing or signing legal documents
▶ representing another before a court or other **tribunal**

The definition of "the practice of law" varies by state. Most states include a definition in their statutes, but the right to interpret that definition lies with the state's highest courts. At one point, the ABA proposed to draft a model definition of "practice of law" to provide guidance to the states. However, in 2003, after much discussion, the ABA's Task Force on the Model Definition of Practice of Law decided it was a matter best left to the individual states.

CASE ON POINT

In a recent case in the California Court of Appeals, the court held that practicing law means more than just appearing in court; practice of the law "includes legal advice and counsel and the preparation of legal instruments and contracts by which legal rights are secured although such matter may or may not be pending in a court."

—*Estate of Condon, 76 Cal.Rptr.2d 922 (1998)*

◼ THE PRACTICE OF LAW IN CYBERSPACE

The Internet presents a unique set of challenges concerning the unauthorized practice of law. In 2006, it was estimated that 180 million Americans use the Internet at least once a month. In the twenty-first century, thriving businesses need a presence on the Internet. They need a Web site to promote their businesses and they need to provide useful information on that Web site to attract potential customers and clients. But what about attorneys? Clearly, most law firms have marked their presence in cyberspace with their own Web sites. These Web sites provide basic information about the law firm and often about the lawyers that comprise that firm. The unauthorized practice of law questions arise when attorneys also provide advice on their Web sites, possibly in an online forum or on a blog. The Internet is not a local or statewide medium. Online legal advice by attorneys licensed to practice law in

Kentucky may be viewed by Kentucky residents but also by individuals in Texas, Connecticut, and Bali. Attorneys who give advice on their Web sites or elsewhere on the Internet can be viewed as practicing law outside of the jurisdictions in which they are licensed to practice—the unauthorized practice of law. Attorneys can try to safeguard against these charges in several ways. Web sites may be established in a manner that requires visitors to register and then limits the information that may be viewed as legal advice to site visitors who are within the jurisdiction of the attorneys' practice. Attorney and law firm Web sites often include disclaimers indicating that the information provided on the Web site is not *legal advice.*

The anonymous nature of the Internet can pose unique problems for unwary consumers who seek online legal advice and services, possibly through a chat room or a blog, without any proof of the *attorney's* credentials. It is possible for anyone to enter an online forum and claim to be an attorney.

◼ PROFESSIONS AT RISK OF ENGAGING IN THE UNAUTHORIZED PRACTICE OF LAW

Certain occupations put individuals at risk for crossing the line with regard to the unauthorized practice of law. Paralegals are, of course, included in this group. The unauthorized practice of law by paralegals is discussed in Part II.

Realtors, accountants, bankers, and other professionals whose work puts them in constant contact with individuals who are entering into contracts or in need of other legal documentation are also at risk for engaging in the unauthorized practice of law. Some jurisdictions have adopted legislation and special rules that apply to individuals in such professions who routinely prepare documents for others incident to their businesses.

For example, it is usually permissible for a realtor to prepare purchase agreements for his or her clients, most realtors receive special training in how to provide that service. However, it is generally not permissible for the realtor to give legal advice concerning title to the property or for the realtor to represent his or her client in a dispute over the property if that dispute should result in legal action.

◼ SELF-REPRESENTATION

In most jurisdictions, **self-representation** is a right granted to individuals. The right of self-representation in federal court is granted by 28 USC 1654. The Supreme Court has held that self-representation in the state courts is a constitutional right in criminal cases. Self-representation in legal matters is on the rise in the United States, especially in the family courts, traffic courts, estate planning, and probate matters and also in matters involving federal agencies. Self-help books and software, availability of information over the Internet, and an attempt by the courts to be more accessible have all contributed to the increase in self-representation. See Exhibit 4-1. The services provided by **mediators, legal document preparers** and independent paralegals have also had a significant impact.

Chapter 4

> **OF INTEREST**
>
> Nolo Press, the largest self-help law publisher in the United States, provides books, forms, and software for wills, estate planning, divorce, business organization, and several other legal topics. According to information on Nolo's Web site, over nine million people have used their products to solve their own legal problems.

In recent years, an abundance of new interactive tools to help laypersons prepare their own documents has again demonstrated the complications technology can bring to the definition of the practice of law. Computer programs have been introduced to help laypeople draft their own wills and estate-planning documents as well as business and real estate documents. While these programs may help alleviate unnecessary legal fees for the educated consumer, problems can arise when the programs are provided by unauthorized and incompetent individuals and when the consumers do not understand the full legal implications of using the documents that they can now prepare for themselves. Several jurisdictions have taken action to regulate this type of self-help legal software. Some states have enacted legislation that specifically addresses the self-help legal software. Texas has added a section to their statute that defines the practice of law to indicate that the "practice of law does not include the design, creation, publication, distribution, display, or sale, including . . . by means of an Internet Web site, of written materials, books, forms, computer software, or similar products if the products clearly and conspicuously state that the products are not a substitute for the advice of an attorney."[6]

In some jurisdictions, corporations may elect self-representation if they are represented by officers who are tending to the business of the corporation. Other jurisdictions allow corporations to be represented only by licensed attorneys.

Exhibit 4-1

Factors Contributing to the Increase in Self-Representation

- Availability of self-help books
- Availability of legal self-help software
- Availability of legal information over the Internet
- Attempts by the courts to be more accessible
- Availability of services of mediators, legal document preparers, and independent paralegals

ENFORCING THE UNAUTHORIZED PRACTICE OF LAW RULES

Methods for enforcing unauthorized practice of law rules are not uniform among the states and neither are the consequences to attorneys and laypersons who are found to be in violation of those rules. Control of the unauthorized practice of law belongs to the judiciary in most states. The courts have the authority to determine who is eligible to practice before them.

In many states, the bar association appoints a committee to oversee the enforcement of unauthorized practice of law rules. The bar association and committee both derive their power from the state's highest court. Most actions against individuals are brought in the courts by a state's bar association.

Disciplinary action by a state bar association may be brought against attorneys who engage in the unauthorized practice of law or who assist in the unauthorized practice of law. The options for sanctions against the attorney include disbarment, suspension or revocation of the attorney's license to practice law, probation, or a reprimand. Because nonattorneys are not members of the bar associations, bar association disciplinary boards have no authority over them. Disciplinary action may only be brought against licensed attorneys who are members of the bar of the state in question. Other tools for enforcing unauthorized practice of law rules include **injunctions, contempt proceedings, criminal prosecution and writs of quo warranto.**

▊ GUIDELINES FOR UTILIZING PARALEGALS

While common sense and general ethical guidelines often dictate how much supervision paralegals require, sometimes the issue is not so clear. Experienced paralegals may have the knowledge to do things they can not legally do, and it is often hard for attorneys to know which tasks can be legally delegated and how much supervision is required. Attorneys may find some assistance in the ABA's Model Guidelines for Utilization of Legal Assistant Services and the guidelines for utilization of paralegals adopted as state statute or as part of the state's court rules.

The ABA's Model Guidelines for the Utilization of Legal Assistant Services, adopted by the ABA in 1991, make it clear that attorneys are responsible for the conduct of legal assistants working under their supervision and that, provided the attorney maintains responsibility for the paralegal's work product, the attorney may delegate any tasks normally performed by attorneys unless the provision of such service by someone other than an attorney is specifically prohibited by statute, court rule, administrative rule or regulation, controlling authority, the ABA Model Rules of Professional Conduct, or by the Model Guidelines.

The Model Guidelines specifically prohibit attorneys from delegating to paralegals responsibility for establishing an attorney-client relationship, for establishing the amount of a fee to be charged for a legal service, or for a legal opinion rendered to a client.

The Model Guidelines do not offer many specifics or much detail on the utilization of paralegals, nor do the guidelines adopted by many states. However, until a consensus is reached on paralegal regulation, guidelines for utilizing paralegals may be the best guidance attorneys have to define the legal possibilities and limits of paralegals.

■ PART II FROM THE PARALEGAL'S PERSPECTIVE

As a paralegal, you have several sources to turn to for information on avoiding the unauthorized practice of law. Although rules concerning the unauthorized practice of law are addressed in the codes of ethics of national, state, and local paralegal associations, the paralegal associations have no legal authority over paralegals. As a paralegal, you must also be aware of the rules concerning the unauthorized practice of law established by the statutes, case law, and attorney codes of ethics in any state in which you work.

A QUESTION OF ETHICS

Suppose you are packing a briefcase for attorney Katherine Laurence for a pretrial hearing scheduled on a criminal misdemeanor case. You have been very involved with the preparation of the case, and you have made sure that all the necessary motions and documents are in her briefcase and that everything is ready to go. Katherine is about to leave the office when the phone rings. It is her daughter's teacher calling with an emergency. Katherine's 10-year-old daughter has fallen while playing soccer and has been seriously injured. She is on her way to the hospital via ambulance. Katherine leaves her briefcase, tells you to "handle it," and rushes out the door.

There are no other attorneys from your firm in the office, and the hearing starts in 20 minutes. You attempt to call the judge's clerk to tell him that Ms. Laurence will not be able to attend the hearing, but you are unable to get through to anyone in the judge's chambers or the clerk's office. What should you do? Should you appear in court on behalf of Ms. Laurence?

Answer and Discussion

In most jurisdictions, appearing in court on behalf of Ms. Laurence would be considered the unauthorized practice of law. There are, however, some exceptions to this rule for nonattorneys who appear on behalf of an employer simply to ask for a continuance of the matter. If you know the rules in your jurisdiction and they permit such appearances, you may want to make the appearance on behalf of Ms. Laurence. Your first item of business would necessarily be to explain to the judge what has transpired and let the judge direct you on how to proceed. If you are unsure of the rules in your jurisdiction and you are unable to reach the judge or judge's clerk by telephone, you may want to go to the courthouse and try to personally locate the judge's receptionist, secretary, or clerk, present him or her with the situation and the documents, and ask that the message be relayed to the judge. If the motion is a very simple, uncontested matter, the judge may ask you to appear on behalf of the attorney or he or she may want to reschedule a date for Ms. Laurence to appear.

The one thing you absolutely cannot do in any jurisdiction is to simply appear in court and represent Ms. Laurence's client without identifying yourself as a paralegal appearing on behalf of Ms. Laurence.

⬛ TRADITIONAL PARALEGALS

While it seems that unauthorized practice of law rules unnecessarily restrict the activities that may be performed by paralegals, there are very few restrictions on the activities and responsibilities that may be assumed by properly supervised **traditional paralegals**. As a paralegal, you can use your knowledge of the law and of legal procedure to assist attorneys in numerous ways. Drafting legal documents and performing other law-related services may at first glance appear to be practicing law. However, if you work under the supervision of an attorney who is ultimately responsible for your actions, you are merely assisting attorneys with their practice of law. Therefore, there is no question of unauthorized practice of law.

According to Guideline 2 of the ABA Model Guidelines for Utilization of Paralegal Services:

> *Provided the lawyer maintains responsibility for the work product,*
> *a lawyer may delegate to a paralegal any task normally performed*
> *by the lawyer except those tasks proscribed to a nonlawyer by*
> *statute, court rule, administrative rule or regulation, controlling*
> *authority, the applicable rule of professional conduct of the*
> *jurisdiction in which the lawyer practices, or these Guidelines.*

Guideline 5 of the NALA's Model Standards and Guidelines for Utilization of Legal Assistants says that paralegals can perform any functions delegated by an attorney unless otherwise prohibited by law.

Guideline 5

Except as otherwise provided by statute, court rule or decision, administrative rule or regulation, or the attorney's rules of professional responsibility, and within the preceding parameters and proscriptions, a legal assistant may perform any function delegated by an attorney, including, but not limited to the following:

1. Conduct client interviews and maintain general contact with the client after the establishment of the attorney-client relationship, so long as the client is aware of the status and function of the legal assistant, and the client contact is under the supervision of the attorney.

2. Locate and interview witnesses, so long as the witnesses are aware of the status and function of the legal assistant.

3. Conduct investigations and statistical and documentary research for review by the attorney.

4. Conduct legal research for review by the attorney.

5. Draft legal documents for review by the attorney.

6. Draft correspondence and pleadings for review by and signature of the attorney.

7. Summarize depositions, interrogatories and testimony for review by the attorney.

8. Attend executions of wills, real estate closings, depositions, court or administrative hearings, and trials with the attorney.

9. Author and sign letters, providing the legal assistant's status is clearly indicated and the correspondence does not contain independent legal opinions or legal advice.

Corporate Paralegals

Paralegals who work for corporations must also be aware of their legal and ethical boundaries. Under most circumstances, a corporation may not designate a nonattorney to represent it in matters of a legal nature. Again, if you work under the direct supervision of attorneys in a legal department, you probably need not be too concerned. However, if you find you are working on legal matters with very little or no attorney supervision, you must consider the possibility that the work you are performing could be considered the unauthorized practice of law.

Government Paralegals

Both federal and state government agencies utilize paralegals in very responsible roles. Many of these paralegals become experts in very specialized areas. In an effort to keep costs low and operate as efficiently as possible, paralegals and other nonlawyers who work for federal and state agencies are often allowed to perform tasks typically considered to be the practice of law. These paralegals and other nonlawyers receive their authority to perform certain functions from state statute or administrative agency rules and regulations. For example, the following is an excerpt from Minnesota Statutes § 518.5513 concerning procedures for child and medical support orders and parentage orders:

> ... *Subd. 2. Role of nonattorney employees; general provisions.*
> *(a) The county attorney shall review and approve as to form and content all pleadings and other legal documents prepared by nonattorney employees of the county agency for use in the expedited child support process.*
> *... (c) Nonattorney employees of the county agency may perform the following duties without direction from the county attorney:*
>
> *(1) gather information on behalf of the public authority;*
>
> *(2) prepare financial worksheets;*
>
> *(3) obtain income information from the Department of Employment and Economic Development and other sources;*
>
> *(4) serve documents on parties;*
>
> *(5) file documents with the court;*
>
> *(6) meet and confer with parties by mail, telephone, electronic, or other means regarding nonlegal issues;*

*(7) explain to parties the purpose, procedure, and function of the
expedited child support process and the role and authority of
nonattorney employees of the county agency regarding nonlegal
issues; and*

(8) perform such other routine nonlegal duties as assigned.

*(d) Performance of the duties prescribed in paragraphs (b) and (c) by
nonattorney employees of the county agency does not constitute the
unauthorized practice of law for purposes of Section 481.02.*

■ FREELANCE PARALEGALS

Freelance paralegals are self-employed paralegals who work for a number of
attorneys, under their supervision, on a temporary or contract basis. Freelance
paralegals must follow the same general guidelines as traditional paralegals. In
addition, they have the added concern of making sure that the attorneys they are
reporting to understand that they must adequately supervise the paralegal's work.
Neither case law nor statutes distinguish paralegals employed by an attorney or
law firm from independent paralegals retained by an attorney or a law firm.[7]

CASE ON POINT

In one case heard in New Jersey, it was decided that it is the amount of
supervision, not the paralegal's employment status–whether the paralegal
was a law firm employee or independent paralegal–that determines the
issue of the unauthorized practice of law.

—In Re: Opinion No. 24 of Committee on Unauthorized Practice of Law, 607 A2d 962

■ INDEPENDENT PARALEGALS

Most of the real controversy surrounding paralegals and the unauthorized practice
of law concerns **independent paralegals**—paralegals who offer their services
directly to the public without attorney supervision. Independent paralegals may also
be referred to as legal document preparers, forms practitioners, or similar names in
different locations. Many of the services offered by independent paralegals are
self-help services. These services include furnishing and completing forms and
offering self-help information written by attorneys. The independent paralegals do
not represent individuals in legal matters; rather, they assist their customers with
self-representation. Whereas it is clear that, in most instances, individuals have the
right of self-representation, the role of a layperson to assist them is less clear.

Independent paralegals are often in danger of crossing the unauthorized
practice of law line. For example, in most jurisdictions, it is legal for independent
paralegals to sell legal forms and printed material drafted by attorneys and

explain legal practice and procedure to the public. However, if the independent paralegal dispenses legal advice, in addition to the legal forms, the paralegal will probably be committing the unauthorized practice of law. In Michigan, the court has ruled that "the advertisement and distribution to the general public of forms and documents utilized to obtain a divorce together with any related textual instructions does not constitute the unauthorized practice of law."[8] However, offering counsel and advice in addition to the forms and documents *is* considered to be the unauthorized practice of law.

If you are considering employment as an independent paralegal, you must be very sure of the precedence for independent paralegals in your state. You must know how the unauthorized practice of law has been defined in your state and be exceedingly careful that your services never meet with that definition. In addition, you must be aware of any registration requirements in your state. For example, beginning in the year 2000, California individuals who render the services of a legal document technician as defined by statute must meet with certain requirements and register with the appropriate county clerk. The California requirement is one of the first of its kind, but there may be new legislation in your state, so you must keep current with any developments regarding paralegal regulation. For the latest developments in your state, keep current with your local paralegal association.

GUIDANCE FROM THE PARALEGAL ASSOCIATIONS

Both the NALA Code of Ethics and Professional Responsibility and the NFPA Model Code of Ethics and Professional Responsibility have provisions specifically prohibiting the unauthorized practice of law by their members. Legal assistants, under the definition adopted by the NALA, work under the supervision of an attorney. In addition, nearly every canon of the NALA's Code of Ethics and Professional Responsibility refers to the necessity for legal assistants to avoid the unauthorized practice of law, especially Canon 3, which is set forth in Exhibit 4-2.

Exhibit 4-2

From the NALA's Code of Ethics and Professional Responsibility

CANON 3

A paralegal must not: (a) engage in, encourage, or contribute to any act which could constitute the unauthorized practice of law; and (b) establish attorney-client relationships, set fees, give legal opinions or advice or represent a client before a court or agency unless so authorized by that court or agency; and (c) engage in conduct or take any action which would assist or involve the attorney in a violation of professional ethics or give the appearance of professional impropriety.

In addition, the NALA provides its Model Standards and Guidelines for Utilization of Legal Assistants-Paralegals to give guidance to attorneys and paralegals on the proper utilization and attorney supervision of paralegals to avoid the unauthorized practice of law. Pursuant to these guidelines, legal assistants should not:

1. Establish attorney-client relationships; set legal fees; give legal opinions or advice; or represent a client before a court, unless authorized to do so by said court; nor

2. Engage in, encourage, or contribute to any act which could constitute the unauthorized practice of law.[9]

Although the NALA Code of Ethics and Professional Responsibility and the NFPA's Model Code of Ethics and Professional Responsibility are not legally binding on the members of those organizations, these documents do give some guidance to paralegals. In addition, the NFPA will issue opinions on questions concerning legal ethics, including the unauthorized practice of law. Exhibit 4-3 sets forth the NFPA's rules concerning the unauthorized practice of law.

Exhibit 4-3

From the NFPA's Model Code of Ethics and Professional Responsibility and Guidelines for Enforcement

1.8 A PARALEGAL SHALL NOT ENGAGE IN THE UNAUTHORIZED PRACTICE OF LAW.

ETHICAL CONSIDERATIONS

EC-1.8(a)   A paralegal shall comply with the applicable legal authority governing the unauthorized practice of law in the jurisdiction in which the paralegal practices.

AVOIDING THE UNAUTHORIZED PRACTICE OF LAW

There are certain activities that all paralegals must be cautious to avoid, and some general rules to follow, to be sure that they are not engaging in the unauthorized practice of law. In general, you will want to:

▶ Always disclose your status as a paralegal, including on letterhead and business cards.

▶ Make sure that legal documents and any correspondence you prepare expressing a legal opinion are reviewed, approved, and signed by your supervising attorney.

▶ Communicate important issues concerning each case or legal matter with your supervising attorney and see that your work is reviewed and approved by an attorney.

▶ Never give legal advice.

▶ Never discuss the merits of a case with opposing counsel.

▶ Never enter into fee agreements for legal services or agree to represent a client (on behalf of your supervising attorney or law firm).

▶ Never represent a client at a deposition, in a court of law, or before an administrative board or tribunal (unless paralegals or other laypersons are specifically authorized to appear by the court's rules or agency regulations).

Disclose Your Status

When meeting or speaking with clients or attorneys, you must always introduce yourself as a paralegal. When signing correspondence, be sure to indicate your title below your signature. By not doing so, it may be assumed that you are an attorney. Merely presenting yourself as an attorney may be considered the unauthorized practice of law.

Law firms often include the names of their paralegal employees on their letterhead and provide business cards for their paralegals. In both instances, it is important that your title is included beneath your name. Omitting your paralegal title could expose you to charges of the unauthorized practice of law.

Including a paralegal's name and title on a law firm's letterhead is not permissible in every jurisdiction. A minority of jurisdictions in the United States, including the state of Georgia, have found it unethical for law firms to include the names of paralegals on their law firm letterhead.[10]

Freelance paralegals and independent paralegals must make sure that in addition to their letterhead and business cards, any marketing materials they use must include their title and clearly indicate that they are not attorneys and not authorized to give legal advice or practice law.

Have Your Work Reviewed and Approved by an Attorney

There are several reasons why preparing legal documents, a task that might otherwise be considered clerical, is usually considered to be the practice of law.

1. The preparation of most legal documents requires a superior knowledge of the law not possessed by most laypeople.

2. The preparation of legal documents can affect the legal rights of those for whom they are prepared.

3. The preparation of legal documents is often accompanied by legal judgment and legal advice as to which legal document to prepare and how the document should be prepared.

As a paralegal, a significant amount of your time may be spent drafting legal documents and correspondence. With very few exceptions, any legal documents you prepare must be reviewed by an attorney. In addition, if you are asked to draft correspondence that gives legal advice to a client, the correspondence should be reviewed and signed by the responsible attorney. After you have been working with the same attorneys for a long time and they attain a high comfort level with your work, the tendency may be to skip over the review process. Be sure to remind the attorneys you work for from time to time (if necessary) that they are ultimately responsible for your work and that they are responsible for reviewing and approving your work product.

Communicate with Your Supervising Attorney

It is important that you communicate clearly with your supervising attorney regarding any matters on which you are working. Your communication can include face-to-face meetings, memos, e-mails, and other methods to keep the attorney apprised of any developments as necessary to allow him or her to adequately direct and supervise your work. The means of communication is not as important as the fact of a clear understanding between you and your supervising attorney.

Do Not Give Legal Advice

It is generally agreed that giving legal advice is considered to be practicing law. Several tests have been applied to determine whether an individual is giving legal advice, and different rules and tests may be applied in different jurisdictions. Generally, someone is giving legal advice if:

1. the knowledge of the information imparted generally requires an advanced legal knowledge and skill.
2. it is intended to advise someone of his or her legal rights.
3. it is not advice normally given by a nonlawyer as part of another business or transaction.

To avoid the unauthorized practice of law, you must avoid giving legal advice. This is a challenge for many paralegals, especially those who meet regularly with clients. Most paralegals come in frequent contact with clients, and conversation involves the exchange of information. Paralegals must be sure that the information they provide does not include their independent legal judgment or advice. When you meet with clients or speak to clients over the telephone to relay information about their cases, you must be sure that you qualify any information you give them that may constitute legal advice by saying that it is the attorney's opinion. If they ask for your opinion or advice on matters that you have not discussed with the responsible attorney, you must defer the question and say that you are unable to give advice but that you will check with an attorney. Never give your opinion as to the merits of a client's case—even when the client asks and you are confident you know the answer.

Chapter 4

Never Discuss the Merits of a Client's Case with Opposing Counsel

Discussing a client's case with opposing counsel can be considered the unauthorized practice of law, even if you identify yourself as a paralegal. In addition, it can have serious negative consequences to your client's case.

Never Agree to Represent a Client or Negotiate or Set Fees on Behalf of an Attorney

Entering into an arrangement to accept a fee for work of a legal nature by anyone other than a duly licensed attorney is considered the unauthorized practice of law. Although paralegals commonly meet with potential clients to gather information prior to the client meeting with an attorney, it is important that the paralegal not discuss fee arrangements with the potential clients or agree (on behalf of the attorney) that the attorney will take on representation of the individuals as clients. Both the attorney and paralegal often handle initial client interviews or the attorney will meet with potential clients either immediately before or after the paralegal meets with them. The State Bar of Michigan has given an opinion that a lawyer should not entrust to a paralegal the full responsibility for conducting the initial interview and passing the information on to the lawyer. The opinion emphasizes the importance of the direct attorney-client relationship necessary to exercise the attorney's trained professional judgment.[11]

Never Represent a Client at a Deposition, in a Court of Law, or Before an Administrative Board or Tribunal without Authorization

In general, it is considered practicing law to appear on behalf of someone else in a court of law or before an administrative board or tribunal. There are, however, several notable exceptions to this rule.

1. Nonlawyers may represent others at administrative hearings if permitted by the administrative agency.
2. In some jurisdictions, it is permissible for nonlawyers to appear in front of the court on behalf of an attorney employer to request a continuance on the attorney's behalf.
3. Some jurisdictions allow law clerks who are supervised by attorneys and certified as to having completed minimum education requirements to appear before certain courts.
4. In some jurisdictions, it is permissible for nonlawyers to appear before the court if the court specifically grants permission.
5. In some jurisdictions, corporations may represent themselves.
6. In most instances, individuals are guaranteed the right to appear pro se.

Many administrative agencies, especially federal agencies, allow paralegals to appear before their tribunals to represent the rights of individuals. Each federal administrative agency has the power to permit representation by paralegals and other laypersons in their proceedings. Many agencies, including the Internal Revenue Service, the Immigration and Naturalization Service, and the Social Security Administration, permit paralegal representation before their agencies. Some agencies, such as the U.S. Patent Office, require special education and **certification** before representation is allowed. The individual states must permit paralegal representation before federal agencies in accordance with the rules of the federal agency. However, the state administrative agencies have their own rules and are not required to permit paralegal representation—many do not. If you are asked to make an appearance in front of an administrative agency, you must make certain that the extent of your involvement is permissible under the agency's rules. Exhibit 4-4 is a list of federal and state agencies that allow nonlawyer representation.

Exhibit 4-4

Federal Agencies Permitting Nonlawyer Representation

As reported in the *National Paralegal Reporter*, Agencies that Allow Nonlawyer Practice, Summer 1999.

Representation is allowed only as permitted by applicable federal statute or regulation by the following agencies:

- Board of Immigration Appeals
- Civil Aeronautics Board
- Comptroller of the Currency
- Consumer Product Safety Commission
- Department of Agriculture
- Department of Health and Human Services
- Department of Justice
- Department of Labor
- Department of Transportation
- Department of Veterans Affairs
- Federal Deposit Insurance Corporation[1]
- Federal Energy Regulatory Commission
- Federal Maritime Administration[2]
- Federal Mine Safety and Health Review Commission
- General Accounting Office
- Internal Revenue Service[3]
- Interstate Commerce Commission[4]
- National Credit Union Administration

Exhibit 4-4 (*Continued*)

Federal Agencies Permitting Nonlawyer Representation

- National Mediation Board
- National Transportation Safety Board
- Occupational Safety and Health Review Commission
- Small Business Administration
- U.S. Customs Service
- U.S. Environmental Protection Agency

State Agencies that Permit Nonlawyer Representation

Representation is permitted only as allowed by applicable state statute or regulation by the following state agencies:

Alaska

Human Rights Commission

California

Labor

Unemployment

Workers Compensation

Illinois

Workers Compensation

Michigan

Unemployment Compensation

Minnesota

Workers Compensation

New York

70% of state agencies and 63% of New York City agencies

Ohio

Workers Compensation

Washington (Seattle, King County)

Nonlawyers are allowed to present ex parte orders that have been agreed on. *Ex parte* refers to orders that are on and for one party only, without contestation by any person adversely interested.

Washington (Tacoma, Pierce County)

Nonlawyers are allowed to present ex parte orders that have been agreed on. *Ex parte* refers to orders that are on and for one party only, without contestation by any person adversely interested.

Wisconsin

Workers Compensation

[1] Only qualified nonlawyers are permitted to represent.
[2] Only registered nonlawyers are permitted to appear.
[3] Nonlawyers must become enrolled agents.
[4] Only registered nonlawyers are permitted to practice.

Some court rules provide that the courts may grant permission to specific individuals to appear in court on behalf of another for specific reasons. Under certain circumstances, paralegals may appear before certain courts on behalf of their attorney-employers when their appearance is more in the nature of a messenger.

If you are ever asked to appear in court or in front of any administrative agency board or tribunal, you must be **certain** that the rules of the court or tribunal permit such appearance. Exhibit 4-5 is a checklist of rules for avoiding the unauthorized practice of law.

Exhibit 4-5

Avoiding the Unauthorized Practice of Law

- Disclose your status as a paralegal.
- Get approval and signature from your supervising attorney for any legal documents and any correspondence you prepare that may express a legal opinion.
- Communicate important issues concerning each case or legal matter with your supervising attorney.
- Never give legal advice.
- Never discuss the merits of a case with opposing counsel.
- Never enter into fee agreements for legal services (on behalf of your supervising attorney or law firm).
- Never agree to represent a client on behalf of an attorney.
- Never represent a client at a deposition, in a court of law, or before an administrative board (unless specifically authorized by the court's rules or agency regulation).
- Make sure that any letterhead or business cards with your name on them indicate that you are a paralegal.

CONSEQUENCES TO THE PARALEGAL FOR THE UNAUTHORIZED PRACTICE OF LAW

There are negative consequences both for the paralegal who is found to be practicing law and for any attorney who is responsible for the paralegal's supervision. Where no harm has been done to anyone, the most likely consequences would be disciplinary action against the responsible attorney for assisting in the unauthorized practice of law by not supervising his or her employees adequately. Under some circumstances, a dissatisfied client can sue the supervising attorney for malpractice. Independent paralegals may have an injunction filed against them to cease their business or they may be cited for **contempt.**

Paralegals who work without attorney supervision, especially paralegals whose actions cause harm to the public, may be in danger of criminal prosecution for the **misdemeanor** crime of practicing law without a license. Additionally, paralegals deemed to be practicing law without a license may be sued for legal malpractice in some jurisdictions. In one case in the state of Washington, the court found that nonlawyers who attempt to practice law are liable for their negligence and must meet the same standard of care as that of a lawyer.[12] Exhibit 4-6 is a summary of possible consequences to the unauthorized practice of law.

Exhibit 4-6

Consequences to Engaging in the Unauthorized Practice of Law

Consequences to the Attorney	Consequences to the Paralegal
Disciplinary proceedings	Injunction
Injunction	Contempt of court
Contempt of court	Criminal prosecution
Criminal prosecution	Disciplinary proceedings brought against supervising attorney
Civil action brought against attorney	Loss of employment
	Civil action brought against paralegal

In 2007, Brian Valery was indicted on criminal charges of impersonating a lawyer and perjury. Valery had impersonated a lawyer at a prestigious New York law firm for more than two years, representing its clients in several important cases. Valery had worked as a paralegal for the firm since 1996, pretending to attend law school at night and then to pass the bar exam in 2004.[13]

CASE LAW INVOLVING PARALEGALS

It is important to know how paralegals and the unauthorized practice of law have been treated by the courts in your state. Following is a sample of some of the outcomes of cases involving paralegals and the unauthorized practice of law in recent years:

▶ In a 2003 case before the Supreme Court of Louisiana, it was determined that two paralegals who basically ran a plaintiff personal injury law firm with little or no attorney control or supervision were engaged in the unauthorized practice of law.[14]

▶ In a 2004 case brought before the Supreme Court of Florida, a company formed to provide legal form preparation services was enjoined from engaging in the unauthorized practice of law and was fined $9,000. This company provided customers with legal assistance in selecting, preparing, and completing legal forms.[15]

▶ In a case heard in the Supreme Court of Ohio in 2005, a nonattorney who provided document preparation services, including preparation of divorce complaints, on behalf of others, and who counseled others on their legal rights was found to be engaged in the unauthorized practice of law and ordered to pay a civil penalty of $40,000.[16]

▶ In 2005, the Cleveland Bar Association charged that a company that provided legal research, document preparation, and other ancillary services was engaged in the unauthorized practice of law. The company was enjoined from representing others in court pursuant to powers of attorney, preparing court documents for another without attorney supervision, and engaging in other acts constituting the practice of law.[17]

▶ In 2006, the Columbus Bar Association in Ohio brought a disciplinary proceeding against a paralegal for the unauthorized practice of law. This paralegal was employed by an attorney for several years and worked under the attorney's supervision. When his supervising attorney was home recovering from a serious injury, the paralegal acted independently in his absence. The paralegal prepared several legal documents, including pleadings in a divorce case, and signed the attorney's name. The paralegal was found to be engaged in the unauthorized practice of law and fined $5,000.[18]

For all the reasons discussed in this chapter, it will be important for you to avoid the unauthorized practice of law throughout your career. To do so, you will need to be up to date on the unauthorized practice statutes, rules of ethics, and case law in your jurisdiction. Remember, all these factors are subject to change with time. To keep current with the rules for avoiding the unauthorized practice of law in your state, consult the current rules of ethics applicable to the attorneys for whom you work or request guidance from your local or national paralegal association.

SPECIAL UNAUTHORIZED PRACTICE OF LAW CONCERNS FOR THE SPECIALTIES

The general advice concerning avoiding the unauthorized practice of law in this chapter concerns all paralegals. Depending on your specialty, you may be faced with some special concerns.

Chapter 4

Litigation Paralegals

In addition to the rules discussed in this chapter to avoid the unauthorized practice of law, litigation paralegals face some unique challenges—most of them concerning the representation of clients.

Making Court Appearances

While litigation paralegals may accompany the attorneys they work with to court to assist with hearings and trials, with very few exceptions, it is generally considered the unauthorized practice of law for paralegals to appear on their own on behalf of a client in court.

Taking Depositions

Paralegals are typically not allowed to take **depositions** under the unauthorized practice of law rules.

Preparing Pleadings

Litigation paralegals are often responsible for drafting pleadings and other litigation-related documents. However, legal documents prepared by litigation paralegals should be reviewed and signed (if an attorney's signature is necessary) by the responsible attorney to avoid the unauthorized practice of law.

Negotiating with Opposing Counsel

Litigation paralegals are often intimately familiar with the merits of a client's case and may be responsible for drafting memorandums and correspondence concerning the settlement of a case. However, it would be considered the unauthorized practice of law for a litigation paralegal to directly negotiate a settlement with opposing counsel.

Estate Planning and Probate Paralegals

Estate-planning and probate paralegals also face some unique challenges, most of them due to the fact that they may work closely with estate-planning clients or the probate court administration.

Giving Legal Advice

Even though you may have heard your supervising attorney explain the tax benefits for establishing a particular type of estate plan several times, for you to advise clients on the type of estate planning they should implement would be considered the unauthorized practice of law. It may be acceptable for you to relay information from the attorney you work for—"As you discussed with Ms. Johnson, she recommends that you transfer your assets to a revocable trust because . . ."—but you want to make sure you are not the one giving the advice.

In *Doe v. Condon*, 532 S.E.2d 879 (S.C. 2000), the court held that a paralegal who gathered client information and answered general estate planning questions during initial client interviews was engaging in the unauthorized practice of law.

Drafting Estate Planning Documents and Probate Court Forms

After a time, drafting estate planning documents and the numerous forms that must be filed with the probate courts can seem routine and even tedious. However, it is important that your preparation of these legal documents is reviewed by an attorney to avoid the unauthorized practice of law.

Real Estate Paralegals

Real estate paralegals often get to be experts on the transfer of real estate within their jurisdictions. Recognizing this, some jurisdictions have even passed special laws that allow paralegals to handle transactions typically reserved for attorneys. However, unless supervised by an attorney, several real estate–related transactions are still considered practicing law.

Giving Legal Advice

Clients who are contemplating purchasing or selling real estate often turn to their attorneys for advice. This advice definitely falls under the realm of practicing law and should be reserved for the attorney.

Preparing Real Estate Transfer Documents

Although real estate paralegals are often responsible for drafting real estate documents, including the documents required to transfer property, these documents should be reviewed by an attorney to avoid the unauthorized practice of law.

Attending Real Estate Closings

Especially when large transactions involving the transfer of commercial real estate are concerned, real estate paralegals are often instrumental at facilitating the closing of the transaction. Real estate closings can involve the review, signing, and exchanging of numerous documents. Unless expressly permitted in the jurisdiction in which you work, facilitating the closing of a real estate transaction without the presence of an attorney may be considered the unauthorized practice of law. You must be aware of the rules in the area in which you work.

In *The Florida Bar v. Pascual,* 424 So.2d 757 (Fla.1982), the court found that a paralegal who represented a party in the purchase and closing of a restaurant without the supervision of an attorney and gave legal advice to the purchaser was engaged in the unauthorized practice of law.

■ CHAPTER SUMMARY

► Anyone who practices law without a license or special permission is considered to be engaged in the unauthorized practice of law.

► The main goal of laws prohibiting the unauthorized practice of law is to protect the public from representation by unqualified and unscrupulous individuals.

► The code of ethics in every state provides that attorneys have an ethical duty to not engage in the unauthorized practice of law and to not assist any individual in the unauthorized practice of law.

► Attorneys are responsible for supervising their nonattorney employees to the extent that their employees will not be practicing law.

► The legislature and the courts in each state define exactly what constitutes the practice of law.

► In addition to representing individuals in a court of law or administrative tribunal, setting fees for legal work, giving legal advice, and preparing or signing legal documents are all activities considered to be practicing law.

► Actions brought against an individual for the unauthorized practice of law are usually brought by a special committee appointed by a state's bar association under the authority of the highest court in a state.

► Injunctions, citations for contempt of court, and criminal prosecution are the tools most often used for enforcing the unauthorized practice of law rules.

► Paralegals may assist in nearly all aspects of an attorney's representation of a client provided that the paralegal's status is disclosed; the attorney establishes the attorney-client relationship; the paralegal is supervised by the attorney; the attorney remains responsible; the paralegal's work becomes the attorney's work product; the paralegal does not exercise unsupervised legal judgment; and the paralegal is instructed in the standards of client confidentiality.

► Paralegals may represent individuals in administrative agency proceedings if the administrative rules and regulations of that particular agency permit such representation.

► To avoid the unauthorized practice of law, paralegals must never give legal advice.

► Paralegals found to be practicing law may have an injunction filed against them to cease their business practice. They may be found in contempt of court or be charged with a criminal offense.

▶ Paralegals who engage in the unauthorized practice of law may be personally liable for any damages they cause by rendering their services.

▶ More guidance on what constitutes the unauthorized practice of law may be forthcoming with any future regulation of paralegals.

■ FREQUENTLY ASKED QUESTIONS

Can I give legal advice on my blog as along as I identify myself as a paralegal?

No. In general, the giving of legal advice by anyone other than a licensed attorney is considered to be the unauthorized practice of law. You could probably share information with other paralegals, such as where to file real estate documents in your county, but to advise others how to proceed in a legal matter would be the unauthorized practice of law. Identifying yourself as a paralegal is a good idea, but not everyone who views your blog may understand the distinction between paralegals and attorneys. They may misunderstand that you are authorized to give legal advice and not understand the limitations placed on you.

Can an attorney from North Dakota represent a client in a South Dakota court as long as the client is also from North Dakota?

No. Not without a South Dakota license or special permission from the South Dakota court or unless the two states have a reciprocity agreement. Attorneys must be licensed in any state in which they practice law, regardless of where their clients reside.

I work for a sole practitioner. Can I run his office for him while he is out of town for two weeks?

Only on a very limited basis. You can answer telephone calls and correspondence, taking messages and letting clients know that the attorney will call them on his return. If anything urgent comes up that requires legal advice or a decision concerning how to proceed with a client's case, you will have to contact the attorney. You cannot advise the attorney's clients in his absence or appear in court on his behalf.

As a paralegal, will I ever be able to appear in court?

Paralegals often attend court hearings and trials with the attorneys they work for to assist them during the proceeding. Under rare and special circumstances, paralegals may appear in court or in front of other tribunals. Certain administrative agencies allow paralegals to appear in front of their boards or tribunals. Court rules of certain courts also allow paralegals or law clerks to appear to request continuances or handle routine motions. You must check the rules of the pertinent court or administrative agency.

As an independent paralegal, can I offer my services to the public to help individuals complete their own bankruptcy forms and represent themselves in bankruptcy court?

Possibly, but you must be very careful here. You will want to check to see if this type of service is permitted in your state. Some states may have a special certification that you can obtain to allow you to perform such services. When independent paralegals offer their services to the public, there is often a fine distinction between assisting individuals to represent themselves and giving them legal advice and representation. While you may be allowed to provide clerical assistance, you will not be allowed to give legal advice.

Can I use a signature stamp with the signature of the attorney I work for to "sign" correspondence and pleadings when the attorney is out?

While it may be convenient to use a signature stamp to execute correspondence and legal documents, it is not advisable. Although some jurisdictions have approved the use of signature stamps for limited purposes, typically it is best to avoid their use. If you are sending out something that requires an attorney's signature, unauthorized practice of law rules probably dictate that the correspondence or document must be prepared, or at least approved, by an attorney. To send out correspondence or documents with a signature stamp in lieu of an attorney's actual signature may imply that the attorney has not reviewed the document. If you are asked by the attorney you work for to use such a stamp, you may want to research the precedence for using signature stamps in your state.

■ **ENDNOTES**

[1] Comment [1] to Rule 5.5 of the *Model Rules of Professional Conduct* (2004).
[2] ABA Commission on Nonlawyer Practice, Nonlawyer Activity in Law-Related Situations: A Report with Recommendations 126 (1995).
[3] *Louisiana State Bar Association v. Edwins,* 540 So.2d 294 (La. 1989).
[4] 7 AMJUR ATTYS §118 (1997).
[5] *The Florida Bar v. Brumbaugh,* 355 So. 2d 1186 (Fla. 1978).
[6] Texas Government Code §81.101 (2005).
[7] *In Re Opinion No. 24 of Committee on Unauthorized Practice of Law,* 607 A2d 962 (NJ 1992).
[8] *State Bar of Michigan v. Cramer,* 249 NW2d 1 (Mich. 1976).
[9] Guideline 2, *Model Standards and Guidelines for Utilization of Legal Assistants-Paralegals,* National Association of Legal Assistants, Inc. (2005).
[10] Georgia State Attorney Disciplinary Board Advisory Opinion No. 21 (September 16, 2977, DR 3-103).
[11] Michigan Ethics Opinion RI-128 (4/21/92).
[12] *Bowers v. Transamerica Title Insurance Company,* 675 P.2d 193 (1983).
[13] Cowan, Alison Leigh. "Case of the Paralegal Who Played a Lawyer Raises Many Questions," *The New York Times,* January 22, 2007.
[14] *In Re: Goff,* 837 So.2d 1201 (La. 2003).
[15] *The Florida Bar v. We the People Forms and Service Center of Sarasota, Inc.,* 883 So.2d 1280 (Fla. 2004).
[16] *Ohio State Bar Association v. Allen,* 837 N.E.2d 762 (Ohio 2005).
[17] *Trumbull County Bar Association v. Legal Aid State Services, Inc.,* 846 N.E. 2d 35 (Ohio 2004).
[18] *Columbus Bar Association v. Thomas,* 846 N.E. 2d 31 (Ohio 2006).

Chapter 5

Confidentiality

"Three may keep a secret if two of them are dead."
– Benjamin Franklin: *Poor Richard's Almanac* (1735)

INTRODUCTION

To receive the best possible legal representation, clients must divulge all relevant facts to their attorneys, even if the information is embarrassing or damaging. To effectively represent the client and possibly counsel the client to refrain from wrongful conduct, the attorney needs the client's full disclosure.[1] Obviously, a client may be reluctant to divulge information if not assured of the attorney's complete confidentiality. For that reason, attorneys have an ethical duty to keep client confidences and secrets. "The confidences communicated by a client to his attorney must remain inviolate for all time if the public is to have reverence for the law and confidence in its guardians."[2] In *Upjohn v. United States,* the Court discusses some of the ways that the **attorney-client privilege** benefits the public. See Exhibit 5-1. Rules and guidelines concerning client confidentiality come from several sources. In this chapter, we will examine the broad ethical rules concerning client confidentiality and the **confidential** relationship, and the more narrow rules concerning attorney-client privilege in the law of evidence. The second part of this chapter focuses on the issue of confidentiality from the paralegal's perspective.

Exhibit 5-1

"The purpose of the privilege (regarding attorney-client communications) is to encourage full and frank communication between attorneys and their clients and thereby to promote broader public interests in observance of law and the administration of justice. The privilege recognizes that sound legal advice or advocacy serves public ends and that such advice or advocacy depends upon the lawyer being fully informed by the client. . . ."

—*Upjohn v. United States (1981)*

◼ PART I: THE ETHICAL DUTY OF CONFIDENTIALITY

With some exceptions, information imparted to attorneys and paralegals in the course of client representation must be kept confidential and may not be disclosed or discussed with others outside of the office. The rule of confidentiality applies not only to information given to the attorney by the client but also information relating to a client's case from other sources. The rules of confidentiality and the exceptions to the rules vary from state to state. It is important to consult the pertinent state code of ethics whenever a question arises.

Model Rule 1.6(a) of the Model Rules of Professional Conduct establishes the attorney's duty with regard to client confidentiality. Pursuant to Rule 1.6, attorneys may not reveal information relating to representation of a client unless the client gives informed consent, the disclosure is implicitly authorized to carry out the representation of the client, or the disclosure is permitted by one of five special exceptions discussed later in this chapter to prevent harm or protect the attorney.

The attorney's ethical duty of confidentiality extends to the attorney's employees and agents, especially paralegals. The rules of professional conduct provide that attorneys are responsible for safeguarding confidential client information against unauthorized disclosure by individuals who are under their supervision.

What Is Protected?

Information learned by an attorney from or about a client during the course of representing that client is presumed to be confidential. The scope of the attorney's ethical duty of confidentiality is very broad and includes all information relating to the representation regardless of its source. Information received by an attorney from conversations with a client, documents produced by a client, and even an outside source regarding the representation of the client all fall under the attorney's duty of confidentiality.

The attorney's duty of confidentiality usually begins with the first meeting with the client. The ethical duty of confidentiality also applies to prospective clients who consult an attorney in good faith for the purpose of obtaining legal representation or advice, even if the attorney declines representation and performs no legal services for the individual.[3]

An attorney or paralegal may never divulge confidential client information, even after the attorney's representation has terminated. The duty of confidentiality continues after the client-lawyer relationship has terminated and even after the client's death.[4] This rule is of special concern for attorneys and paralegals who leave one law firm to work for another. The attorney or paralegal may never divulge confidential information learned through previous employment—especially if it would be to the detriment of former clients. At times, attorneys or paralegals who go to work for a new law firm find they have confidential information about previous clients that could affect clients in the new law firm. Such situations may cause a conflict of interest and disqualify the attorney or paralegal from working on certain files in the new law firm. Conflicts of interest are discussed in Chapter 6.

Confidentiality and the Corporate Client

The attorney's ethical duty of confidentiality extends to corporate clients in much the same way that it applies to individual clients. The duty of confidentiality and the attorney-client privilege can extend to officers and directors of the corporation as well as to employees at various levels who are acting on behalf of the corporation. The attorney-client privilege also applies to the corporate entity. In effect, this rule prevents attorneys from testifying against their corporate clients in a court of law or from disseminating confidential information about the corporation.

Exceptions

As with most important rules of ethics, there are exceptions to the rule of confidentiality. Two important exceptions relate to the attorney's ability to better serve the client and are considered to be in the client's best interests:

1. A lawyer may divulge confidential information if the client gives informed consent.

2. A lawyer may divulge confidential information when the disclosure is impliedly authorized to carry out the representation.

After explanation from their attorneys, clients often give their express permission to disclose information concerning their representation to third parties to further their own interests. For example, a client may authorize his or her attorney to discuss confidential financial records with the client's accountant.

An attorney is implicitly authorized to make disclosures about a client when appropriate in carrying out the representation, except to the extent that the client's instructions or special circumstances limit that authority.[5] If attorneys did not have implied authorization to discuss their clients' matters with others, it would be most difficult for them to practice law. For example, while litigating a case for a client, it is often necessary to disclose certain information to negotiate a satisfactory settlement.

In addition, it may be in the client's best interest for his or her attorney to consult with other attorneys within the law firm who may have past experience in similar situations or a certain expertise that will assist the attorney's representation. Attorneys and paralegals within a firm may discuss a client's case among themselves unless circumstances warrant otherwise. If an attorney or paralegal needs to consult with an attorney outside of the firm, the client's permission must be obtained. It is usually considered proper for an attorney to give limited information to outside agencies for bookkeeping, accounting, data processing, photocopying, and similar reasons, as long as the agency is selected with due care and is warned concerning the confidential nature of the information.

In addition to these two exceptions that are considered to be in the client's best interests, there are exceptions to the rules concerning client confidentiality that may be adverse to the client's interests but are allowed to protect the public or the integrity of the court. These rules vary among the states and have been the topic of much controversy in recent years. Rule 1.6(b) of the ABA's Model Rules of Professional Conduct, as amended provide that in addition to the two exceptions discussed above, lawyers may reveal information relating to the representation of a client to the extent the lawyer reasonably believes necessary to prevent death or bodily harm or, under certain circumstances, prevent or rectify substantial injury to financial or property interests. Also under the Model Rules, attorneys may reveal client information to secure legal advice about the attorney's compliance with the rules or to establish a claim or defense on behalf of the attorney if a controversy arises between the client and attorney or if the attorney faces civil or criminal charges based on the attorney's representation of the client. Attorneys may also be required to reveal client confidences to comply with other laws or if directed by a court order.

To Prevent Death or Physical Injury

Under Rule 1.6(b)(1) of the Model Rules of Professional Conduct, an attorney *may* divulge confidential information to prevent the client from taking an action that the attorney is reasonably certain would result in the death or substantial bodily harm of another. If a client confesses murder to his or her attorney, the attorney has no right or duty to disclose that information. If, on the other hand, the client convincingly tells the attorney that he or she is going to commit murder after their meeting, the attorney may disclose that information to prevent the reasonably certain death of the intended victim. The attorney must divulge no more information than absolutely necessary to prevent the crime from being committed.

Many jurisdictions that have adopted the Model Rules have not adopted this rule verbatim. Some states allow an attorney to divulge confidential information to prevent *any* future crime, and some *require* attorneys to divulge confidential information to prevent certain crimes.

An attorney whose client consults him about intentions for future criminal behavior must attempt to counsel the client from committing such a crime.

To Prevent, Rectify, or Mitigate Loss Caused by Client's Past Crime or Fraud

Model Rule 1.6(b)(2) provides that under certain circumstances, an attorney may reveal confidential information to prevent a financial loss to a third party. This is a new exception under the Model Rules, recommended by the ABA Task Force on Corporate Responsibility in 2003, partly in response to the Enron bankruptcy and related scandals.[6] For example, suppose that an attorney discovers her client, a CEO of a public corporation, intends to submit falsified corporate financial statements to the SEC. The misinformation is intended to attract investors who would probably end up paying too much for the stock and possibly losing their investment. The attorney may take any steps necessary to prevent the release of the falsified financial statements and prevent the financial loss to investors, including disclosing otherwise confidential information.

Model Rule 1.6(b)(3) applies when the client has already committed the fraud or crime, but there still remains a possibility to prevent, mitigate, or rectify the losses suffered by third parties. If, for example, the attorney learns that financial statements already submitted by the client were falsified and greatly overstated the corporation's income, the attorney may reveal that information to prevent further losses being suffered by the corporation's investors.

Under the Model Rules, both exceptions concerning the financial loss of a third party due to the crime or fraud of the client are limited to substantial injury and situations where the client used the attorney's services to further the crime. The drafters of this new rule stated that it was their belief that "the interest of society, and the bar, in assuring that a lawyer's services are not used by a client in the furtherance of a crime or a fraud justifies an exception to the important principle of confidentiality." [7]

To Obtain Legal Advice Concerning the Attorney's Ethical Responsibilities

Because an attorney's obligation to follow the applicable rules of ethics is so important and because circumstances can make those rules difficult to apply to certain situations, attorneys may divulge confidences to seek legal advice concerning their obligations under the pertinent rules of ethics.

To Establish a Defense to a Legal Claim or Disciplinary Charge Against the Lawyer

Where a legal claim or disciplinary charge alleges complicity of the attorney in a client's misconduct or other misconduct of the attorney involving representation of the client, the lawyer may respond to the extent the lawyer reasonably believes necessary to establish a defense.[8] If an attorney is involved in a civil action that he or she must personally defend due to the representation of a client, the attorney may divulge such information as necessary to defend him or herself. Attorneys may divulge only as much information as necessary for their defense.

An attorney entitled to a fee is also permitted to divulge the minimum information necessary to prove the services rendered to collect that fee.

To Comply with Other Law or Court Order

Model Rule 1.6(b)(6) provides that an attorney may reveal information relating to the representation of a client to comply with other law or a court order. Some exceptions to the rule of confidentiality provided by other law include:

1. an attorney may divulge information to prevent making a false statement of fact or law to a court or other tribunal or to correct a false statement of material fact or law previously made to the tribunal by the attorney.[9]

2. an attorney may divulge information to prevent **perjury** or fraud on the court.[10]

3. an attorney may divulge information under certain circumstances when ordered to do so by a court of law.

4. an attorney has a legal obligation to report to the IRS any cash receipts from clients in excess of $10,000.[11]

While the rules of most states are based on the Model Rules of Professional Conduct, there are several significant differences among the states with regard to client confidentiality. Exhibit 5-2 gives examples of how states may adopt their own rules concerning confidentiality. Note the different requirements for attorneys to reveal confidences to prevent a crime in these states pursuant to the Texas Disciplinary Rules of Professional Conduct 1.05(c)(7) and California Rules of Professional Conduct Rule 3-100(b). It is always important to be familiar with the rules of ethics concerning confidentiality in the state in which you work.

Exhibit 5-2

From the Texas Disciplinary Rules of Professional Conduct

1.05 Confidentiality of Information

(c) A lawyer may reveal confidential information:

    (1) When the lawyer has been expressly authorized to do so in order to carry out the representation.

    (2) When the client consents after consultation.

    (3) To the client, the client's representatives, or the members, associates, and employees of the lawyer's firm, except when otherwise instructed by the client.

    (4) When the lawyer has reason to believe it is necessary to do so in order to comply with a court order, a Texas Disciplinary Rule of Professional Conduct, or other law.

    (5) To the extent reasonably necessary to enforce a claim or establish a defense on behalf of the lawyer in a controversy between the lawyer and the client.

    (6) To establish a defense to a criminal charge, civil claim or disciplinary complaint against the lawyer or the lawyer's associates based upon conduct involving the client or the representation of the client.

    (7) When the lawyer has reason to believe it is necessary to do so in order to prevent the client from committing a criminal or fraudulent act.

    (8) To the extent revelation reasonably appears necessary to rectify the consequences of a client's criminal or fraudulent act in the commission of which the lawyer's services had been used. . . .

(e) When a lawyer has confidential information clearly establishing that a client is likely to commit a criminal or fraudulent act that is likely to result in death or substantial bodily harm to a person, the lawyer shall reveal confidential information to the extent revelation reasonably appears necessary to prevent the client from committing the criminal or fraudulent act.

(f) A lawyer shall reveal confidential information when required to do so by Rule 3.03(a)(2), 3.03(b), or by Rule 4.01(b).

From the California Rules of Professional Conduct

Rule 3-100. Confidential Information of a Client

(A) A member shall not reveal information protected from disclosure by Business and Professions Code section 6068, subdivision (e)(1) without the informed consent of the client, or as provided in paragraph (B) of this rule.

(B) A member may, but is not required to, reveal confidential information relating to the representation of a client to the extent that the member reasonably believes the disclosure is necessary to prevent a criminal act that the member reasonably believes is likely to result in death of, or substantial bodily harm to, an individual.

(C) Before revealing confidential information to prevent a criminal act as provided in paragraph (B), a member shall, if reasonable under the circumstances:

    (1) make a good faith effort to persuade the client: (i) not to commit or to continue the criminal act or (ii) to pursue a course of conduct that will prevent the threatened death or substantial bodily harm; or do both (i) and (ii); and

    (2) inform the client, at an appropriate time, of the member's ability or decision to reveal information as provided in paragraph (B).

(D) In revealing confidential information as provided in paragraph (B), the member's disclosure must be no more than is necessary to prevent the criminal act, given the information known to the member at the time of the disclosure.

(E) A member who does not reveal information permitted by paragraph (B) does not violate this rule.

Chapter 5

⊕ ATTORNEY-CLIENT PRIVILEGE

In addition to the ethical rule of client confidentiality, the attorney-client relationship is subject to the attorney-client privilege, which includes the work product rule.

The attorney-client privilege is a privilege found in **evidence law** that governs the use of information in a court proceeding. An attorney who is called on to testify or provide **evidence** concerning the representation of a client may claim the attorney-client privilege and refuse to testify or provide such evidence. The burden of proof concerning the attorney-client privilege is usually on the party claiming the privilege, but the court will make the final determination as to whether the testimony being sought is protected by the privilege. The attorney-client privilege provides that the attorney may not be called on to give testimony concerning confidential information disclosed to the attorney by the client during the course of representation. Exhibit 5-3 is a comparison between the ethical rule of confidentiality and the attorney-client privilege.

Exhibit 5-3

Ethical Rule of Confidentiality vs. Attorney-Client Privilege

Ethical Rule of Confidentiality	Attorney-Client Privilege
Found in the pertinent code of ethics	Found in evidence law
Concerns all actions of the attorney regarding confidential information concerning the client	Concerns judicial and other proceedings in which an attorney may be called as a witness or required to provide evidence concerning a client
Protects all information the attorney has relating to a client, regardless of its source	Concerns communications made by the client in a confidential setting for the purpose of securing legal advice or assistance
Applies to past wrongdoings and the contemplation of certain future wrongdoings	Applies to past wrongdoings—not to contemplation of future wrongdoings
With limited exceptions, prevents all disclosures of confidential information	Does not prevent disclosures outside the judicial process or information received from sources other than the client

The attorney-client privilege generally continues even after the client's death. This rule was upheld in a 1998 U.S. Supreme Court decision, when the court held that deputy White House counsel Vincent Foster's attorney, James Hamilton, could not be compelled to turn over notes from a meeting between Foster and Hamilton. The notes in question, which had been subpoenaed as directed by independent prosecutor Ken Starr, were from a July 1993 meeting during which confidential matters were discussed, including various investigations of staff firings in the White House travel office. Mr. Foster committed suicide just nine days after the meeting.

In its ruling, the Supreme Court held that: "Knowing that communications will remain confidential even after death encourages the client to communicate fully and frankly with counsel. While the fear of disclosure, and the consequent withholding of information from counsel, may be reduced if disclosure is limited to posthumous disclosure in a criminal context, it seems unreasonable to assume that it vanishes altogether. Clients may be concerned about reputation, civil liability, or possible harm to friends or family. Posthumous disclosure of such communications may be as feared as disclosure during the client's lifetime."[12]

Because the attorney-client privilege has the effect of keeping the truth from the court, the scope of the privilege is more limited than the attorney's ethical duty of confidentiality and applies only in judicial and other proceedings in which an attorney may be called as a witness or required to provide evidence concerning a client. The privilege applies only to communications made between a client and an attorney or agent of the attorney in a confidential setting for the purpose of securing legal advice or assistance. It does not prevent disclosures outside the judicial process or information received from sources other than the client.

Waiver of the Attorney-Client Privilege

The attorney-client privilege may be waived expressly or implicitly—but only by the client. The client owns the privilege. The attorney may not waive it. When the privilege is waived, it is given up by the client and the attorney may disclose the confidential information in question.

The attorney-client privilege is waived expressly when the client, either verbally or in writing, gives the attorney permission to disclose confidential information otherwise covered by the privilege. A client may do this for several reasons when he or she feels that it is to the client's advantage to disclose the information to the public or to certain individuals. For example, a client may permit her attorney to disclose confidential information in court if the client feels it is in her best interest to do so.

An implied waiver of the attorney-client privilege may be given by certain actions taken by the client. For example, if a client goes public with information otherwise covered by the privilege, the client has implicitly waived the privilege. It may also be considered a waiver of the attorney-client privilege if a client divulges otherwise confidential information to a third party. However, it is generally not considered a waiver of the attorney-client privilege if the client divulges confidential information in front of a paralegal or another agent of the attorney.

> ### OF INTEREST
> Because paralegals are agents of the attorneys they work for, most communications between a paralegal and a client for the purposes of assisting the attorney to provide legal advice and services to the client are considered privileged.

Work Product Rule

Before a case proceeds to trial, there is a period of **discovery.** Discovery is a "means for providing a party, in advance of trial, with access to facts that are within the knowledge of the other side, to enable the party to better try her case."[13] The discovery process may include **interrogatories, requests for production of documents, depositions,** and other means prescribed by applicable law. In federal court, the various instruments of discovery serve to "narrow and clarify the basic issues between the parties and as a device for ascertaining the facts, or information or as to the existence or whereabouts of facts, relative to those issues."[14]

Although the discovery process is far reaching, not all information in an attorney's possession is discoverable. The **work product rule** provides that an attorney's work product is privileged and not subject to discovery. Three criteria have been recognized as necessary to invoke the work product rule. The material in question must be:

1. documents and tangible things otherwise discoverable.

2. prepared in anticipation of litigation.

3. by or for another party or that party's representative.[15]

The work product rule generally includes memoranda and other documents prepared by an attorney in preparation of litigation. The exact documentation that falls under the work product rule depends on the circumstances of each case and the importance of the documentation to the case.

Under certain circumstances, the inadvertent disclosure of documents can result in a waiver of the attorney-client privilege under the work-product rule, especially when that inadvertent disclosure is considered to be extremely careless or negligent. Exhibit 5-4 is a summary of conditions under which the attorney-client privilege may be applied.

Exhibit 5-4

Conditions for Applying the Attorney-Client Privilege

- The communication must be between individuals subject to the privilege (including the client, attorney, and attorney's agents).
- The communication must be made in a confidential setting.
- The communication must be for the purpose of securing legal advice or assistance.

CASE ON POINT

In a case heard in Massachusetts, the court held that the attorney-client privilege was waived due to the attorney's gross negligence when he inadvertently produced a box of over 3,200 pages of privileged material.

—*Amgen V. Hoechst Marion Roussel, Inc., 190 F.R.D. 287 (Mass. 2000)*

PART II: FROM THE PARALEGAL'S PERSPECTIVE

The issue of client confidentiality is of special concern to paralegals because the privilege of confidentiality clearly extends to the lawyer's employees and law firm staff, especially paralegals. Paralegals are often in a position to receive confidential information and must at all times resist the temptation to disclose this information, either to the media, as a matter of convenience when working on a client's file, or as a source of interesting gossip with friends and family. Breaching a client's confidentiality can have serious consequences to paralegals and to the attorneys they work for.

A QUESTION OF ETHICS

You are reviewing the Answers to Interrogatories received on the *Burns v. Value Auto* case when you find something amiss on page 32. There is an extra page stuck in the document, upside down and backward. A yellow Post-it on the extra page reads "Please mark 'Confidential' and file in the Value Auto file." A quick glance at the extra page tells you that it is correspondence from Tim Jensen, the president of Value Auto, to his attorney—the opposing counsel in the *Burns v. Value Auto* case. The correspondence was apparently stuck in among the documents unintentionally.

This is really intriguing; there may be something that could benefit your client in this letter. What do you do?

Answer and Discussion

While court rulings on inadvertent disclosure may vary depending on the jurisdiction and the circumstances, and while you will want to check with your supervising attorney, your safest course of action is to fold the letter (without reading it) and put it in an envelope returning it to the opposing counsel. You or your supervising attorney should call opposing counsel to let them know the letter is on its way back. Although some courts have ruled that an unintentional disclosure of attorney-client communications waives the attorney-client privilege, when an attorney (or paralegal) inadvertently receives materials that appear to be confidential and not intended for him or her, the recipient should refrain from examining the materials, notify the sending attorney, and abide by the sending attorney's instructions.[16] Rule 4.4 of the Model Rules of Professional Conduct indicates that attorneys who receive documents inadvertently shall promptly notify the sender.

THE PARALEGAL'S ETHICAL DUTY OF CONFIDENTIALITY

Both national paralegal associations recognize the importance of maintaining client confidentiality in their codes of ethics.

The NALA's Rules

The paralegal's ethical duty to maintaining client confidences is set forth in Canon 7 of the NALA Code of Ethics and Professional Responsibility, which must be adhered to by all members of NALA. See Exhibit 5-5.

Exhibit 5-5

From the NALA's Code of Ethics and Professional Responsibility

CANON 7

A paralegal must protect the confidences of a client and must not violate any rule or statute now in effect or hereafter enacted controlling the doctrine of privileged communications between a client and an attorney.

The NFPA's Rules

Canon 1.5 of the NFPA's Model Code of Ethics and Professional Responsibility, set forth in Exhibit 5-6, establishes the NFPA's rule with regard to confidentiality.

Exhibit 5-6

From the NFPA Model Code of Ethics and Professional Responsibility and Guidelines for Enforcement

1.5 A PARALEGAL SHALL PRESERVE ALL CONFIDENTIAL INFORMATION PROVIDED BY THE CLIENT OR ACQUIRED FROM OTHER SOURCES BEFORE, DURING, AND AFTER THE COURSE OF THE PROFESSIONAL RELATIONSHIP.

ETHICAL CONSIDERATIONS

EC-1.5(a)   A paralegal shall be aware of and abide by all legal authority governing confidential information in the jurisdiction in which the paralegal practices.

EC-1.5(b)   A paralegal shall not use confidential information to the disadvantage of the client.

EC-1.5(c)   A paralegal shall not use confidential information to the advantage of the paralegal or of a third person.

EC-1.5(d)   A paralegal may reveal confidential information only after full disclosure and with the client's written consent; or, when required by law or court order; or, when necessary to prevent the client from committing an act that could result in death or serious bodily harm.

EC-1.5(e)   A paralegal shall keep those individuals responsible for the legal representation of a client fully informed of any confidential information the paralegal may have pertaining to that client.

EC-1.5(f)   A paralegal shall not engage in any indiscreet communications concerning clients.

Ethical Consideration 1.5(a) is of the utmost importance to paralegals. It reaffirms that paralegals are subject to the code of ethics and case law in any jurisdiction in which they work. As discussed previously, although most states in the country have adopted the significant provisions of the ABA's Model Rules of Professional Conduct, there are many variations from the Model Rules among the states, especially in the area of attorney-client confidentiality.

As a paralegal, you will often be in a position to learn client confidences and secrets, many of which could be potentially harmful or damaging to a client. Ethical Consideration 1.5(b) of the NFPA's Model Code provides that you must never use this information to the client's disadvantage. You must never disclose any confidential information that could be to the disadvantage of a client unless required by law.

Paralegals may find themselves in a position to learn confidential information that could be used to their advantage. Ethical Consideration 1.5(c) of the NFPA's Model Code provides that confidential client information must never be used to the advantage of the paralegal. For example, a paralegal could be in a position to learn inside information on a corporation that could affect the price of the stock. For a paralegal to act on that confidential information by buying or selling stock of that corporation or recommending it to a friend would not only be unethical, but it would also be illegal.

OF INTEREST

In 2002, a paralegal in Manhattan was sentenced to 2½ years in jail for his attempt to sell trial strategy documents to the opposing counsel.

—*U.S. Department of Justice Press Release (January 30, 2002)*

Remember that the NFPA's Model Code of Ethics and Professional Responsibility has no binding authority and may vary from a state's code of ethics and state law. You must always be aware of and adhere to the state code of ethics and state law applicable to attorneys.

To provide the client with the best possible representation, the attorney must be aware of all the pertinent facts. The rules of attorney-client confidentiality are designed to encourage the client to make full disclosures to the attorney, even if the information is embarrassing or damaging to the client. The paralegal must not keep confidential client information from the attorney. In fact, Ethical Consideration 1.5(e) of the NFPA's Model Code specifically provides that the paralegal has a duty to keep the attorney apprised of any pertinent confidential information learned about the client.

At times, a paralegal may be in a position to learn confidential information that is almost overwhelmingly intriguing. Whether it is to your mother, your best friend, or the *Inquirer*, you must always resist the temptation to talk about a client or client's case outside of the office.

PARALEGALS AND THE ATTORNEY-CLIENT PRIVILEGE

Courts have found that paralegals are also subject to the attorney-client privilege. In a case heard in Kentucky in 2000, the court found that the attorney work product prepared by a paralegal on the corporate counsel's staff was protected "with equal force" as any trial preparation material prepared by an attorney in anticipation of litigation.[17]

PRACTICAL CONSIDERATIONS

A study of all the pertinent rules of ethics and laws still will not tell you everything you need to know concerning client confidentiality. In addition, you need common sense and an understanding of the practical issues you will face in keeping your client's confidential information confidential and avoiding any inadvertent disclosures. Courts have found that an attorney-client privilege can be waived if the privileged information is not treated with care to keep it confidential. That task often falls to paralegals.

Keeping Communications Confidential

Modern law offices are usually designed with privacy and confidentiality in mind. Even so, you must be careful that confidential information is not accidentally leaked by conversations that may be overheard.

In the Office

Even though it is permissible to discuss confidential client information with associates within the office, such conversations should be confined to those with a need to know. Idle gossip around the water cooler with coworkers who have nothing to do with a particular client can lead to leaks and trouble.

All client conferences should be held in private offices or in a private conference room with the door shut. You should always avoid confidential discussions with a client in common areas of the office, especially areas such as the reception area where other clients could overhear.

If you work for a law firm or other type of organization with a receptionist who is located in a common reception area, the receptionist must be aware of the need to keep client names and other information confidential. Callers should be announced quietly—out of earshot of anyone who may be waiting in the reception area.

Outside the Office

Not all confidential meetings and conversations will take place in the office. There will always be the need to meet at a client's office, at the office of the opposing counsel, or even a business lunch. Caution must always be used when discussing confidential matters outside of the office. You must use extra caution that no confidential information is overheard. Keep the use of names and specifics to a minimum when your conversation may be overheard.

Cell Phones

Cell phones are usually considered to be private and secure. However, it is possible that cell phone conversations can be overheard. If you are using a cell phone for a confidential and sensitive conversation, it is advisable that you let the party you are speaking to know so that they will not say anything they do not want overheard.

Fax and E-mail

Communications by fax and e-mail are accepted almost as a necessity in the modern law office. If you are operating the fax machine, always double-check the telephone number being used. If you fax documents to the wrong number, they cannot be taken back. You may want to limit the use of the speed dial and redial features to give yourself time to think things through before the actual transmission of documents. Before you send a fax, you must picture in your mind the receiving fax machine. If your transmission is going to another office, will it go to a fax machine where it can be picked up by anyone who may be near the machine? If so, you may want to call ahead to see that the recipient is standing by, ready to receive your message. Many law firms and law departments include a message on their fax cover sheet indicating that the transmission is confidential and should be forwarded to the intended party immediately.

Many law firms use e-mail to communicate with each other in the office, with attorneys in other offices, and with clients. If you are ever in a position to transmit confidential client information by e-mail, you must use the proper security measures to assure that the information does not land in the wrong hands. This includes always using a secure password and turning off your computer screen when you are not using your computer. Always stop and think before hitting the send button, especially if your e-mail software automatically completes the e-mail address for you. Make sure you are sending your e-mail to the correct address.

Most law firms have invested heavily in technology to protect the confidentiality of their clients, making e-mail a relatively secure means of communication. If you are using your personal computer and software outside of the office, you must be equally sure client confidentiality is protected.

Talking to the Press

This section may be more appropriately called *Not Talking to the Press*. If a reporter requesting information on a particular client or case contacts you, your only response can be "No comment!" You can take a message and refer the call to the supervising attorney. You will probably not want to give out the attorney's name or phone number unless you have discussed the situation in advance. Never talk to the press concerning a client or a case without the permission of the supervising attorney.

Protecting Confidential Files and Documents

Just as important as protecting confidential conversations and messages is protecting confidential files and documentation. Files and confidential documents must always be kept in a secure location to prevent loss, theft, or the inadvertent breach of confidential information.

Securing Files after Hours

All client files should be locked in fireproof file cabinets at night to prevent loss by fire or theft or a breach of confidence. If there are no fireproof file cabinets within the attorney or paralegal offices, the files should be kept in a safe central location.

Chapter 5

Keeping Confidential Information Out of Sight

Never leave confidential information in plain sight. If you meet with clients in your office, you must be certain that no confidential information is left lying about on your desk or cabinets. You must also be certain that confidential documents are not visible on your computer screen. Be sure to take a quick look over your office before admitting a client or anyone else to your office to make sure that all confidential information is secure.

Shredding Confidential Materials When Necessary

The manner in which confidential client documents are disposed of can affect their protection under the attorney-client privilege. Drafts of confidential documents and other information that are to be disposed of should be shredded whenever possible. Confidential documents should not land in trashcans that will eventually be emptied into a central location.

Double Checking Everything That Leaves the Office

When you are sending information out of the office, especially if you are sending large volumes of documents to opposing counsel, such as a response to a request for a production of documents, you must always double-check to see that nothing is inadvertently sent out of the office or sent to the wrong person. If necessary, review your correspondence and your secretary or assistant's outgoing mail, with the rules of confidentiality in mind.

Dealing with Outside Services

Exceptions to the ethical codes of conduct allow for the utilization of outside services, such as billing services, photocopying services, and file storage services. Only the minimum information required should be given to these types of services. When using such outside services, you must be certain that you use a reliable service that employs individuals who are aware of the importance of confidentiality. Under certain circumstances, outside vendors may be requested to execute confidentiality agreements, promising their confidentiality. See Exhibit 5-7 for a summary of tips for keeping client information and documents confidential.

Exhibit 5-7

Tips for Keeping Client Information and Documents Confidential

Be sure you never meet with clients in a part of the office where your conversation could be overheard.

Keep office conversations concerning clients on a need-to-know basis—foregoing idle gossip.

Be sure client meetings held outside the office take place in a location where your conversation cannot be overheard.

Double check addresses on all correspondence leaving the office—including e-mail.

Double check any e-mail attachments you send out to make sure you do not send out the wrong document in error.

Check all fax phone numbers and dial carefully.

When holding meetings in your office, make sure no confidential information is visible on your desk, cabinet, or computer screen.

Do not talk to the press.

Lock all files in fireproof file cabinets at the end of the day.

Shred confidential materials you are disposing of.

When dealing with outside photocopy, billing, file storage, or similar services, make sure you are dealing with reputable services. Get signed confidentiality agreements when necessary.

SPECIAL CONSIDERATIONS FOR SPECIALISTS

The rules of confidentiality and the attorney-client privilege extend to every area of law. However, the area of law in which you practice will have a practical effect on how you apply the rules.

Litigation Paralegals

Litigation paralegals are often very involved in the discovery process, especially gathering and assembling documents for the discovery process. Document production can involve the review and production of numerous boxes of documents. If you are assigned such a task, you must be very sure that you are familiar with the pertinent work product rules. If in doubt, be sure to ask your supervising attorney.

You must also be sure to be especially vigilant whenever documents are sent to the opposing counsel to be sure that nothing is inadvertently disclosed. All documents leaving the office should be double checked.

If you are assisting an attorney in a courtroom setting, make sure that all of your conferences with your client are held in a private location where you cannot be overheard.

Personal Injury Paralegals

In addition to the special concerns that all litigation paralegals face, personal injury paralegals often deal with confidential medical records of clients or the opposing party. The rules of confidentiality that protect your clients can sometimes make it difficult to represent them too. Paralegals who request medical records, either their client's records or medical records of an opposing party, must have the proper authorization. Authorization for release of medical records must be given in accordance with the regulations of the federal **Health Insurance Portability and Accountability Act (HIPAA).** Privacy Rules under HIPPA require healthcare providers to obtain authorizations that contain very specific information before they can release any medical information about a patient. Personal injury paralegals must be familiar with the rules of confidentiality, the attorney-client privilege, and the HIPAA Privacy Rules.

Corporate Paralegals

Special attention to client confidentiality must be given by the corporate paralegal working in the securities or merger and acquisition areas. Rumors regarding mergers and acquisitions can have a devastating effect on the outcome of the proposed transaction as well as an effect on the price of the stock of either or both parties involved. Likewise, unauthorized leaks of information from a law firm that represents publicly held corporations, or corporations that are planning public offerings, can have significant financial implications for the client. All information regarding a publicly held corporation must be closely monitored and released only with forethought. If information passed on to third parties regarding a publicly held corporation is considered "inside information," anyone buying or selling stock of the subject corporation based on that information could be guilty of insider trading and subject to civil lawsuits or even criminal prosecution under federal securities laws.

Family Law Paralegals

Family law paralegals often find themselves working with clients who seek the attorney's assistance to obtain a divorce. In most instances, even if the divorce is very amicable, the attorney will only be representing one of the parties. The parties themselves may, at times, forget that fact. If you work as a family law paralegal, you must be sure to remember who it is, your attorney is representing. Never share information that may be considered confidential with the other party.

Criminal Law Paralegals

Criminal law paralegals can find themselves in some interesting ethical dilemmas. You must always remember the basic rules of confidentiality when working in the criminal law setting and never discuss anything you learn from a criminal representation outside of the law office. If you are ever in a position to hear a client confess to a crime, that confession will probably need to remain confidential. Discuss it *only* with the responsible attorney.

■ CHAPTER SUMMARY

▶ With a few exceptions, attorneys and paralegals have an ethical duty to keep confidential information learned from and about the client during the course of representation.

▶ The rule of confidentiality begins with the client's first meeting with the attorney and lasts indefinitely.

▶ The attorney-client privilege is a privilege found in evidence law that governs the use of information in court proceedings.

▶ The attorney-client privilege protects communications made for the purpose of securing legal advice or assistance.

▶ The rules for confidentiality are prescribed by state law and by the code of ethics that is binding on attorneys in each state.

▶ The attorney's ethical duty of confidentiality extends to the attorney's employees, especially paralegals.

▶ Confidential information may be divulged with the client's permission and when disclosure is implicitly authorized.

▶ In some instances, confidential information may be divulged to prevent the commission of a crime.

▶ Confidential information may be disclosed to establish a claim or defense in a controversy between an attorney and client.

▶ Confidential information must be divulged to rectify or prevent a fraud on the court.

▶ Both national paralegal associations recognize the importance of client confidentiality and include provisions requiring paralegals to maintain client confidentiality in their codes of ethics.

▶ Confidential client information may be discussed as necessary with other attorneys and paralegals within the office. Client permission is usually required to release confidential information to attorneys outside of the office who may be consulted.

▶ Care must be taken that confidential conversations with or about a client are never overheard either within the office or outside of the office.

▶ Written confidential information that must be disposed of should be shredded.

■ FREQUENTLY ASKED QUESTIONS

A couple of years ago, I was involved in a very interesting murder case that got a lot of publicity. I just got a call from an author who will be writing a book about the crime and the trial who would like to interview me. Since we no longer represent the client, is it okay to grant an interview with the author?

No. The rules of confidentiality outlast the attorney's representation of the client. In fact, an attorney or paralegal may never divulge confidential client information, even after the client's death.

Is it okay to send copies of financial documents from our files to our client's accountants?

It depends on the working relationship between the attorney, client, and the accountant. If they are working on an ongoing transaction, such as the purchase of a business, it would be understood that the attorney and accountant would share information. If, however, it is an unfamiliar accountant calling to request financial information concerning one of your clients, you should obtain the client's permission first.

Is information given to the attorney by the client still considered confidential and privileged if I attend the meeting?

Yes. Although, under certain circumstances, the attorney-client privilege may be waived if the client divulges otherwise confidential information in the presence of a third party, there is generally no waiver of the privilege when information is shared in the presence of a paralegal or another agent of the attorney.

Is it okay to discuss client cases with other paralegals in the law firm?

While idle gossip around the water cooler is not a good idea, it is often necessary and advisable to discuss your clients' cases with others in your firm to get their help or advice.

Is it okay to send a client an e-mail containing confidential information?

Yes, as long as you take proper precautions. First, make sure you are sending from a secure computer. Most law firms have the proper security software installed on all computers in the law firm. Also, you will want to make sure that you are sending the confidential information to a computer that is secure. You should check with your clients to make sure that they have sole and private access to their e-mails. Always be sure to verify the e-mail address.

■ ENDNOTES

[1] Model Rules of Professional Conduct, Rule 1.6 (2004).
[2] *U.S. v. Standard Oil Co*, 136 F. Supp. 345, 355 (S.D. N.Y. 1955).
[3] The ABA Commission on Ethics and Professional Responsibility, Formal Opinion 90-358 (1990).
[4] Model Rules of Professional Conduct Rule 1.6 (2004).
[5] Model Rules of Professional Conduct Rule 1.6 (2004).
[6] Report of the ABA Task Force on Corporate Responsibility, March 31, 2003.
[7] Report of the ABA Task Force on Corporate Responsibility, March 31, 2003.
[8] Model Rules of Professional Conduct Rule 1.6 (2004).
[9] Model Rules of Professional Conduct, Rule 3.3 (2004).
[10] Model Rules of Professional Conduct, Rule 3.3 (2004).
[11] 26 U.S.C.A. §6050I.
[12] *Swidler & Berline et al. v. the United States*, 118 S.Ct. 2081 (1998).
[13] *Ballentine's Legal Dictionary and Thesaurus*, Lawyers Cooperative Publishing (1995).
[14] *Hickman v. Taylor*, 329 U.S. 495 (1947).
[15] *Gold Standard v. American Resources*, 805 P.2d 164 (Utah 1990).
[16] The ABA Commission on Ethics and Professional Responsibility, Formal Opinion 92-368 (1992).
[17] *Wal-Mart Stores, Inc. v. Dickinson*, 29 S.W.3d 796 (Ky. 2000).

Chapter 6

Conflict of Interest

*"Lack of loyalty is one of the major causes of
failure in every walk of life."*
– Napoleon Hill

■ PART I: CONFLICTS OF INTEREST

Of the utmost importance in any attorney-client relationship are the duties of
loyalty and confidentiality owed to the client by the attorney. An attorney must
not represent a client unless he or she can do so with undivided loyalty.
"Loyalty to a client prohibits undertaking representation directly adverse to that
client without that client's consent."[1] When the interests of the client conflict
with the interests of the attorney or other clients represented by the attorney,
it is referred to as a **conflict of interest.** Conflicts of interest may arise from
an attorney's responsibilities to another client or to a former client or from the
attorney's own interests.[2]

If a conflict of interest will arise from representation of a new client, the
attorney should decline that representation. If a conflict of interest arises during
the representation of a client, the attorney must withdraw from representation.
When interpreting conflict of interest rules, courts must consider the attorney's
duty of loyalty to the client, the economic interests of the attorney, and the
public's interest in the availability of legal services.[3]

An attorney with a conflict of interest who does not voluntarily withdraw
may be disqualified from representing a client by court order on motion brought
by opposing counsel. Consequences of impermissible conflicts of interest can
include compensatory damages awarded in civil malpractice lawsuits, loss of
fees, loss of clients, reprimands, and other sanctions meted out by the state
attorney disciplinary board.

OF INTEREST

Conflict of interest is the third-most common and the second-most costly error for which malpractice claims are filed.

—*LawPro Magazine*, *"Conflicts of Interest," March 2003*

Not only attorneys are subject to ethical rules concerning conflicts of interest. It is also possible for paralegals to become involved in conflicts. It is, therefore, very important that paralegals are familiar with the rules of ethics concerning conflicts of interest. The first part of this chapter is devoted to the rules concerning conflicts of interest. Our discussion includes the basic rules, client consent to permit representation notwithstanding conflicts, and the rules that may apply in special situations. The second part of this chapter focuses on conflicts of interest from the paralegal's perspective, including the rules of the paralegal associations and practical considerations for avoiding conflicts of interest. Exhibit 6-1 is a summary of situations in which a conflict of interest may arise.

Exhibit 6-1

Conflicts of Interest

A Conflict of Interest can arise when . . .

- The interests of two clients are **directly adverse**
- The attorney's representation of one client could be **materially limited** by
  1. The attorney's representation of **another current client**
  2. The attorney's representation of a **former client**
  3. A **business interest of the attorney**
  4. A **personal interest of the attorney**

CONCURRENT CONFLICTS OF INTEREST

When the attorney's representation of a current client may be compromised by the attorney's responsibilities to another client, a former client, a third party, or by the attorney's personal or business interests, the attorney has a **concurrent conflict of interest.** In states that follow Rule 1.7(a) of the ABA's Model Rules of Professional Conduct, an attorney is considered to have a concurrent conflict of interest if the representation of one client would be directly adverse to another client the attorney represents or if there is a significant risk that the attorney's representation of one client will be materially limited by the attorney's responsibilities to another client, a former client or a third person, or by a personal interest of the attorney. Exhibit 6–2 illustrates how the state of Arizona defines a concurrent conflict of interest. Arizona is one state that follows the example of the ABA's Model Rule 1.7(a).

Exhibit 6-2

From the Arizona Ethics Rules

ER 1.7 Conflict of Interest: Current Clients

(a) Except as provided in paragraph (b), a lawyer shall not represent a client if the representation involves a concurrent conflict of interest. A concurrent conflict of interest exists if

  (1) the representation of one client will be directly adverse to another client; or

  (2) there is a significant risk that the representation of one or more clients will be materially limited by the lawyer's responsibilities to another client, a former client or a third person or by a personal interest of the lawyer.

The attorney's duty of loyalty to a current client generally prohibits the representation of two clients with interests that are directly adverse. Typically, an attorney could not represent both the husband and wife in a marriage dissolution because their interests are directly adverse.

Even if the potential clients do not have directly adverse positions, if there is a significant risk that the attorney's responsibilities to one client would be materially limited by the attorney's responsibilities to another client, a former client, or a third person, the attorney has a conflict of interest and must decline representation. The attorney's responsibilities to a client are materially limited if the attorney's independent professional judgment is clouded. For example, if the attorney represents a partnership and the partners would like to hire a new partner to manage the business, the attorney may have a conflict if asked to negotiate and prepare an employment agreement between the partnership and the new partner—unless the new partner is represented by separate counsel. The attorney's judgment may be clouded by his current representation and past association with the partnership. The attorney may not be able to negotiate an employment agreement that would be in the best interests of both the partnership and the new partner/employee.

> ### CASE ON POINT
> An attorney in Ohio was suspended indefinitely for several violations of Ohio's Code of Professional Responsibility, including DR5-105, which provides that an attorney must refuse to accept employment if the interests of another client may impair the independent professional judgment of the lawyer. The attorney in this case represented both the wife (complainant) and husband (defendant) in a domestic abuse case, leading to a plea bargain for the defendant.

Disciplinary Counsel v. Brown, 737, N.E.2d 516 (Ohio 2000)

There are several instances where an attorney's personal interests may present a significant risk that the attorney's representation will be materially limited. A personal relationship between the attorney and opposing counsel is one such personal interest. If an attorney is related by blood or marriage to opposing counsel, there may be a significant risk that confidential client information may be revealed or that the attorneys' loyalty or judgment may be affected by the relationship. Under most circumstances, an attorney must decline representation if related to counsel for the adverse party. However, at times, the representation may be permissible if each client gives informed consent. Model Rule 1.8, discussed later in this chapter, concerns several other personal interests that may present a conflict.

█ FORMER CLIENT CONFLICTS OF INTEREST

As with the ethical duty to client confidentiality, the attorney's duty of loyalty to the client begins with the initial meeting and outlasts the attorney's representation of the client. It is therefore possible for an attorney to have a conflict of interest involving a current or prospective client and a former client.

Rule 1.9 of the Model Rules, which has been followed closely by many states, prevents an attorney from successively representing a client with interests materially adverse to a former client in the same or substantially related matter.

The rules regarding successive representation are not quite as strict as those concerning the simultaneous representation of clients who may have adverse interests. Rule 1.9 concerning former clients provides that an attorney must decline representation of a new client if the following tests are met:

1. The subject matter of the new representation is the same or substantially related to the representation of the former client; and

2. The new representation is materially adverse to the interests of a former client.

To illustrate, suppose that an attorney has been requested to represent the widow of an airplane crash victim in a wrongful death suit against the airline. However, the attorney had defended that same airline against a similar suit by a passenger who survived the same crash. The attorney would have to decline the representation because (1) the new representation (of the widow) is materially adverse to the interests of the former client (airline), (2) the subject matter (wrongful death or personal injury due to airplane crash) is the same as the subject matter of the previous representation, and (3) the attorney learned confidential information through his former representation of the airline that could be used to the airline's disadvantage in the potential representation of the widow.

Attorneys may not oppose a former client in the same or a substantially related matter. However, it may be permissible for an attorney to oppose a former client in a different matter that is unrelated to the matter in which the attorney represented the former client. Such representation may be permissible so long as the attorney did not learn anything in representing the former client that may be used as a detriment to the former client. For example, prior defense of the airline in a personal injury suit stemming from an airplane crash would probably not preclude the attorney from opposing his former client (the airline) in a wrongful dismissal suit brought by a former employee—so long as the attorney learned nothing through prior representation that would constitute an unfair advantage in the second suit.

The conflict of interest rules may sometimes appear to be complicated and confusing—it is difficult to draft rules to cover such a multitude of possible situations that may involve conflicts. It is important to remember that all the rules are designed to ensure that the attorney's duties of confidentiality and loyalty to each client remains intact. If any representation involves a breach of either of those duties, it is likely a conflict of interest.

Even if it is established that the interests of a new client may be materially adverse to those of a former client, the attorney may take on the representation if the former client consents after consultation in accordance with the pertinent rules.

CONSENTING TO REPRESENTATION

A conflict of interest can arise without any actual wrongdoing on the part of the attorney. For example, it is possible for an attorney to represent two clients with marginally conflicting interests and still give each client the best possible representation. Even though a concurrent conflict of interest exists, such representation may be permissible if the representation is not otherwise prohibited by law and

1. all affected clients consent, in writing, after being fully informed of the conflict
2. the attorney has a reasonable belief that he or she can provide competent and diligent representation to each affected client
3. the representation does not involve the assertion of a claim by one client against another client who are both represented by the attorney in the same litigation or proceeding.

The attorney has a special duty to the client to use independent judgment when assessing the facts surrounding the potential representation and conflict. The attorney must fully advise the clients of all circumstances surrounding the potential conflict and any foreseeable consequences. If the attorney would be required to divulge confidences to fully advise all parties, the attorney should not seek the consent. The attorney must not attempt to persuade the client to waive the attorney's disqualification and consent to the representation.

Exhibit 6-3 is a checklist for obtaining proper consent for representation notwithstanding a conflict of interest.

Exhibit 6-3

Checklist for Obtaining Consent to Representation
Notwithstanding a Conflict of Interest

- The lawyer can provide competent and diligent representation to each affected client.
- The representation is permitted under law.
- The representation does not involve the assertion of a claim by one client against the other in the same litigation.
- The client is fully advised of all circumstances surrounding the potential conflict.
- The client is fully advised of any foreseeable consequences of the representation.
- No client confidences are divulged to obtain the consent.
- No persuasion is used to obtain the consent.

IMPUTED DISQUALIFICATION

It is assumed that in the practice of law, an attorney may share client confidences with others in the attorney's **firm.** For that reason, the rule of **imputed disqualification** provides that all members of a law firm are disqualified from representing a potential client if one member of the firm is disqualified because of a conflict of interest. This situation most often arises when attorneys switch law firms.

Specific rules regarding imputed disqualification are set by each state in the code of ethics that attorneys must abide by. Rule 1.9(b) of the Model Rules provides that if an attorney has learned confidential information about a client represented by the attorney or the attorney's previous law firm, the attorney's new firm may not undertake a new representation of a client with materially adverse interests in the same or substantially related matter. For example, suppose an attorney works for a law firm that specializes in medical malpractice defense. Dr. Hartman is one of the firm's clients that the attorney has represented. If the attorney leaves that firm and goes to another firm, no attorney in the new firm may accept representation of a client who is seeking to sue Dr. Hartman.

Exhibit 6-4 is a list of situations that may cause potential conflicts of interest. There are exceptions to this rule. If the former client gives informed, written consent, the new representation may be permissible. Also, under certain circumstances, the attorney with the conflict may be screened from the new client and that client's case, allowing the other attorneys in the firm to undertake representation.

Exhibit 6-4

Checklist for Potential Conflicts of Interest with Current Clients and Current and Past Clients

A conflict of interest may occur if the potential client has interests directly adverse to

- a current client of the attorney
- a current client of the attorney's law firm
- a past client of the attorney
- a past client of the attorney's law firm
- a past client of an attorney or paralegal with whom the attorney is currently associated
- clients whose representation may be materially limited by the attorney's representation of another current or past client.

Screening and Erecting Ethical Walls

Many jurisdictions permit exceptions to the imputed disqualification rule when a **screening** process is properly implemented. Also referred to as erecting an **ethical wall** or **Chinese Wall**, screening refers to a policy within a law firm to screen or shut out a disqualified attorney within the firm from representation of the client presenting the conflict. An effective screen usually provides that the disqualified attorney

1. does not participate in the matter
2. does not discuss the matter with any member of the firm
3. represents through sworn testimony that he or she has not shared any confidential information with a member of the firm
4. does not have access to any documentation concerning the matter
5. does not share in any fees from the matter.

In some cases, the rule of imputed disqualification has been applied to law firms when it is a paralegal who has switched sides, creating a potential conflict of interest. However, adequate screening of the paralegal is typically sufficient to avoid disqualification of the paralegal's new law firm.

CONFLICTS IN CIVIL LITIGATION

Simultaneous representation of clients with conflicting interests in a civil suit is prohibited. Obviously, an attorney cannot represent both the plaintiff and defendant to the same lawsuit. However, under certain circumstances and with informed consent, an attorney may represent parties whose interests may conflict,

Chapter 6

such as co-plaintiffs or co-defendants. Attorneys must be cautious of representing more than one party in civil litigation, even if their interests initially appear to coincide. Throughout the course of litigation, it may become apparent that the parties' interests conflict by way of incompatibility in positions against the opposing party or conflicting interests with regard to settling the matter. For example, it is inadvisable for a personal injury attorney to represent both the driver and passenger of an automobile for damages they sustained when their car was hit by another car whose driver ran a red light. Although it may appear at the outset of the case that the interests of the two clients coincide, it is possible that facts could come to light during the trial that would cause a conflict of their interests. What if the attorney learns through representation of the driver client that the driver client had been drinking prior to the accident and may have been at least partially at fault?

Simultaneous representation of multiple clients may be acceptable if it is clear that the attorney may adequately represent the interests of each client and each client consents after consultation in accordance with the applicable rules of ethics.

CONFLICTS IN CRIMINAL MATTERS

It is usually inadvisable for an attorney to represent more than one defendant in a criminal matter. "The potential for conflict of interest in representing multiple defendants in a criminal case is so grave that ordinarily a lawyer should decline to represent more than one co-defendant."[4] Problems presenting a conflict of interest for the attorney may arise if the best defense of one client implicates the other client. However, in instances where defense of multiple clients is clearly in the best interests of the defendants and all clients properly consent after consultation, representation of **co-defendants** may be permissible.

Conflicts in Nonlitigation Matters

An attorney may represent multiple clients in nonlitigation matters if the clients have a mutual interest and if the clients agree after consultation. It is not uncommon for a client to request his or her attorney to represent the client and another in the purchase and sale of a home, in documenting a loan between them, or in a similar type of transaction that they do not perceive to be adversarial. If the attorney has a long-standing relationship with one of the parties and there are still unresolved issues between the parties, the attorney must decline such representation. The attorney cannot represent the best interests of both clients with undivided loyalty under such circumstances. If, however, the parties have already reached a complete agreement and simply need the attorney to document the transaction, it may be permissible. Examples would be assisting two clients with the formation of a partnership or drafting an employment agreement. In this instance, the attorney must carefully consider the potential for conflicting interests between the parties, and the clients must be made fully aware of the potential conflicts. Another example would be the representation of both a husband and wife in an amicable marriage dissolution. Under most circumstances, the attorney may represent *either* the husband or wife and advise the spouse to seek other representation.

DETECTING CONFLICTS OF INTEREST

Law firms are getting larger, more specialized, and are merging at an unprecedented rate. All these factors make it crucial to have proper procedures in place for detecting conflicts of interest. Conflicts of interest may not always be obvious to the attorney taking on representation of a new client. Law firms must have a procedure in place to assure that none of the attorneys in the firm take on representation of a new client who may have interests conflicting with the interests of a current or former client of the firm or with current attorneys or paralegals. Formal procedures are typically in place in law firms to prevent conflicts of interest within a law firm. For example, when an attorney opens a new file, he or she will conduct a law firm database search by client and by adverse party to make sure there is no conflict. It is the responsibility of every attorney and paralegal to assure that they do not unknowingly become involved in a conflict of interest situation that could prove inconvenient and costly to the client when discovered too far into the representation. "To determine whether a conflict of interest exists, a lawyer should adopt reasonable procedures, appropriate for the size and type of firm and practice, to determine in both litigation and non-litigation matters the persons and issues involved."[5] Exhibit 6-5 is an example of a form that may be completed by attorneys in a law firm when taking on a new representation. Depending on the size of the firm, memos such as Exhibit 6-5 may be circulated to all attorneys and paralegals whenever a new file is opened, or the information from the form may be entered into a database, and reports with the data from all new representations may be circulated periodically.

Consider the two following scenarios: In the first scenario, a well-established client of the law firm brings in a new litigation case concerning a property development project gone wrong. The firm does a conflict of interest check and realizes immediately that one of the firm's attorneys was formerly in-house counsel for the potential defendant in the matter. The responsible attorney immediately tells the firm's client that the firm will be unable to represent the client on this particular matter. As an alternative, the attorney with the conflict may be screened. The client understands and consents to the screening or seeks other counsel for the matter.

In the second scenario, the conflict goes undetected until two weeks before the trial, when the opposing counsel files a Motion to Disqualify the firm. The supervising attorney must talk to the client and admit that the conflict was not detected. For the firm to withdraw at this point will be a great hardship to the client, and the firm may lose all the client's future business.

Exhibit 6-5

New Litigation Client Conflict of Interest Check Form

Client(s)'s Name(s) _____

Date of Initial Contact _____

Supervising Attorney(s) _____

Assigned Paralegal(s) _____

Type of Matter _____

Parties Involved _____

Names of all Plaintiffs or Potential Plaintiffs (include all maiden and corporate names where appropriate):

_____

_____

_____

_____

Names of all known Attorneys and Law Firms Associated with the Plaintiffs:

_____

_____

_____

_____

Names of all Defendants or Potential Defendants (include all maiden and corporate names where appropriate):

_____

_____

_____

_____

■ THE ORGANIZATION AS A CLIENT

An attorney representing a corporation or another business organization has a duty of loyalty to the organization itself and must act to protect the interests of the organization. The attorney may not represent officers, directors, or others associated with the firm if the interests of the individual conflict with the interests of the organization.

If an attorney becomes aware of actions being taken by officers, directors, agents, or others that are harmful to the organization the attorney represents, the attorney must act according to prescribed ethical rules to protect the organization.

Rule 1.13(b) of the Model Rules provides that the measures to be taken by the attorney should proceed as is reasonably necessary in the best interest of the organization, including, if warranted by the seriousness of the matter, referral to the highest authority that can act on behalf of the organization as determined by applicable law. Any measures the attorney chooses to take should be taken "to minimize disruption of the organization and the risk of revealing information relating to the representation to persons outside the organization."[6]

SPECIAL RULES CONCERNING GOVERNMENT LAWYERS

Attorneys who represent government agencies must generally abide by the rules of ethics that apply to attorneys in private practice. In addition, some special rules apply—especially to those attorneys who leave government employment for private practice.

Attorneys who work for government agencies become very familiar with the policies and procedures of their governmental employers. Those same attorneys often take their specialized knowledge with them and use it in private practice. Although government attorneys owe the same duty of loyalty and confidentiality to their client (the government agency that employs them), much of the information learned during their representation is not considered confidential, and it is not improper for an attorney to disclose that information during a subsequent representation of a client.

An attorney who leaves a government position for private practice must be certain to never use confidential information learned through government employment to the unfair advantage of a client.

CONFLICTS INVOLVING THE ATTORNEY'S BUSINESS AND PERSONAL INTERESTS

The lawyer must not have any interests that would adversely affect the interests of a client, although the possibility of a conflict does not, in itself, preclude representation. "The critical questions are the likelihood that a conflict will eventuate and, if it does, whether it will materially interfere with the lawyer's independent professional judgment in considering alternatives or foreclose courses of action that reasonably should be pursued on behalf of the client."[7]

Several types of situations and actions may arise that could cause a conflict of interest because of the attorney-client relationship. If any of these situations or actions are associated with one attorney in a law firm, they are associated with all attorneys in the firm and may disqualify the entire firm, not just the individual attorney, with the conflict. Rule 1.8 of the Model Rules provides for the following ten types of situations or actions that may cause a conflict of interest:

1. Entering into certain business transactions that may involve or affect a client.

2. Using information relating to the representation to the disadvantage of the client.

3. Preparing instruments giving the attorney, or a person close to the attorney, a gift from the client, except where the client is related.

4. Making or negotiating an agreement giving the attorney literary or media rights regarding the representation—prior to the conclusion of the representation.

5. Providing most types of financial assistance to the client.

6. Accepting compensation for representing the client from someone other than the client.

7. Making certain aggregate settlements of claims or aggregate plea bargains when representing multiple clients.

8. Entering into certain agreements limiting the attorney's liability for malpractice.

9. Acquiring an interest in a cause of action or the subject of litigation in a matter relating to the attorney's representation of the client.

10. Having a sexual relationship with a client, unless a consensual sexual relationship existed between them when the lawyer-client relationship commenced.

Business Transactions

An attorney who chooses to transact personal business with a client must be very careful to not create a conflict of interest (or even the appearance of one). Some of the considerations to be taken into account when attorneys and clients transact business together include whether:

1. the transaction is fair and reasonable to the client.

2. the client fully understands the terms of the transaction.

3. the client has the opportunity to seek independent counsel.

4. the client consents in writing to the business transaction.

For example, suppose a client consults with her attorney when her business runs into financial trouble. The client is contemplating the sale of the business, and her attorney decides that he would like to buy it. The attorney would definitely have a conflict of interest if he were to continue representing the client in seeing to its successful sale and purchase. If the client, after being fully consulted, decides that she would like to sell her business to the attorney, the client should immediately retain a new attorney to represent her interests in the transaction.

Information Relating to the Representation

Rule 1.8(b) states that an attorney "shall not use information relating to representation of a client to the disadvantage of the client unless the client consents after consultation, except as permitted or required by Rule 1.6 or Rule 3.3."[8] This rule emphasizes the importance of the proper treatment of confidential information learned by an attorney through representation of a client and the attorney's duty of loyalty to the client.

Gifts to Lawyer

Attorneys may not draft wills or other instruments that grant a substantial gift from the client to the attorney, unless the attorney and client are related. This rule would prevent an unethical attorney from taking advantage of an elderly client with no living relatives but would not prevent an attorney from drafting a last will and testament for his or her parents in which the attorney is named as a beneficiary. An attorney may accept a gift from a client if the transaction meets general standards of fairness.[9]

Literary or Media Rights

Rule 1.8(d) states that "Prior to the conclusion of representation of a client, a lawyer shall not make or negotiate an agreement giving the lawyer literary or media rights to a portrayal or account based in substantial part on information relating to the representation." An attorney is thereby prohibited from accepting literary rights or media rights as compensation for their representation from a client. If an attorney were allowed to sell literary or media rights based on his or her representation of a client prior to the conclusion of that representation, the attorney's personal financial interests may be influenced by the outcome of that representation. For example, it may be a more interesting story if the matter were to go through a lengthy trial as opposed to an amicable settlement. This rule attempts to abolish any conflict of interest that may arise when the attorney's financial interests and the client's interests differ.

Financial Assistance to the Client

It is generally unethical for an attorney to encourage a client or potential client to initiate a lawsuit by enticing them with financial assistance other than the advance of litigation expenses. An exception to this rule is that an attorney may pay court costs and expenses of litigation on behalf of an indigent client.

Fees Paid from a Source Other Than the Client

It is unethical for an attorney to accept payment of a client's fees from someone other than the client if the attorney allows the individual paying the fees to affect the attorney's professional judgment, or the attorney-client relationship in any way. If an attorney accepts payment of legal fees from a source other than the client, the attorney must be sure that the source of the fee payment does not influence or jeopardize the attorney's representation of the client's best interests.

Settlements and Pleas on Behalf of Two or More Clients

An attorney must not accept a settlement or plea bargain on behalf of two or more clients as a "package deal" if it is not in the best interests of all affected clients and unless the clients all agree after consultation.

Potential Malpractice Claims

When an attorney agrees to represent a client, the attorney may not ask the client to enter into an agreement whereby the client promises not to sue the attorney for malpractice for the representation if the outcome is not to the client's satisfaction. Furthermore, if a client has a claim of malpractice against the attorney, the attorney should not settle with the client unless the client is represented by an independent counsel, or unless the attorney has informed the client of the advisability for the client to seek the advice of an independent counsel.

Interest in Cause of Action

With few exceptions, it is unethical for an attorney to acquire an interest in the client's cause of action or the subject matter of litigation. The long-standing rule against an attorney acquiring an interest in a client's litigation is designed to prevent conflicts that might impair the attorney's exercise of independent judgment on a client's behalf. Attorneys may, however, file a lien against property of the clients in connection with legal fees earned by the attorney. Rules for filing an attorney's lien are usually established by state law. Another very common exception to this rule is the contingency fee arrangement.

Sexual Relations

Lawyers are prohibited from having sexual relations with a client unless a consensual sexual relationship predates the client-lawyer relationship.[10] This is a new rule that has been adopted by several jurisdictions to prevent the unfair exploitation of the client, who may be vulnerable in the relationship. Exhibit 6-6 is a checklist of potential conflicts of interest involving an attorney's personal/business interests.

Exhibit 6-6

Checklist for Potential Conflicts of Interest Involving Attorney's Personal/Business Interests

- Having a personal relationship with or being related to an adverse party, the opposing counsel, or anyone associated with the matter.
- Entering into business transactions with the client.
- Receiving a substantial gift from the client or someone else involved in the matter.
- Drafting documents on behalf of a client granting the attorney or paralegal a financial interest (other than reasonable attorney's fees).
- Providing financial aid to the client.
- Receiving legal fees from a source other than the client.
- Negotiating a settlement or plea bargain on behalf of two or more clients.

- Entering into an agreement with the client providing that the client will not sue the attorney for legal malpractice in the future.
- Acquiring a financial interest in the client's case.
- Having a sexual relationship with the client.

■ THE ATTORNEY AS A WITNESS

A conflict of interest can arise when an attorney who is acting as an advocate in a trial also serves as a witness. Attorneys are generally prohibited from representing clients in a matter where the attorney is likely to be called as a witness, unless the matter to which the attorney will testify is an uncontested matter or relates to the nature and value of the legal services provided to the client. There are also exceptions to the rule against representing a client where the attorney may be called as a witness when the disqualification of the lawyer may cause a substantial hardship on the client.

According to the Model Code, "[t]he roles of an advocate and of a witness are inconsistent; the function of an advocate is to advance or argue the cause of another, while that of a witness is to state facts objectively."[11]

■ FROM THE PARALEGAL'S PERSPECTIVE

As a paralegal, you must be aware of and abide by the ethical rules concerning conflicts of interest that govern attorneys. Your personal interests must not conflict with those of a client of an attorney you are assisting. In addition, you must not be put in the position of assisting a client who has an interest adverse to a client of your current or former employer. If you work for a law firm or legal department in a traditional role under the supervision of an attorney, you usually need only be concerned with potential conflicts between clients of your current employer and any former employers. If a paralegal has a conflict of interest, the whole firm may be disqualified from representation of a client, unless proper measures are taken to rectify the situation. Courts have found that paralegals should be held to the same standards as attorneys, although if such a conflict does exist, it is usually a sufficient remedy to screen the paralegal from involvement with that client and all confidential information relating to that client.

Chapter 6

CASE ON POINT

In a 1998 lawsuit brought by users of a contraceptive against the contraceptive distributors in Texas, the attorneys for one of the plaintiffs were disqualified on motion by attorneys for the defendant shortly before trial when it was determined that a paralegal working for the plaintiff was previously employed by one of the distributors—a defendant in the case.

—*In Re: American Home Products Corp., 985 S.W. 2d 68 (Texas 1998)*

A QUESTION OF ETHICS

Ben Meyers has just begun his first week at his job as a litigation paralegal, with the firm of Wendell & Jacobson, when he is confronted by a potential problem. Ben was assigned to work on the *Ace Manufacturing v. Diamond Supply* file, a case name that he recognizes from his last job. At his previous position, Ben's employer represented Ace Manufacturing. Ben was not directly involved with the case, although he did help out one of the other paralegals at his last firm by summarizing a few depositions. Now, at Ben's new job with Wendell & Jacobson, they are representing Diamond Supply; Ben has been asked to oversee the entire litigation process. Ben has a feeling that this might be considered a conflict of interest, but he is not really sure. He is still on probation at his new job and does not want to rock the boat. Should Ben tell his new employer of his past involvement with the file?

Answer and Discussion

Yes. Even the appearance of conflict of interest such as this could cause serious problems for Ben's new employers. At the least, they would be embarrassed if they knew nothing of Ben's prior involvement and his former employer called them on it. At worst, the counsel for Ace Manufacturing could file a motion to disqualify Ben's law firm from representing Diamond Supply in the action against Ben's former employer, and if it is not handled correctly, Wendell & Jacobson could lose their client.

 THE PARALEGAL AND IMPUTED DISQUALIFICATION

To disqualify an entire law firm from representing a client because a paralegal has a conflict of interest stemming from prior employment could restrict the mobility and employability of a paralegal who has worked for large litigation law firms. The ABA and the courts have recognized this as being unnecessarily restrictive to paralegals and have recommended that "any restrictions on the nonlawyer's employment should be held to the minimum necessary to protect confidentiality of client information."[12] The ABA recommends the following:

> *A law firm that employs a nonlawyer who formerly was employed by another firm may continue representing clients whose interests conflict with the interests of clients of the former employer on whose matters the nonlawyer has worked, as long as the employing firm screens the nonlawyer from information about or participating in matters involving those clients and strictly adheres to the screening process described in this opinion and as long as no information relating to the representation of the clients of the former employer is revealed by the nonlawyer to any person in the employing firm. In addition, the nonlawyer's former employer must admonish the*

nonlawyer against revelation of information relating to the representation of clients of the former employer.[13]

The NALA's Rules

The NALA's Code of Ethics and Professional Responsibility does not specifically address conflicts of interest for the paralegal. However, Canon 8 states that "A legal assistant must do all other things incidental, necessary, or expedient for the attainment of the ethics and responsibilities as defined by statute or rule of court."

The NFPA's Rules

The NFPA addresses conflicts of interest in Section 1.6 of its Model Code of Ethics and Professional Responsibility, set forth in Exhibit 6-7.

Exhibit 6-7

From the NFPA's Model Code of Ethics and Professional Responsibility and Guidelines for Enforcement

1.6 A PARALEGAL SHALL AVOID CONFLICTS OF INTEREST AND SHALL DISCLOSE ANY POSSIBLE CONFLICT TO THE EMPLOYER OR CLIENT, AS WELL AS TO THE PROSPECTIVE EMPLOYERS OR CLIENTS.

ETHICAL CONSIDERATIONS

EC-1.6(a)   A paralegal shall act within the bounds of the law, solely for the benefit of the client, and shall be free of compromising influences and loyalties. Neither the paralegal's personal or business interest, nor those of other clients or third persons, should compromise the paralegal's professional judgment and loyalty to the client.

EC-1.6(b)   A paralegal shall avoid conflicts of interest that may arise from previous assignments, whether for a present or past employer or client.

EC-1.6(c)   A paralegal shall avoid conflicts of interest that may arise from family relationships and from personal and business interests.

EC-1.6(d)   In order to be able to determine whether an actual or potential conflict of interest exists a paralegal shall create and maintain an effective recordkeeping system that identifies clients, matters, and parties with which the paralegal has worked.

EC-1.6(e)   A paralegal shall reveal sufficient non-confidential information about a client or former client to reasonably ascertain if an actual or potential conflict of interest exists.

EC-1.6(f)   A paralegal shall not participate in or conduct work on any matter where a conflict of interest has been identified.

Chapter 6

Exhibit 6-7 *(Continued)*

From the NFPA's Model Code of Ethics and Professional Responsibility and Guidelines for Enforcement

EC-1.6(g) In matters where a conflict of interest has been identified and the client consents to continued representation, a paralegal shall comply fully with the implementation and maintenance of an Ethical Wall.

The NFPA has given the opinion that if it is determined that a conflict of interest exists, the paralegal is prohibited from participating in or conducting work on the matter and an ethical wall must be implemented and maintained. The NFPA further lists the following steps to erect and adhere to the ethical wall:

1. Prohibit the paralegal from having any connection with the matter.

2. Ban discussions with or the transfer of documents to or from the paralegal.

3. Restrict access to files.

4. Educate all members of the firm, corporation, or entity as to the separation of the paralegal (both organizationally and physically) from the pending matter.[14]

PRACTICAL CONSIDERATIONS

The consequences of an undisclosed conflict of interest involving a paralegal and a client of the law firm employer can have devastating effects for the client, the supervising attorney, the law firm, and the paralegal. If, as a paralegal, you have any question concerning a possible conflict of interest you may be involved in, you must report it to your supervising attorney immediately.

Here are some steps you can take to be certain that you are not involved improperly in a conflict of interest situation:

1. Keep a current list of client names and the matters on all files on which you work. This may be as simple as keeping copies of your billing records.

2. When you leave your position in a law firm, take a list of the clients on whose files you have worked and the matters to compare with any files you may be assigned to in the future. This list should be kept confidential. The only information to be disclosed from this list would be the name of a former client whose file you have worked on (or opposing party) if a conflict of interest arises.

3. Keep current with your firm's conflict of interest procedures. Law firms commonly circulate weekly lists of new clients and new matters that the firm is representing. This list should be checked against your current list of clients and any lists from previous employers.

4. If your firm takes on a client with whom you have a personal interest, either a financial interest or a personal relationship, that information should be reported to your supervising attorney as soon as possible.

5. If you ever suspect that you may possibly be involved in a conflict of interest situation, report it to your supervising attorney or other appropriate individual in your law firm or law department immediately.

SPECIAL CONSIDERATION FOR SPECIALISTS

As discussed throughout this chapter, the rules concerning conflicts of interest may be applied to paralegals as well as attorneys. Because it is the responsibility of the attorney to accept or decline client representation, the main concern of the paralegal, regardless of specialty, is in detecting any possible conflict of interest that affects the paralegal directly and to report that possible conflict to the responsible attorney. Due to the adverse nature of litigation, litigation paralegals are most often faced with conflict of interest issues.

Litigation Paralegals

Litigation paralegals will have conflict of interest problems most often when they change jobs frequently. Especially if you change from one firm to another in the same city, chances are at some point you could run into a conflict of interest situation. As a paralegal, you must be sure that you are included in all procedures for conflict checking in your law firm. You should carefully review all memos circulated concerning new firm clients to be sure that you have not worked with attorneys who have represented adverse interests to any new clients. If you do come across a conflict, a potential conflict, or even the possible appearance of a conflict, you must notify the responsible attorney immediately.

CHAPTER SUMMARY

▶ When the interests of the client conflict with the interests of the attorney or other clients represented by the attorney, it is referred to as a conflict of interest.

▶ Loyalty to a client prohibits undertaking representation directly adverse to that client without that client's consent.

▶ Paralegals may be held to the same standards as attorneys concerning conflicts of interest.

▶ An attorney may not represent a client with interests materially adverse to those of a former client in the same or substantially related matter unless the former client consents after consultation.

▶ All members of a law firm are disqualified if one member of the firm is disqualified to represent a client due to a conflict of interest under the rule of imputed disqualification.

▶ Under certain circumstances, imputed disqualification can be avoided if proper screening procedures are established.

▶ An attorney must not have any personal or business interests that conflict with the interests of a client.

▶ An attorney may enter into a business transaction with a client only if every safeguard is taken to assure that the transaction is fair and reasonable to the client.

▶ An attorney must not use confidential information learned through representation of a client to the client's disadvantage.

▶ It is an attorney's duty to ensure the ethical conduct of paralegals and to prevent conflicts of interest arising from the paralegal's other employment or interests.

▶ When paralegals find themselves in a conflict of interest situation, it is most often due to a change of employers.

■ FREQUENTLY ASKED QUESTIONS

Is it possible for attorneys to represent two clients with adverse interests?

Yes. It is possible as long as the representation is not prohibited by law and the attorney believes that he or she will be able to provide competent and diligent representation to each client. If that is the case, the attorney can represent both parties if the representation does not involve one client suing the other and if both clients give informed written consent.

I would like to have the attorney I work for draft wills for my parents. I will probably be the main beneficiary under their wills. Is this a conflict of interest for the attorney or for me?

No. There should be no conflict of interest here for either the attorney or you. It is permissible for attorneys to prepare instruments giving the attorney a gift when the client is related. It should be permissible for the attorney to prepare documents for your parents in which you are a named beneficiary.

I have just started a new job in a litigation law firm and discovered that one of the firm's clients was the plaintiff in a lawsuit in which my previous firm represented the defendant. Will my new firm be disqualified from representing this client?

Your new firm will probably not be disqualified, but you may be screened from cases involving the client presenting the conflict. It is important that you disclose your past involvement with the firm's client as soon as possible.

The law firm I work for has just initiated a lawsuit on behalf of a client against a small business of which my husband is a part owner. Could this be a conflict of interest? Do I need to disclose my husband's involvement with the defendant business?

Again, this should not be a problem for the firm you work for as long as you are screened from any involvement with the lawsuit against your husband's business. You must disclose your husband's association with the defendant business.

How can I be sure that when I switch jobs to go to a new law firm, I will not have any conflicts of interest?

There is no way to be sure that you will not have any conflicts of interest in the new firm, but you can take precautions to be sure that you recognize any potential conflicts and address them immediately. When you leave your current firm, you should take with you a list of the firm's clients, even those that you have not worked with directly. This list should remain confidential, to be used only to check for conflicts of interest with the new firm's clients. Always immediately disclose any possible conflicts you may discover.

▇ ENDNOTES

1   Model Rules of Professional Conduct Rule 1.7 (2004).
2   Model Rules of Professional Conduct Rule 1.7 (2004).
3   Model Rules of Professional Conduct Annotation to Rule 1.7 (2004).
4   Model Rules of Professional Conduct Rule 1.7 (2004).
5   Model Rules of Professional Conduct Rule 1.7 (2004).
6   Model Rules of Professional Conduct Rule 1.13(b) (2004).
7   Model Rules of Professional Conduct Rule 1.7 (2004).
8   Model Rules of Professional Conduct Rule 1.8(b) (2004).
9   Model Rules of Professional Conduct Rule 1.7 (2004).
10 Model Rules of Professional Conduct Rule 1.8(j) (2004).
11 Model Code of Professional Responsibility, EC 5-9 (1983).
12 The ABA Commission on Ethics and Professional Responsibility, Informal Opinion 88-1526 (1988).
13 The ABA Commission on Ethics and Professional Responsibility, Informal Opinion 88-1526 (1988).
14 The NFPA Informal Ethics and Disciplinary Opinion No. 95-3 (1995).

Chapter 7

The Ethics of Legal Fees and Financial Matters

*"The man who does not work for the love of work
but only for money is not likely to make money nor
find much fun in life."*

– Charles M. Schwab

PART I: FINANCIAL DEALINGS BETWEEN ATTORNEYS AND THEIR CLIENTS

Any time both attorneys and clients are concerned with financial matters, attorneys must use the utmost care to follow the pertinent rules of ethics—many of which are designed to protect the client. With regard to safekeeping of a client's funds and trust accounting, the attorney has a fiduciary duty to the client. When it comes to assessing fees for legal services and billing clients, attorneys must deal fairly with the client—taking into consideration their unequal positions.

The rules of ethics of each state include very specific rules for financial dealings between attorneys and their clients. The rules prescribe guidelines for safekeeping of a client's property, establishing reasonable fees for legal services, fee agreements, and fee-splitting arrangements. Regardless of these safeguards, a high proportion of ethical complaints against attorneys concern financial matters, either mishandling of money held by attorneys on behalf of clients or excessive or unfair billing.

Part I of this chapter explores the rules of ethics governing financial dealings between attorneys and their clients, especially legal fees, the safekeeping of client funds, and requirements for client trust accounting. Part II of this chapter focuses on these same issues from the paralegal's perspectives and takes a look at the recoverability of paralegal fees.

■ LEGAL FEES AND BILLING

Attorneys have an ethical duty to bill their clients fairly and receive no excessive or unfair payment from their clients. They must not use coercion to extract or increase fees at any point during the representation. There is a decided inequality in bargaining positions between the attorney and client (who may be unaware of his or her legal rights) that must be taken into consideration by attorneys when negotiating legal fees. Attorneys owe their clients the "obligation to deal fairly and in good faith when negotiating a fee and when ultimately charging and collecting a fee."[1]

Reasonable Fees

Attorneys' fees must be reasonable. Several factors are considered when determining the reasonableness of attorneys' fees, including the time and labor involved, the difficulty of the questions involved, and the skill required to perform the legal service properly. Reasonableness also depends on the fee customarily charged in the locality for similar legal services, the time limitations imposed on the attorney, and several other matters set forth in the rules of professional conduct. Factors that determine reasonableness often include

- ▶ the time and labor required of the attorney for the representation.
- ▶ preclusion from other employment.
- ▶ the customary fee charged for similar representation.
- ▶ the results obtained for the client.
- ▶ the time limitations.
- ▶ the nature and length of the professional relationship between the attorney and client.
- ▶ the experience, reputation, and ability of the attorney.
- ▶ whether or not the fee charged is contingent or fixed.

Time and Labor

One of the most important factors in determining the reasonableness of attorneys' fees is the time and labor required of the attorney and the attorneys' firm. The time and labor will depend, in large part, on the novelty and difficulty of the question at hand. For example, if a client raises a legal issue that the attorney, and possibly even the courts, has never addressed before, it will take much more time, and more highly skilled time, and warrant a higher fee than pursuing a routine legal matter similar to that handled by the attorney before.

Preclusion from Other Employment

Whether an attorney's representation of a client precludes the attorney from accepting other employment will have an impact on the reasonableness of the fee charged. At times, an attorney may be presented with a legal matter or representation that will preclude him or her from accepting other employment. When this is the case, it is reasonable that the attorney be fairly compensated for foregoing other representations.

Customary Fee

When the reasonableness of a fee is considered, it will be taken into account what fee is typically charged for a similar matter in the locality for similar services. Fees vary from region to region, and attorneys are allowed to bill whatever is customary within their areas.

Results Obtained

When an attorney achieves exemplary results for a client, this can be taken into consideration when determining the reasonableness of the fee.

> **CASE ON POINT**
>
> In a case heard in Idaho in 2001, the court found that attorney's fees charged in excess of $100,000 for "mismanaging a $500,000 estate" were excessive, especially since the attorney indicated he could resolve the matter for $5,500.

—*Idaho State Bar v. Frazier, 28 P.3d 363 (Idaho 2001)*

Although a higher rate of attorney's fees may be reasonable when the attorney is able to reach beneficial results for the client, the attorney may not justify a higher fee just because the client has the ability to pay it. Courts have found that "A client's ability to pay cannot justify a charge in excess of the value of that service."[2]

Time Limitations

The time limitations placed on legal services by a client can have an effect on the reasonableness of the attorneys' fees. For example, suppose the president of a corporation presents her attorney with a proposed multimillion-dollar merger in November and declares that she wants it to be a *done deal* by the end of the year. Such a request would mean that the attorney may have to hire additional help, put other matters on hold, and work days, nights, and weekends to get the transaction completed on time. It would be reasonable for the attorney to charge above-average fees under these strict time constraints.

Nature and Length of the Professional Relationship

The nature and length of the professional relationship between the attorney and client can also have a bearing on the reasonableness of the attorneys' fees. For example, compare the representation of an established corporate client in a civil suit versus the one-time representation of an out-of-town corporation. When it comes to representing the established client, the law firm may already have pertinent corporate documents on hand. The attorneys and law firm staff will know who to contact at the corporation for the information they need, and they will have established procedures for coordinating litigation. In representing the out-of-town corporation, a significant amount of time may be spent just getting to know the corporation, the pertinent individuals at the corporation, and how to approach the situation. Much more time will be spent transporting documentation and information between the corporation and the law firm as well as communicating with the new client. It is reasonable that the law firm should charge the out-of-town corporation more than the established client for similar representation.

Experience, Reputation, and Ability of the Attorney

It is reasonable for experienced attorneys with excellent reputations to expect more for their time than newer attorneys of lesser ability.

OF INTEREST

Former Enron CEO Jeffrey Skilling incurred attorney's fees of approximately $70 million for his defense in the Enron scandal. His top attorney billed at a rate of $800 per hour for his services.

Contingent Fees

Attorneys are paid on a **contingent fee** basis when they agree to represent a client and to accept a percentage of the recovery secured for the client as their fee. If the attorney is unable to secure any recovery for the client, the attorney receives no compensation for his or her time. A contingent fee that calculates to more than the attorney's usual per hour rate is usually considered reasonable because the attorney is taking a risk that the client will not collect anything, and thereby, the attorney will not get paid. In addition, attorneys working on a contingent basis may be required to put in a significant amount of time before they ever see any fee from their clients.

CASE ON POINT

In a 2002 employment class action suit against Microsoft, plaintiffs' attorneys were awarded a $27.1 million contingent fee. The court found that the fee was justified, in part because the case was "extremely risky" and counsel "achieved exceptional results." The $27.1 million attorney fee was only 28% of the settlement fund awarded to the plaintiffs.

—*Vizcaino v. Microsoft Corporation, 290 F.3d 1043 (9th Cir. 2002)*

A contingent fee may be found to be unreasonable in the event that a relatively small amount of work is done on the case or if the case does not involve any real risk to the attorney. It may also be found to be unreasonable if it is grossly disproportionate to the fees charged by other attorneys in the area.[3] Exhibit 7-1 is a summary of the factors considered when determining the reasonableness of attorneys' fees.

Exhibit 7-1

Factors for Determining Reasonableness of Attorneys' Fees

Time and labor

Preclusion from other employment

Customary fee

Results obtained

Time limitations

Nature and length of the professional relationship

Experience, reputation, and ability of the attorney

Contingency of fees

Payment of Fees

There are numerous methods used for the payment of legal fees, including a flat fee, a contingent fee, and general and special retainers. The method of payment chosen will depend on several circumstances, including the type of services rendered, the past relationship between the attorney and the client, the financial circumstances of the client, and the estimated length of time the services will take.

Perhaps the most important aspect of the payment of fees is that there is a clear understanding between the attorney and the client as to how fees will be billed, how payment will be made, what services will be rendered for the fees, which costs and expenses incurred during the representation will be included in the fee, and which will be billed additionally. This understanding should be put in a written agreement signed by the client at the onset of the representation and amended, if necessary, when circumstances change.

General Retainer

When a client hires an attorney, the client is said to have retained the attorney. A **general retainer** refers to the situation where a client hires an attorney for a specific length of time rather than for a specific project. During the time the attorney is under general retainer, the attorney may not accept any representation that may be contrary to the interests of the client who has retained the attorney. The attorney agrees to make legal services available to the client during the general retainer period. The attorney may bill additional amounts for special projects taken on during the general retainer term, per agreement with the client. The general retainer is not considered advance payment; rather, it is considered to be earned when paid.

For example, a corporation may have a law firm on general retainer on an annual basis to answer general legal questions that arise during the year. The officers and managers of the corporation would be free to call their attorneys during the year with legal questions without worrying about additional legal expenses. However, if the corporation becomes involved in a significant lawsuit during the year, the corporation would enter into another agreement with the law firm for representation on this particular matter. An additional agreement regarding payment of fees for that lawsuit would have to be entered into.

Special Retainer

A special retainer refers to employment of an attorney for a specific case or legal project. For example, when a client and attorney enter into an agreement whereby the attorney agrees to represent a client in a divorce proceeding, the attorney is on a special retainer.

Flat Fee

Attorneys can be hired to perform certain legal services on a flat fee basis. This means that the client will not be billed by the hour but rather by the service performed, regardless of the time it takes. Bankruptcy proceedings, simple wills, and divorces are services that are often performed on a flat fee basis. For example, attorneys who specialize in estate planning may tell clients at the first meeting that they will prepare simple will for $250. The $250 will include all the services rendered in connection with the will.

Contingent Fees

Contingent fees arrangements, whereby the attorney receives a portion of the settlement obtained on behalf of the client, are usually considered to be reasonable and ethical. Contingent fee arrangements allow individuals to retain attorneys without having to invest heavily in attorneys' fees before they collect anything. Such arrangements offer access to the legal system to those who may otherwise not be able to afford it.

A contingent fee of 25% to 40% of the total amount collected on behalf of the client is customary. The drawback to attorneys who accept representation on a contingent fee basis is that if the attorney collects nothing for the client, the attorney receives no compensation for his or her time.

Contingent fee arrangements must be fully explained to the client, and contingent fee agreements must be made in writing and signed by the client.

Impermissible Contingent Fees

Subsection (d) of Rule 1.5 of the Model Rules of Professional Conduct and provisions of the codes of ethics of most states prohibit contingent fee arrangements based on securing a divorce or upon the amount of alimony, support, or property settlement in a domestic relations case. Subsection (d) also prohibits attorneys from charging a contingent fee in a criminal matter. Contingent fees are prohibited in criminal matters because they cause a potential conflict of interest for the attorney, who may not get paid if his or her client makes a plea bargain or accepts some other type of arrangement that may be in the client's best interest. Contingent fees in domestic relation cases are prohibited because they may give incentive to attorneys to discourage reconciliation between divorcing parties.

FEE AGREEMENTS

Whenever an attorney takes on a new client representation, the attorney must discuss the fee arrangement with the client and obtain the client's agreement for payment—preferably in writing. The attorney should communicate to the client the scope of the representation and the basis or rate of the fee and expenses for which the client will be responsible.[4]

Model Rule 1.5(b) provides that when the lawyer has not regularly represented the client, the basis or rate of the fee shall be communicated to the client, preferably in writing, before or within a reasonable time after commencing the representation.

New clients should have it clearly explained to them how the firm calculates their billing. They should understand if the billing will be done on an hourly basis or contingent basis or charged a flat fee. If the client will be billed on an hourly basis, the attorney should explain to the client the billing rates of various individuals who will be working on the client's file, including paralegals. It should also be clearly communicated to the client that there may be additional charges for reimbursement to the firm for expenses incurred during the course of the representation.

New clients are typically asked to enter into a written fee agreement that includes information discussed concerning the basis for the billing and the client's obligation to pay. A written fee agreement reduces the likelihood of a misunderstanding that could lead to a dispute concerning fees. Exhibit 7-2 is a checklist of important information to be included in fee agreements.

Exhibit 7-2

Checklist for Drafting Attorney Fee Agreement

Name and address of the attorney and the law firm.

Name and address of the client(s).

Purpose of the attorney-client relationship.

Hourly rate for the primary attorney.

Terms for paying of the attorney fees.

Statement concerning reasonableness of fees based on the attorney's experience, preclusion from other employment, customary fee, time limitations, etc.

Hourly rate of all attorneys and paralegals in the firm who may render services for the client under the agreement.

Identification of possible costs and expenses that may be charged to the client.

Client authorization to employ investigators and experts on behalf of the client and at the client's expense.

Means for compensation of the attorney should the client dismiss the attorney.

Signature of both attorney and client.

 ## FEE DISPUTES

Unfortunately, disputes concerning attorneys' fees at times lead to court actions. Most often, these are actions brought by the attorney to enforce payment of fees. If the client has not paid a bill for legal fees, it may be because the client feels the fees were unreasonable. The courts have the final authority to approve attorneys' fees. As a part of their inherent authority to regulate the practice of law, the court has the power to decide on the reasonableness of attorneys' fees, even if the attorney and client have entered into a written fee agreement.

Often, fee disputes arise when clients feel that they have not received the services for which they are being billed. The attorney must be able to prove that proper, competent services were rendered, resulting in a reasonable fee. An attorney will not be allowed to recover fees if the attorney demonstrated incompetence, negligence, or divided loyalty toward the client.

With increasing frequency, attorneys include arbitration clauses in their fee agreements that provide for **mediation** or arbitration in the event of a fee dispute. The ABA endorses fee arbitration with its Model Rules for Fee Arbitration, and some courts have created arbitration procedures for fee disputes. Arbitration proceedings are usually much quicker than court proceedings, providing a benefit to both the attorney and the client. In addition, unlike most court proceedings, arbitration proceedings can be kept confidential.

 ## DIVISION OF FEES WITH OTHERS

Referral fees and agreements between attorneys to share fees are usually acceptable, as long as the client is fully informed (and agrees to the arrangement) and as long as the particular agreement is permitted by the rules of ethics in the pertinent jurisdiction.

Failure to fully inform the client and obtain the client's approval concerning a proposed fee-splitting agreement can cause the agreement to fail. According to the Supreme Court of Minnesota: "Each client has a right to choose the attorney that he/she prefers and to be knowledgeable about the specifics of his/her case, especially those terms regarding the payment of fees. To allow attorneys to proceed with fee-splitting arrangements without the client's written agreement or knowledge would put the client at a severe disadvantage in the lawyer-client relationship."[5]

Attorneys are prohibited from sharing fees with nonlawyers (except under special circumstances), and they are generally prohibited from forming a partnership with a nonlawyer if any of the partnership's activities include the practice of law. The intention of these rules is to protect the attorney's professional independence of judgment. The concern of the drafters of these rules is that if attorneys share fees with nonlawyers, there is the risk that the attorney's actions will be controlled by the nonlawyer, who may place his or her interests before the interests of the client.

It is not permissible for an attorney to share fees with a paralegal or to pay a referral fee to anyone other than another attorney. Attorneys may, however, make contributions to compensation or retirement plans, even though the plan is based, at least in part, on the profits of the attorney or law firm.

CLIENT TRUST ACCOUNTS

When attorneys receive money or property that belongs to clients or third parties, the attorney must hold those funds in a client trust account. Each state has its own rules concerning the handling of client funds and client trust accounts. Pursuant to Rule 1.15 of the Model Rules of Professional Conduct, attorneys must hold property of clients or third persons in a separate trust account maintained in the state where the attorney's office is situated.

Funds that Must Be Held in Trust

The practice of many attorneys requires them to hold funds belonging to their clients or to third parties from time to time. Following are some examples of the types of funds that must be held in a client trust account:

- ▶ advance payment of legal fees and costs
- ▶ client funds that may be used in the event of a settlement of a lawsuit
- ▶ personal injury settlement checks
- ▶ payments of child support or alimony by a client or for the benefit of a client
- ▶ funds for real estate closings
- ▶ client funds to pay income taxes
- ▶ estate funds held during the probate process
- ▶ funds associated with merger or acquisition closings

Required Recordkeeping

Attorneys must keep exact and proper books and records of all funds held in trust. The code of ethics in some jurisdictions provides specific instructions for how the funds must be accounted for and which type of records must be kept. Records must be kept in the state where the attorney's office is located, unless otherwise agreed to by the client, and they must be kept for the prescribed number of years after the account is closed (typically five).

Commingling of Funds

The only funds that may be deposited in any type of client trust accounts are funds in which the client has an interest. Attorneys may not deposit any of their own personal funds or general business funds into client trust accounts. To mix an attorney's funds with client funds so that the funds lose their individual ownership identity is considered **commingling of funds.** Under the Model Rules of Professional Conduct, Rule 1.15(b), it is permissible for an attorney to deposit his or her own funds only as necessary to pay any banking fees or administrative expenses associated with the administration of the client trust account. "The commingling of a lawyer's funds with those held in trust for clients subjects client funds to many unacceptable risks, including attachment by creditors and misappropriation or conversion of the funds (whether intentional or not) by the lawyer."[6]

Advance Fees

In most jurisdictions, all fees received in advance of the work completed must be held in a client trust account. As the fees are earned, the client is billed and the money is transferred from the client's trust account to the attorneys' general account. Attorneys should notify clients in writing when they are disbursing money from their client trust accounts for payment of fees. The notification should include the time, amount, and purpose of the withdrawal as well as a complete accounting of the client trust account.

Advance fees must be held in a client trust account is to ensure that the funds are there should the client be entitled to a refund of fees. Legal fees are generally refundable to the client if the anticipated legal services are not performed or if the attorney is otherwise discharged from service.

Fees paid to attorneys as a general retainer are not considered advance fees and need not be deposited in a client trust account.

> **CASE ON POINT**
> In 2001, an Iowa attorney was suspended for three months, in part for neglecting to deposit advances for court costs and retainers into a trust fund.

—*Iowa Supreme Court Board of Professional Ethics v. Adams, 623 N.W.2d 815 (IOWA 2001)*

Interest Earned on Client Trust Accounts

If an attorney holds substantial funds in a client trust account for a significant amount of time, the attorney may be required to hold the funds in an interest-bearing account, with the interest payable to the client. When client funds entrusted to attorneys are of a small amount to be held for a short period of time, attorneys may be required under their state's code of ethics to hold the money in Interest on Lawyers Trust Accounts (IOLTA). IOLTAs are a special type of trust account designed for the pooling of the funds of several clients when those funds individually are too small to generate the interest income required for the administrative costs associated with setting up a separate bank account. Attorneys pool all such funds together by depositing them in an IOLTA, thus creating a large enough sum to earn interest. Any interest earned on an IOLTA is donated to nonprofit organizations that provide for the delivery of legal services to low-income individuals. The principal in such accounts remains the property of the individual clients.

Although there were some legal challenges to IOLTAs in the 1990s, in 2003, the U.S. Supreme Court found that state laws requiring the use of IOLTAs were neither unethical nor illegal. State laws concerning IOLTAs vary. It is important to be familiar with the laws concerning IOLTAs in any jurisdiction in which you work.

OF INTEREST

Nationally, IOLTAs generated over $148 million in 2000 to help low-income people in communities throughout the United States to resolve everyday disputes, like spousal and child abuse, domestic relations, child support, and consumer and housing problems.

—*Commission on Interest on Lawyers' Trust Accounts, www.abanet.org*

Disputed Amount

If the attorney and client are in dispute as to the amount in a client trust account to which the attorney is entitled and to which the client is entitled, the attorney must disburse the amount that is not disputed and hold the disputed portion in trust until the matter is resolved.

Misappropriation of Client Funds

Improper use of client funds by an attorney for any unauthorized purpose is considered **misappropriation.** This includes not only **conversion,** or stealing the funds, but also unauthorized temporary use for the attorney's personal benefit. Misappropriation may occur when the attorney pays the funds of one client to another client, if the attorney keeps unearned advance fee, or if the client's funds are used for the attorney's personal purposes.

Often, attorney disciplinary actions result not from the outright theft of client funds by an attorney but when attorneys *borrow* client funds with the intention of repaying them at a later date. Even if the funds are fully repaid, the attorney has still misappropriated them. Courts have held that "a lawyer's subjective intent, whether it be to borrow or to steal, is irrelevant to the determination of the appropriate discipline in a misappropriation case."[7]

Misappropriation of a client's funds is a very serious breach of ethics that typically results in disbarment of the attorney and often in criminal prosecution. The need to maintain public confidence in the bar has caused the bar associations and the courts to deal quite severely with attorneys who misappropriate client funds. As stated by the District of Columbia Court of Appeals, "in virtually all cases of misappropriation, disbarment will be the only appropriate sanction unless it appears that the misconduct resulted from nothing more than simple negligence."[8]

■ PART II: FROM THE PARALEGAL'S PERSPECTIVE

Attorneys have the ultimate ethical responsibility for most financial matters, including billing and handling client funds. This does not mean, however, that paralegals are unaffected by the ethical rules concerning billing and other financial matters. Quite the opposite is true. Because clients are generally billed for the time paralegals spend working on their files, paralegals must be familiar with the rules of ethics concerning billing and fee splitting. In addition, because paralegals are often responsible for the bookkeeping and recordkeeping associated with accounting for client funds, it is imperative that they are familiar with the ethical rules applicable to attorneys concerning client funds as well as the rules for the bookkeeping and recordkeeping of client funds.

A QUESTION OF ETHICS

Maria Sanchez is an immigrant from Monterrey, Mexico. She has been in the United States most of her life and is a U.S. citizen. Maria is a paralegal for a Houston, Texas, law firm that specializes in immigration law. Maria's paralegal education, dedication, and her ability to speak both English and Spanish fluently have made her a real asset to the firm. Recently, Maria's cousin Paula immigrated to the United States from Mexico. Maria's law firm assisted Paula with her immigration and all her related legal needs. Maria was proud of the fine job her law firm did for her cousin and that she was able to bring some business to her law firm. Maria personally thanked one of the partners of the firm for helping her cousin. He responded by saying that it was a pleasure and that if she had any other friends or relatives who were in need of immigration assistance, the firm would give Maria a bonus of 10% of the fees the firm earns for each client she brings in to the firm. Maria is excited about the prospect, not only could she help certain of her relatives, but she can earn a substantial bonus on a continuing basis. Is there a problem here?

Answer and Discussion

Yes, definitely. It is unethical for attorneys to share legal fees with nonattorneys. Although it may seem harmless for paralegals to be paid on a commission basis or to receive bonuses based on client fees received, both situations are considered to be fee splitting and are prohibited by the rules of ethics.

PARALEGALS AND BILLING

Most law firms bill clients based on time spent by attorneys and paralegals on each client's file. Attorneys and paralegals have set billing rates, and clients are billed accordingly. Paralegal billing rates are usually based on the market as well as the paralegal's experience and level of expertise. According to a recent national survey, the median paralegal billing rate in 2005 was $150 per hour. Paralegal clerks billed a median rate of $95 per hour, while the national median billing rate for paralegal case managers was $210 per hour.[9] It is very important to a law firm's bottom line that every individual with billing authority, including paralegals, closely track his or her **billable hours** and meet his or her set requirements for billable hours.

It will be the ethical responsibility of the attorneys in your firm to determine a fair and reasonable amount to bill each client based on several factors, including your time spent on the file. It will be your ethical responsibility to keep accurate time records, reflecting the amount of time spent on each client's file and the work done for that client. If you work in a corporate legal department, you may also be required to track your time carefully so that the legal expenses associated with the legal department can be allocated to the appropriate corporate project and/or department within the corporation.

Paralegals who work in law firms are required to closely account for their time spent on client matters and work a requisite number of billable hours. Billable hours are hours and fractions of hours that are spent working on a client's file that will later be billed to that client. In addition to their billable hours, paralegals may be assigned several administrative responsibilities that are considered nonbillable. Nonbillable time includes time spent on training, continuing education, marketing, form file maintenance, billing, miscellaneous administrative matters, pro bono work, and personal matters. Exhibit 7-3 is a checklist of tips for effective timekeeping.

Exhibit 7-3

Tips for Effective Timekeeping

Track all of your time meticulously.

Keep copies of all timesheets.

Do not procrastinate when it comes to recording your time—you will be surprised how much you may forget after several interruptions.

Record *all* your billable hours. If you have spent too much time on a certain matter, the billing attorney can adjust the amount.

Budget your time carefully based on your annual billable hour requirements.

Do not forget to allow time for vacations and holidays.

Manage your time carefully!

Pressure can be high, especially in large law firms, for paralegals to meet their annual billable hour goals. Your raise, bonus, and possibly continued employment can depend on it. You must always remember to be meticulous with your timekeeping and, most importantly, to be honest. Do not let billing pressures compromise your ethics.

OF INTEREST

According to a 2005 national survey, paralegals bill a median 1,426 hours per year.

—*Law Office Management & Administration, Rep 5, October 2006*

PARALEGAL FEE RECOVERABILITY

It is not uncommon in matters that are litigated for attorneys' fees to be awarded to the prevailing party. Attorneys' fees may be awarded to the prevailing party, and the losing party required to pay, if the award of attorneys' fees is approved by statute, prior agreement, or if it is deemed lawful and equitable by the court. If the court awards attorneys' fees, the court generally must approve the amount of fees. "In addition to establishing entitlement to attorney fees, the party requesting them must also establish they are reasonable."[10]

The legal fees awarded by courts include the attorney's fees for his or her time plus certain allowable costs. Most, but not all, courts have allowed legal fees that include fees for paralegal time. There is still a certain amount of controversy surrounding the collection of legal fees for paralegal time spent on behalf of a client, and some courts have disallowed the recovery of fees for paralegal time at market rate but considered the paralegal's salary to be overhead for the attorney.

Both state and federal statutes address the awarding of legal fees to the prevailing party under certain circumstances. Federal statutes and several state statutes specifically provide for the award of paralegal fees as well. These statutes acknowledge the importance of the paralegal to providing affordable legal services.

Missouri v. Jenkins was the landmark case concerning paralegal fee recovery. In this case, the prevailing plaintiffs in a school desegregation case sought recovery of their attorneys' fees, which included paralegal time. The U.S. Supreme Court approved the fees charged for paralegal time at market rates. The court held that permitting market rate billing for lower cost paralegals encourages the cost-effective delivery of legal services and, by reducing the spiraling cost of civil rights litigation, furthers the policies underlying civil rights statutes.[11]

CASE ON POINT

In a 2005 case heard in Kansas, the court approved paralegal fees at an hourly rate of $250.

—*Theno v. Tonganoxie Unified School District No. 464, 404 F. Supp. 2d 1281, 1286 (D. Kan. 2005)*

Paralegal fees are usually found to be recoverable so long as the work performed by the paralegal is considered legal in nature, the work performed by the paralegal is supervised by an attorney, the time spent by the paralegal on the particular matter in question is clearly documented, the paralegal is considered by the court to be qualified by education and experience, and the paralegal fees charged are charged at the prevailing market rate in the area. Many courts have approved the recovery of paralegal fees in recognition of the contribution of paralegals in controlling the cost of legal services.

The petitioner for the award of attorney's fees has the burden of establishing the time expended by paralegals is time for which recovery of attorney's fees is appropriate. "The party seeking fees has the burden in the trial court to represent sufficiently specific evidence of his entitlement."[12]

This is typically done by providing the court with detailed time records—making it imperative that you keep accurate and detailed records of all your billable time.

In some recent court cases involving the reasonableness of attorneys fees, courts have held that work that could have effectively been done by a law firm's paralegal could not be billed at the hourly billing rate of a partner. Decisions like this emphasize the importance in utilizing paralegals to keep client fees reasonable.

FEE SPLITTING WITH ATTORNEYS

Rule 5.4 of the Model Rules of Professional Conduct, which prohibits sharing legal fees with nonlawyers, includes paralegals in that definition. It is considered unethical for attorneys to split legal fees with paralegals. This rule is intended, in part, to prevent solicitation of clients by paralegals and to avoid encouraging the unauthorized practice of law by paralegals. You may participate in a retirement or profit-sharing plan established by your employer, but you must be wary of any arrangement that involves a percentage of legal fees collected or any bonuses for bringing in new clients to the firm. Both of these situations have been found to be unethical. In a case heard before the Supreme Court of California, an attorney was disciplined for entering into a fee-splitting arrangement with a paralegal in his employ who was paid a set percentage for cases in which the paralegal was involved. The attorney involved was suspended from practice for two years for violation of the fee-splitting rule and other rules of ethics.[13]

◼ TRUST ACCOUNTING

Paralegals are often responsible for trust accounting functions. As a paralegal, you may find that your work on probate, real estate, personal injury, or other types of files requires you to set up and maintain trust accounts to hold and distribute funds on behalf of clients. For example, if you are working on a probate file, distributions from the estate may be run through a trust account.

Any attorney who delegates work to you involving trust accounting will have the ultimate responsibility for the funds and for overseeing the proper accounting of the funds. An attorney's duty to preserve client funds is nondelegable. However, as a paralegal, you must be aware of the ethical rules for handling client funds. You can help assure that the responsible attorney complies with ethical rules concerning supervision by providing periodic reports concerning any trust accounting matters to the responsible attorney and by having all books readily accessible to him or her.

Some of the tasks associated with the responsible and ethical handling of trust accounts may include:

▶ notifying clients of any disbursements or withdrawals from the trust accounts.

▶ preparing statements of the accounts for clients for approval by the supervising attorney.

▶ reconciling monthly bank statements to trust account registers and calculating interest.

▶ keeping the trust account journal current.

▶ preparing deposits and writing checks from the account (for the attorney's signature).

◼ CHAPTER SUMMARY

▶ Attorney's fees must be reasonable based on the attorney's time and labor, preclusion from other employment, customary fee, results obtained, time limitations, nature and length of the professional relationship, experience, reputation and ability of the attorney, and whether the fee is a contingent fee.

▶ Contingent fees are fees earned by an attorney based on a percentage of the award the attorney can obtain for the client. If the client collects nothing, the attorney is not compensated for his or her time.

Chapter 7

► Fee agreements should be detailed, should be discussed thoroughly with clients, and should be in writing.

► Attorneys are prohibited from splitting fees with nonattorneys under most circumstances.

► Attorneys have a fiduciary duty to clients and third parties with regard to the safekeeping of funds belonging to the client or third party.

► Any funds that an attorney holds for a client or third party must be kept in a separate client trust account.

► The attorney's funds must not be commingled with the client's funds. They must be kept separate.

► Advance fees must be kept in trust until they are earned.

► IOLTAs are client trust accounts for pooled small deposits of funds that will not be held for a significant period of time. Interest earned on IOLTAs is paid to a special nonprofit organization that promotes access to legal services for everyone.

► Improper use of client funds for any unauthorized purpose is considered a misappropriation of funds.

► Paralegal time is usually billed at market rate based on the time spent on the behalf of each client.

► Paralegal fees are usually recoverable but not in every instance and in every jurisdiction.

► Paralegals must not enter into fee-splitting agreements with attorneys.

■ FREQUENTLY ASKED QUESTIONS

Do all retainers our law firm receives need to go into a trust account?

General retainers do not need to be deposited into trust accounts. General retainers are considered earned when received. All special retainers, however, need to be deposited into client trust accounts, with amounts withdrawn and paid to the law firm as earned.

The attorneys I work for would like to establish a profit-sharing plan. Can I participate or is that considered fee sharing?

Yes. Profit-sharing and 401(k) plans are not considered to be fee splitting under most circumstances.

Is it okay for me to receive a commission equal to 10% of the fees our law firm collects for each client I refer to our firm?

No. To receive a commission on any referrals or on any files on which you work would be considered to be fee splitting with the attorney. Fee splitting is impermissible under the rules of ethics of every state.

How do I know if I should set up an IOLTA or a regular trust account for a particular client?

You must consult the rules concerning IOLTAs in your jurisdiction to answer that question definitively. In most jurisdictions, if the amount to be held in trust on the client's behalf is not large enough to earn interest sufficient to cover the administrative and banking costs associated with setting up a separate account, the funds should be deposited into an IOLTA.

As a paralegal, can I also be the law firm's bookkeeper and accept full responsibility for opening and maintaining a trust account, including signing the checks?

You can be the bookkeeper and maintain the firm's books, including the client trust accounts. However, attorneys will typically sign client trust account checks, as they have the ultimate responsibility for the funds. The attorney's duty to preserve client funds is nondelegable.

■ ENDNOTES

1 *Morse v. Espeland,* 696 P.2d 429 (Mont. 1985).
2 *Drake v. Becker,* 303 N.E. 2d 212 (Ill. App. 3d 1973).
3 *Teche Bank & Trust Co. v. J.B. Willis,* 631 So. 2d 644 (La. Ct. App. 1994).
4 Model Rules of Professional Conduct, Rule 1.5(b) (2006).
5 *Christensen v. Eggen,* 577 N.W.2d 221 (Minn. 1998).
6 *In re Anonymous,* 698 N.E.2d 808 (Ind. 1998).
7 *In Re: Warhaftig,* 524 A2d 398 (N.J. 1987).
8 *In re Micheel,* 610 A2d 231 (D.C. 1992).
9 "Paralegal Pay New Benchmarks from AW and IMPA," *Law Office Management & Administration*, Rep 5, October 2006.
10 *McGreevy v. Oregon Mutual Insurance Company, 951 P.2d 798 (Wash. Ct. of App., Div. 3 1998).*
11 *Missouri v. Jenkins,* 491 U.S. 274 (1989).
12 *In re Marriage of Nasir J. Ahmad and Carolyn A. Ahmad,* 555 N.E. 2d 439 (Ill. 1990).
13 *Gassman v. State Bar,* 553 P.2d 1147 (Cal. 1976).

Chapter 8

Advertising and Solicitation

"I'm not an ambulance chaser because I'm usually there before the ambulance."

— Melvin Belli, a.k.a. "The King of Torts"

PART I: ATTORNEY ADVERTISING AND SOLICITATION

Not too many years ago, advertisement of legal services by attorneys was considered unprofessional and unethical and thus was strictly prohibited. Obviously, as demonstrated by the television, newspaper, and other advertisements that are prevalent today, this is no longer the case.

However, advertising and soliciting by attorneys are strictly regulated by the code of ethics of each state. To thwart *ambulance chasers*, the aggressive in-person **solicitation** of individual clients by both attorneys and paralegals is still prohibited.

Part I of this chapter examines the rules of ethics concerning advertising and solicitation. Part II of this chapter focuses on the topic from the paralegal's perspective and takes a look at the rules for including information about paralegals in law firm advertising and permissible advertising by freelance and independent paralegals.

ADVERTISING ACCEPTANCE

Advertising legal services benefits members of the legal community in increased clientele and revenues, but it also benefits the community. The public's need to be informed about available attorneys, their services, and their prices for services is a very strong argument in favor of advertising. For the public to benefit, the advertising must be informative, truthful, and not misleading.

The first permitted advertising of legal services was very limited in scope and media. Over time, restrictions on advertising content have been liberalized, as has the form of media that can be used. In every instance, the change was first brought about by a challenge of a state rule leading to a decision by the U.S. Supreme Court.

The prohibition on attorney and law firm advertising was first lifted with the 1977 Supreme Court decision of *Bates v. State Bar of Arizona*, 433 U.S. 350 (1977). The U.S. Supreme Court deemed attorney advertising to be commercial speech and applied First Amendment protection. See Exhibit 8-1. The court affirmed an attorney's constitutional right to advertise legal services. All states were forced to follow suit.

Exhibit 8-1

First Amendment to the Constitution of the United States of America

Congress shall make no law respecting an establishment of religion, or prohibiting the free exercise thereof; or abridging the freedom of speech, or of the press; or the right of the people peaceably to assemble, and to petition the Government for a redress of grievances.

The *Bates* opinion also acknowledged states' rights to regulate and restrict attorney advertising, as long as it was within the guidelines established by the court. In his *Bates* opinion, Justice Harry Blackmun listed some of the permitted regulations that may be established by the states, including restricting false and misleading advertising and claims about the quality of legal services.

Again in 1980, the U.S. Supreme Court heard an important case concerning advertising by attorneys and law firms. In this case, *In re: R.M.J.*, an attorney had been disbarred for violating Missouri's Rules of Professional Conduct restricting attorney advertising. The Supreme Court found that the Missouri rules were too restrictive and reversed the judgment of the Supreme Court of Missouri. In his opinion, Justice Lewis Powell emphasized that the states retain authority to regulate advertising but also stated

> . . . *although the States may regulate commercial speech, the First and Fourteenth Amendments require that they do so with care and in a manner no more extensive than reasonably necessary to further substantial interests. The absolute prohibition on appellant's speech, in the absence of a finding that his speech was misleading, does not meet these requirements.*[1]

U.S. Supreme Court decisions have lead the way to the freedom to advertise, followed by corresponding changes to the ABA's Model Code or Model Rules and the codes of ethics of each state. The state codes of ethics cannot be in conflict with decisions from the U.S. Supreme Court. If they are, they are subject to being challenged and being overturned by the state courts or the U.S. Supreme Court.

The U.S. Supreme Court has made several decisions concerning attorney advertising and solicitation since the *Bates* decision. In every instance, the court has had to weigh the interests of several competing groups. On the one hand are the public's need for information and the attorneys' First Amendment rights to freedom of speech. On the other hand is the bar's desire to maintain public respect and dignity and the right of the states to protect their consumers. These considerations will undoubtedly continue to be paramount in any future decisions concerning attorney advertising and soliciting. Exhibit 8-2 is a timeline of some of the more important decisions and events concerning attorney advertising.

Exhibit 8-2

Timeline of Attorney Advertising

1908	The ABA's Canons of Professional Ethics prohibited attorney advertising of any kind.
1977	The U.S. Supreme Court lifted the total ban on attorney advertising in its *Bates* decision. The Court found that attorney advertising was protected under the First Amendment as commercial speech. Weighing the interest of the individual states and the interests of the attorneys, the court found that states could not place a total ban on attorney advertising, but they could restrict it.
1978	The ABA amended its Model Code of Professional Responsibility to conform to the *Bates* decision. The amendment listed 25 categories of information that could be included in advertising by attorneys and law firms.
1978	In *Ohralik v. Ohio State Bar*, the Supreme Court upheld a ban on in-person solicitation, indicating that the same First Amendment protections that applied to attorney advertising did not apply to in-person solicitation.
1978	The U.S. Supreme Court decision in *In Primus* provided that in-person solicitation may be permitted under certain circumstances when the attorney's motive is political or ideological. The court ruled that when the motive behind the solicitation is political expression, the First Amendment is applied much more broadly than if the motive is purely commercial.
1980	The U.S. Supreme Court handed down a decision in the *In R.M.J.* case that emphasized the limits of the states' authority to restrict attorney advertising. The Court affirmed the states' right to restrict misleading advertising and other types of advertising contrary to substantial state interests. However, the court ruled that the First and Fourteenth amendments require that states restrict attorney advertising with care and in a manner no more extensive than reasonably necessary to further substantial interests.
1983	The Model Rules of Professional Conduct are adopted by the ABA. Unlike the prior Model Code, the Model Rules do not dictate the information that may be contained in attorney advertising but provide that advertising must not be false or misleading.
1988	The U.S. Supreme Court ruled that a Kentucky rule prohibiting all targeted direct mail solicitation by attorneys for pecuniary gain was unconstitutional and that states may not categorically prohibit attorneys from soliciting business by sending truthful and nondeceptive letters to potential clients known to face particular legal problems.
1989	The Model Rules of Professional Conduct are amended to provide for restricted direct mail solicitation by attorneys.

1990	The U.S. Supreme Court ruled on *Peel v. Attorney Registration and Disciplinary Commission of Illinois*, holding that consistent with the First Amendment, states may not categorically prohibit attorneys from advertising their certifications as specialists by bona fide organizations.
1995	The NFPA issued Ethics Opinion 95-6 to explain that it is ethical for freelance paralegals, also known as contract paralegals, to advertise their services, as long as several conditions listed in the opinion are met.
1995	In *Florida Bar v. Went For It*, the U.S. Supreme Court upheld a rule of the Florida Bar mandating a 30-day waiting period after an accident or disaster before a solicitation letter can be sent to the victims of the accident.
2002	The Model Rules of Professional Conduct were amended to provide for advertising through "written, recorded or electronic communication, including public media" to reflect the use of the Internet for advertising and the rapid changes in technology.

CURRENT RULES REGULATING AND RESTRICTING ADVERTISING

The Model Rules adopted by the ABA, as well as the rules of most states, permit most types of attorney and law firm advertising, as long as that advertising is not false or misleading. However, there is still a lot of variance among the specific provisions of the state's codes of ethics concerning advertising and solicitation. The rules of ethics addressing advertising generally include

▶ prohibition of false and misleading advertising.

▶ restrictions on the payment of referral fees.

▶ restrictions on advertising certifications and areas of practice.

▶ restrictions on law firm names and letterhead.

▶ restrictions on solicitation of clients.

Law firm marketing has become a big business in the United States. According to a recent survey, law firms are spending an average of 1.8% of their annual revenues on marketing their services.[2]

FALSE AND MISLEADING ADVERTISING

The Supreme Court has held that "Truthful advertising related to lawful activities is entitled to the protections of the First Amendment. But when the particular content or method of the advertising suggests that it is inherently misleading or when experience has proved that in fact such advertising is subject to abuse, the states may impose appropriate restrictions."[3]

The ABA's Model Rules and the rules of all jurisdictions provide that advertising must not be false or misleading. Exhibit 8-3 illustrates how this rule has been adopted by the state of Massachusetts.

Exhibit 8-3

Code of Ethics Provisions Box

From the Massachusetts Rules of Professional Conduct

Rule 7.1 Communications Concerning a Lawyer's Services

A lawyer shall not make a false or misleading communication about the lawyer or the lawyer's services. A communication is false or misleading if it contains a material misrepresentation of fact or law, or omits a fact necessary to make the statement considered as a whole not materially misleading.

◼ Misrepresentation and Misleading Advertising

Advertising that contains material misrepresentation of fact or law is relatively easy to determine because it deals with concrete information and statements that are usually easily proved or disproved. Misleading advertising, on the other hand, is somewhat more difficult to define. What is considered misleading, as opposed to informative, can be subjective, and the definition varies among the states. For example, although it is not an untrue statement, in the *R.M.J.* case, it was found misleading to advertise that an attorney is a member of the U.S. Supreme Court Bar because the general public is unfamiliar with requirements of admission.[4]

Creating Unjustified Expectations

Advertising may be considered false and misleading if it causes the recipient of the material to have unjustified expectations. If the advertising material would cause the recipient to have the expectation of a favorable verdict (when this is not realistic), unrealistic expectations are created. Advertisements concerning results obtained on behalf of other clients, such as winning favorable verdicts or collecting large settlements, may be prohibited in some states under this category because it may cause the potential client to expect the same or a similar outcome.

Comparison Statements

Advertising that compares the skill or quality of legal services rendered by one attorney to the skills and legal services rendered by another may also be considered misleading and is generally prohibited. However, factual statements, such as "the largest law firm in the city," may be permissible.

Fees

Advertised statements concerning fees charged by attorneys are generally acceptable, provided they are not false or misleading. For example, it is not inherently misleading to advertise fees or prices charged for *routine* legal services.[5] It is also permissible to say that legal services are offered at "very reasonable prices" if the prices charged are within the low range of prices for similar services commonly charged in the attorney's geographical area.[6] However, advertising claiming that no fee will be charged unless the client recovers damages has been considered misleading unless the advertisement includes a statement that the client will be responsible for costs and expenses of litigation (when that is the case).[7] Advertisements for fixed fees for certain representations, where there are hidden costs, are also considered misleading.

Dignity in Advertising

Most members of the legal profession would agree that truly tasteless and undignified advertising is embarrassing and reflects poorly on the entire legal community. At one time, the codes of ethics of most jurisdictions contained statements indicating that all advertising must be dignified. However, good taste and dignity in advertising are purely subjective and nearly impossible to regulate, and those provisions have now been mostly eliminated.

▣ ADVERTISING MEDIA

Most current advertising rules focus on content rather than the media used for disseminating the information. Therefore, those rules apply to all types of printed advertising as well as television and advertising on the Internet. Model Rules 7.2(a) provides that a lawyer may advertise services through "written, recorded or electronic communications, including public media."[8]

Print Advertising

Print advertising, including directory advertising and advertisements in newspapers and other periodicals, has been an important form of advertising for attorneys since advertising was first permitted. Despite other, newer forms of advertising, print advertising remains a mainstay—especially with smaller law firms. According to a 2005 survey by Martindale-Hubbell of nearly 1,000 small law firms, the firms spent an average of approximately 24% of their marketing budgets on yellow pages advertising (including online yellow pages). Larger firms spend an average of 13% of their marketing budgets on directories.

    The rules of many states require that copies of all advertising, including a record of the content and use of the advertising, must be kept for two years. Some states require copies of all advertising by attorneys and law firms to be submitted to a committee of the bar association prior to, or simultaneous with, its release to the public. This requirement is not included in the Model Rules.

Another typical requirement for print advertising provides that all attorney advertising must be labeled "Advertising" or "Advertising Material." This is to avoid any confusion on the part of the public who may mistake attorney advertising for some other type of document that may require their attention or require them to contact the lawyer or law firm in question.

In addition, all advertisements must include the name of at least one attorney responsible for its content.

Television Advertising

Initially, television advertising was prohibited in most jurisdictions. However, television has become one of the most prevalent forms of communication, and its power to reach the public is unequaled by other forms of media. Because it is the primary source of information for many people of low to moderate income, and especially to those who are illiterate, bans on television advertising have been found to be too restrictive and have been overturned. As stated by the Supreme Court of Connecticut, "A total ban on advertising through the electronic media would not only exceed the state's legitimate interest in protecting potential consumers, but its overinclusiveness would also keep a great deal of information from consumers, thereby hindering their ability to make an informed choice."[9]

Although television advertising by attorneys is generally allowed in each state, some states place restrictions on such advertising. In Iowa, for example, the Rules of Professional Conduct regarding television advertising provide that "no visual display shall be allowed except that allowed in print as articulated by the announcer."[10] In addition to print advertising and television advertising, attorneys and law firms may use other types of media to communicate their advertising, including billboards and, with increasing frequency, Web sites and blogs on the Internet.

Internet Advertising

In a recent survey by the ABA, 100% of the responding attorneys in law firms with at least 50 attorneys indicated that their law firms had Web sites. The code of ethics of each state applies to Internet advertising and e-mail communications as well as print advertising. However, the rules were not always written with the Internet in mind. One unique problem presented by Internet advertising is its global reach. Advertising by an Indiana attorney may be seen by potential clients in surrounding states and throughout the world. Typically, the attorneys must abide by the rules of ethics that apply to their home jurisdictions.

CASE ON POINT

In 1997, a former attorney, known as The Father of Modern Spam, was disbarred for sending out spam advertising to thousands of e-mail addresses and listservs.

—*In re Canter, No. 95-831-O-H (Judgment of the Hearing Committee, February 25, 1997)*

Some states have amended their codes of ethics to specifically address Internet advertising and the unique problems such advertising presents. Florida Rules of Professional Conduct, for example, set forth specific requirements for advertising on the Internet. According to Rule 4-7.6 of the Florida Rules of Professional Conduct:

All World Wide Web sites and home pages accessed via the Internet that are controlled or sponsored by a lawyer or law firm and that contain information concerning the lawyer's or law firm's services:

(1) shall disclose all jurisdictions in which the lawyer or members of the law firm are licensed to practice law;

(2) shall disclose 1 or more bona fide office locations of the lawyer or law firm, in accordance with subdivision (a)(2) of rule 4-7.2; and

(3) are considered to be information provided upon request and, therefore, are otherwise governed by the requirements of rule 4-7.9.

SPECIALIZATION

Attorneys often find it beneficial to advertise their areas of specialty in their marketing materials. Because the main purpose of advertising is to attract business, they want to be sure to attract the right kind of business. Attorneys are generally permitted to indicate in advertising and other communications the areas of law in which they specialize. If an attorney practices only in certain fields, he or she may say so. It is generally permitted for an attorney to use the word **specialist** or to indicate that he or she practices a specialty. The words *specialist* and *specialty* must not be used in a way that could be misleading.

Any advertising or communication concerning an attorney's fields of law must not be misleading. In a recent case before the Ohio Supreme Court, an attorney was publicly reprimanded for indicating that he was specializing in medical malpractice when, in fact, the attorney had little experience in the field and could not reasonably be considered a specialist.[11]

Rule 7.4 of the Model Rules concerning fields of practice specifically permits attorneys to state they are certified as a specialist in a particular field of law if the attorney has been certified by an organization that has been approved by an appropriate state authority or that has been accredited by the ABA and if the name of the certifying organization is clearly identified in the communication. Rule 7.4 also provides special rules for indicating specialties by attorneys in patent practice or admiralty practice.

Most states have adopted rules similar to Model Rule 7.4. Others allow attorneys to state that their practices are *limited to* or *concentrated in* particular fields. These rules allow attorneys to describe their practices without implying a formal recognition of a certification or specialization in a field of law.

LAW FIRM NAMES AND LETTERHEAD

Attorneys must choose the names of their law firms carefully so that they are not misleading. The name of the firm may include the name of any practicing attorneys of the firm and the names of any deceased partners. The name of the firm may also be a trade name if it is not misleading and does not imply a connection to a government entity. If the law firm has offices in more than one state, the letterhead must indicate the jurisdictional limitations of any attorneys who are listed on the letterhead but not necessarily licensed to practice law in the state in which the letterhead is being used.

Attorneys must be careful that the name of their firm does not imply a **partnership** or other organization where none exists. For example, if John Simons is a sole practitioner who rents office space from a law firm, his letterhead may not indicate John Simons & Associates. This name would tend to mislead the public into thinking that John Simons has a working relationship with the other attorneys in his office building. If any nonlawyers are included on law firm letterhead, the status of the nonlawyer must be clearly indicated.

■ SOLICITATION

Although the rules and views expressed by the bar and the courts concerning advertising have changed dramatically since 1977, the general prohibition on in-person solicitation remains intact.

Rule 7.3 of the Model Rules of Professional Conduct, which serves as a model for most states, prohibits direct contact to solicit prospective clients when the attorney's motivation is his or her own pecuniary gain. Direct contact with the potential client includes in-person contact, contact by telephone, or "real-time electronic contact," such as instant messaging and chat rooms. E-mail communications may be permitted as long as they comply with all other rules concerning solicitation.

Solicitation of clients is prohibited to protect the public because the potential for abuse is considered great. It is generally agreed that in-person and live telephone solicitation of a potential client puts too much pressure on that individual, who may be experiencing extreme stress, loss, or grief. The comments to Model Rule 7.3 justify this ban on in-person solicitation as follows:

> "The prospective client, who may already feel overwhelmed by the circumstances giving rise to the need for legal services, may find it difficult fully to evaluate all available alternatives with reasoned judgment and appropriate self-interest in the face of the lawyer's presence and insistence upon being retained immediately. The situation is fraught with the possibility of undue influence, intimidation, and over-reaching."[12]

There is generally an exception to the prohibition against direct contact to solicit prospective clients when the prospective client is another attorney, a family member, a close personal friend, or someone who has a prior professional relationship with the attorney. For example, if an attorney hears her sister would like to purchase a new home, the attorney would not be out of line if she were to call her sister to see if her sister would like her representation in that purchase.

Under no circumstances may an attorney use direct contact to solicit a potential client if the potential client has let the attorney know of his or her desire not to be solicited by the attorney or if the solicitation involves coercion, duress, or harassment.

When direct solicitation of a potential client is permitted, the attorney must make it clear that the solicitation is considered advertising. For example, under Model Rule 7.3(c), every written, recorded, or electronic communication to prospective clients who are known to be in need of legal services in a particular matter must include "Advertising Material" on the outside of any envelope used and at the beginning and ending of any electronic communication sent.

Solicitation Not for Profit

Although direct contact solicitation is generally banned when the attorney's financial gain is a significant motive, such solicitation may be permitted when the attorney's motive is political or ideological. When the motive behind the solicitation is political expression, the First Amendment is applied much more broadly than if the motive is purely commercial. In *In re Primus*,[13] a case heard before the U.S. Supreme Court in 1978, at issue was the reprimand of a South Carolina attorney for violating the rules of South Carolina regarding solicitation of clients. The attorney in this case, who was representing the local branch of the American Civil Liberties Union (ACLU), spoke to a group of African-American women who had allegedly been sterilized as a condition of their continued receipt of public medical assistance. The attorney advised the women of their legal rights and later informed one of the women by letter that free legal assistance was available from the ACLU. The Supreme Court held that solicitation of possible litigants by the attorney for a nonprofit organization that engages in litigation as a form of political expression and political association constitutes expressive and associational conduct entitled to First Amendment protection that may be regulated only with narrow specificity.

Direct contact with individuals who are potential clients in a federal class action is generally permitted under the Federal Rules of Civil Procedure.

Prepaid or Group Legal Services Plan

Prepaid legal service plans are offered as a benefit to employees. Participants in these plans typically pay premiums to cover certain legal services that may be required in the future. It is generally found to be acceptable for attorneys to solicit the business of such plans. The reason behind this is that the attorneys are not soliciting individuals who will become their clients. They are not soliciting individuals who have been injured, are distressed, or in immediate need of legal services. Rather, they are soliciting the individuals who will administer the plan.

■ REFERRAL FEES AND THIRD-PARTY SOLICITATION

Attorneys are generally prohibited from paying referral fees to third parties and from paying third parties to solicit business on their behalf. While attorneys frequently obtain new business through the referrals of acquaintances and past clients, it is unethical for the attorneys to pay referral fees to laypeople for referrals. However, attorneys are encouraged to use the services of certain types of not-for-profit lawyer referral agencies that specialize in assisting members of the public to find an appropriate attorney, and attorneys are permitted to pay them a customary fee for their services.

Solicitation by Third Parties

The rules of ethics prohibit attorneys from hiring another to solicit new clients for the attorney. For example, personal injury attorneys may not hire runners to listen to police scanners for car accidents, then solicit business from the accident victims on behalf of the attorney. It would also be unquestionably wrong for an attorney to send a paralegal to funerals in an attempt to solicit probate business from widows and widowers.

> ### CASE ON POINT
>
> In a case in Ohio, an attorney was suspended indefinitely for entering into an agreement with third parties to solicit business on his behalf. In that case, an individual hired by the attorney would listen to his police scanner and appear at the scene of accidents, offering to transport the accident victims to see the attorney and a chiropractor he also contracted with.

—*Cincinnati Bar Association v. Rinderknecht, 679 N.E. 2d 669 (OHIO 1997)*

Solicitation Letters

Solicitation of individuals by mail is generally acceptable, although it is regulated by the states. Letters sent to a target group of individuals known to need legal services is permissible advertising. In *Shapero v. Kentucky Bar Association*,[14] a case that came before the U.S. Supreme Court in 1988, the court ruled that a Kentucky rule prohibiting all targeted direct mail solicitation by attorneys for pecuniary gain was unconstitutional. The court held that states may not categorically prohibit attorneys from soliciting business by sending truthful and nondeceptive letters to potential clients known to face particular legal problems.[15]

Solicitation letters are viewed in a different light than in-person or live telephone solicitation for the following reasons:

- ▶ The recipient of a targeted solicitation letter is not faced with the coercive presence of an attorney.
- ▶ The recipient of a targeted solicitation letter, unlike someone who is faced with in-person solicitation, need not give an on-the-spot answer. They are allowed time to consider all options.

▶ The recipient of a targeted solicitation letter always has the option of ignoring the letter and throwing it away.

▶ Where copies of targeted solicitation letters are submitted to a state agency for approval either prior to or when the letter is sent out, they can be scrutinized for fraudulent or misleading statements, unlike statements made during an in-person solicitation.

▶ The contents of written communications concerning an attorney's proposed services are documented with copies, and there can be no question as to exactly what was communicated to the potential client.

The solicitation letter is strictly regulated by state rules. One state rule that was recently challenged in the U.S. Supreme Court is a Florida Bar rule that prohibits attorneys from using direct mail to solicit personal injury or wrongful death clients for 30 days after the accident. In *Florida Bar v. Went For It*,[16] the Court upheld the 30-day waiting period rule because (1) the bar has a substantial interest in protecting the privacy and tranquility of personal injury victims; (2) a study presented by the bar shows that the Florida public views direct mail solicitations immediately following an accident to be intrusive on their privacy; and (3) the rule is sufficiently narrow in scope.

> **CASE ON POINT**
>
> In a 2004 case in New York, an attorney was suspended for one year for sending a solicitation letter to a hospitalized comatose patient in the days immediately following a collision between her automobile and a train. The court held that any "reasonable attorney" would know that "the letter would reach the patient and her family at a time when they were unable to exercise reasonable judgment in retaining an attorney."

—*In re Shapiro, 7A.D.3d 120 (4th Department 2004)*

Following are some of the types of restrictions that may be placed on written solicitations:

▶ Attorneys may be required to observe a 30-day waiting period following an accident or disaster before sending targeted direct mail to victims or their relatives.

▶ All mailings to potential clients must be labeled as "Advertising" or "Advertising Material" on the envelope and on the communication itself.

▶ The solicitation letter must not involve duress, coercion, or harassment.

▶ No solicitation letter may be sent to a prospective client who has made it known to the attorney that he or she does not want to be solicited by the attorney.

▶ A copy of all solicitation letters must be submitted to a state advertising committee or similar agency for approval before being sent.

⬛ PART II: FROM THE PARALEGAL'S PERSPECTIVE

Paralegals are involved in advertising and soliciting in several ways. As a paralegal, you must be aware of the rules of ethics concerning advertising and soliciting that will relate to your work. The rest of this chapter focuses on the issues concerning advertising and solicitation that directly affect paralegals. However, you must remember to always proceed with caution because these rules vary significantly between states and are frequently revised.

A QUESTION OF ETHICS

Suppose you have just started your first paralegal position at a small general practice law firm. The firm consists of five attorneys, two part-time law clerks, two secretaries, and one receptionist. You are the first paralegal the firm has hired. On your first day, your supervising attorney approaches you and asks that you call the stationery supplier and the telephone directory sales representative. Your supervising attorney wants you to have your own business cards, have your name added to the firm letterhead, and to have the firm's Web site administrator add your name to the directory on the firm's Web site.

You are flattered that they want to include you—and so soon—but you are unsure as to how to proceed. Is it even ethical to have the firm use your name in such a way?

Answer and Discussion

Probably, but you must do your research to be sure. Most jurisdictions allow the names of paralegals to be included on law firm letterhead and on firm business cards. Your name can probably also be included in the telephone directory advertisement. You must do your research to be sure your proposed actions are permissible within your jurisdiction. If it is acceptable to use your name in such a manner, you must remember that everywhere your name appears, your title must be included so as not to mislead the public into mistaking you for an attorney. Also, you must be sure that any advertisement that includes your name is not false or misleading.

Traditional Paralegals

If you work as a traditional paralegal, you will need to know your state's rules concerning inclusion of paralegals on letterhead and advertising. It is also possible that you may be involved in various marketing efforts by your firm. Exhibit 8-4 lists some of the activities you may ethically be involved in to promote your law firm.

Exhibit 8-4

What You *Can* Do to Promote Your Law Firm

- Refer friends and relatives to your law firm—when appropriate and NOT for compensation.
- Become active in your paralegal association.
- Network!
- Assist with law firm marketing plans and help with the placement of advertising.
- Encourage the attorneys and management of your firm to sponsor worthwhile community events that you are involved in.

Letterhead

The names of paralegals are often included on law firm letterhead. Most jurisdictions, but not all, permit this so long as the paralegal's title is clearly indicated by his or her name.[17] Some jurisdictions, however, have issued opinions stating that the very use of a paralegal's name on letterhead is misleading and causes the potential for public confusion and potential for the paralegal to engage in the unauthorized practice of law.

Reasoning behind the general acceptability for listing paralegals on law firm letterhead with their titles is that it is useful information that may help to clear up any misunderstandings that clients may have as to who they are dealing with at the law firm.

ABA Informal Opinion 89-1527 provides that "the listing of nonlawyer support personnel on lawyers' letterheads is not prohibited by these or any other Rules so long as the listing is not false or misleading."[18]

As a paralegal, you must be sure that you use law firm letterhead only for law firm business. Any correspondence on law firm letterhead indicates that it is done with the authority of the law firm. Even if your name is on the letterhead, you must be careful to never use law firm letterhead for personal correspondence.

Business Cards

If you work as a traditional paralegal, your employer will most likely furnish you with business cards with your name, title, and the firm or corporate name of your employer. You must be sure that any business card you use indicates your nonlawyer status.

Advertisements

ABA Informal Opinion 89-1527 provides that the names and titles of paralegals may be included in written advertisements "provided the designation is not likely to mislead those who see it into thinking that the nonlawyers who are listed are lawyers or exercise control over lawyers in the firm."[19]

CLA and RP Designations

In addition to including your paralegal title on any letterhead, business cards, or advertising that includes your name, you may also wish to include your Certified Legal Assistant (CLA), Certified Paralegal (CP), or Registered Paralegal (RP) designation. The NALA and the NFPA have their own sets of rules and guidelines for using their designations. To date, there have been no challenges to this practice. See Exhibit 8-5 for the NFPA's rule for fully disclosing your title as a paralegal.

Exhibit 8-5

From the NFPA's Model Code of Ethics and Professional Responsibility and Guidelines for Enforcement

1.7 A PARALEGAL'S TITLE SHALL BE FULLY DISCLOSED.
ETHICAL CONSIDERATIONS

EC-1.7(a)   A paralegal's title shall clearly indicate the individual's status and shall be disclosed in all business and professional communications to avoid misunderstandings and misconceptions about the paralegal's role and responsibilities.

EC-1.7(b)   A paralegal's title shall be included if the paralegal's name appears on business cards, letterhead, brochures, directories, and advertisements.

EC-1.7(c)   A paralegal shall not use letterhead, business cards or other promotional materials to create a fraudulent impression of his/her status or ability to practice in the jurisdiction in which the paralegal practices.

EC-1.7(d)   A paralegal shall not practice under color of any record, diploma, or certificate that has been illegally or fraudulently obtained or issued or which is misrepresentative in any way.

EC-1.7(e)   A paralegal shall not participate in the creation, issuance, or dissemination of fraudulent records, diplomas, or certificates.

Freelance Paralegals

Freelance paralegals depend on the business of attorneys for their livelihood. Although word of mouth is often used to communicate the availability of a freelance paralegal's services, many freelance paralegals would not have work if it was not for effective advertising. According to the NFPA, the right of freelance paralegals to solicit attorneys—the consumers of their services—outweighs the state's right to restrict freelance paralegals' rights to advertise.[20] In 1995, the NFPA issued Ethics

Opinion 95-6, which says that it is ethical for freelance paralegals, also known as contract paralegals, to advertise their services, albeit with several conditions:

- ▶ Freelance paralegals should be sure their advertising is aimed at attorneys, who will be responsible for their work, not at the public.
- ▶ Any advertising by a paralegal should clearly indicate the nonattorney status of the paralegal.
- ▶ Any advertising by a freelance paralegal should in no way indicate that the freelance paralegal offers legal advice or services to the public.
- ▶ Paralegal advertising should comply with attorney advertising guidelines and the code of ethics in the pertinent jurisdictions.
- ▶ Paralegal advertising must not be false or misleading in any manner.
- ▶ Paralegal advertising should include the paralegal's name, address, and phone number.
- ▶ Paralegal advertising should avoid statements that may infer the nature or success of results which may be obtained.
- ▶ Advertising concerning a freelance paralegal should avoid comparisons to other paralegals.

As stated by the NFPA, the overall consideration in promoting freelance paralegals should include maintaining and preserving the dignity of and proper decorum in the legal profession.

Independent Paralegals

Independent paralegals can advertise any legal services they can provide without engaging in the unauthorized practice of law. The advertisements used by independent paralegals must make it clear that the services being offered are being performed by a paralegal (not a lawyer) and do not include giving legal advice or other activities considered to be the practice of law. If independent paralegals do advertise their services, they must be sure that their advertisements are not false or misleading. Exactly what can be advertised in each state varies, as does the definition of the unauthorized practice of law and the activities that may be performed by independent paralegals who do not work under the supervision of an attorney.

In one case heard before the Supreme Court of South Carolina, an independent paralegal's advertisement describing himself as a paralegal was found to be misleading and was not entitled to First Amendment protection because as defined in South Carolina, paralegals work under the supervision of attorneys, but the defendant did not. The court found that "to legitimately provide services as a paralegal, one must work in conjunction with a licensed attorney. Robinson's advertisement as a paralegal is false since his work product is admittedly not subject to the supervision of a licensed attorney."[21]

■ SOLICITATION

Attorneys are prohibited from engaging paralegals to solicit clients for them. If you work for a law firm as a traditional paralegal, you must not solicit business on behalf of your supervising attorney or law firm in contravention to the codes of ethics in place for attorneys in your jurisdiction. "Solicitation, whether in person or by hired proxy, is misconduct warranting appropriate discipline."[22] It is unethical for attorneys to violate their codes of ethics through the actions of others. Therefore, if the circumstances dictate that it is not permissible for the attorney to solicit potential clients, it is not permissible for you to do so on their behalf.

Also, you must avoid any situation in which you are paid referral fees or otherwise compensated for bringing business to your supervising attorney or law firm. Payment of referral fees to laypersons is generally prohibited. The rules do not prohibit you from referring acquaintances to your supervising attorney or any attorney you are acquainted with. Rather, they prevent you from doing so for money.

■ CHAPTER SUMMARY

▶ Attorney and law firm advertising must be permitted under the code of ethics of each state. However, the states have the authority to restrict that advertising under certain conditions.

▶ Under most circumstances, in-person solicitation is considered unethical and prohibited by the code of ethics of each state.

▶ Most changes in the model codes and the state codes of ethics concerning advertising have been brought about by U.S. Supreme Court decisions.

▶ In the 1977 *Bates* decision, the U.S. Supreme Court deemed attorney advertising to be commercial speech and entitled to limited First Amendment protection. The court also affirmed the right of the states to restrict attorney advertising, especially where false and misleading advertising is concerned.

▶ Attorneys currently advertise through numerous types of media, including newspaper and periodical advertisements, mailed announcements, television and radio advertisements, and Web sites and Internet advertisements.

▶ Current rules restricting attorney advertising focus on the content rather than the media. All states prohibit advertising that may be false or misleading.

▶ Attorney advertising, including targeted mailings, must be labeled "Advertising."

▶ It is generally unethical for an attorney to pay a layperson for referrals.

▶ In-person solicitation of a potential client is generally prohibited unless the attorney's motive for the solicitation is not monetary; the potential client is a friend, family member, or former client; or the solicitation is in connection with a federal class action as permitted by federal rules.

▶ Paralegal names and titles may be included on law firm letterhead, on business cards, and in law firm advertising in most jurisdictions.

▶ Freelance paralegals may advertise to their potential customers (attorneys), as long as they follow the general rules prohibiting false and misleading advertising.

► Independent paralegals may advertise any of the services they can legally provide in their jurisdictions. Their advertisements must not be misleading, and they must make it clear that the independent paralegal is not offering legal advice or any other services that would constitute the practice of law.

■ FREQUENTLY ASKED QUESTIONS

The attorneys I work for have asked me to place an advertisement for the firm in a local magazine. Do I need to have the copy approved by anyone other than the attorneys I work for? Do I need to save a copy of that advertising?

You will need to consult the rules of your state on this. The rules of some states require that you submit a copy of all advertising to a committee of the bar association either before or when it is published. Most states also require that copies of your advertising be kept for a certain number of years.

If I witness an accident, can I suggest to the accident victims that they contact the personal injury attorneys I work for?

No. In-person solicitations are generally prohibited because it is felt that such a solicitation puts too much pressure on individuals who are already in a stressful situation. Unless the victim of the accident is a family member or close personal friend, such a solicitation would probably not be permitted.

As a freelance paralegal, can I advertise my services to attorneys?

If you are a paralegal who provides services on a contract basis to attorneys, working under their supervision, it is generally acceptable to advertise to attorneys. You will want to make sure that your advertising makes it clear that you are a paralegal, not a licensed attorney, and that you work under attorney supervision. You must also follow the rules prohibiting false and misleading advertising discussed in this chapter.

The new divorce lawyer I work for has paid me a $75 bonus for referring my sister and has offered me $50 for every new client I refer to the firm. Is this permissible?

No. This type of referral fee is not permissible. Although it is acceptable to refer your sister to the attorney you work for legal services, you do not want to be put in a position where you are expected to solicit business for that attorney. It is unethical for you to accept any compensation for bringing new business into the firm.

Is it okay to send a letter to the families of plane crash victims to offer them the assistance of our law firm?

It is probably permissible as long as all the rules in your state concerning solicitation by mail are followed. Unlike in-person solicitation, solicitation letters are generally permitted because they are thought to put less pressure on the potential client. Most states have placed certain restrictions on solicitation letters. There may be restrictions on the time period during which such letters may be sent and what the content of those letters may be.

■ ENDNOTES

1. *In re the Matter of R.M.J.*, 455 U.S. 191 (1982).
2. Hazelton, Linda. "Follow the Money," *The Law Marketing Portal,* April 13, 2004.
3. *In re the Matter of R.M.J.,* 455 U.S. 191 (1982).
4. *In the Matter of R.M.J.,* 455 U.S. 191 (1982). [To be admitted to the bar of the Supreme Court, the applicant must have been admitted to practice in the highest court of a state, commonwealth, territory, or possession or of the District of Columbia for the three years immediately preceding the date of application and must have been free from any adverse disciplinary action whatsoever during that three-year period, and the applicant must appear to the court to be of good moral and professional character.]
5. *Bates v. State Bar of Arizona,* 433 U.S. 350 (1977).
6. *Bates v. State Bar of Arizona,* 433 U.S. 350 (1977).
7. *Zauderer v. Office of Disciplinary Counsel of the Ohio Supreme Court,* 471 U.S. 626 (1985).
8. Model Rules of Professional Conduct, Rule 7.2(a) (2006).
9. *Grievance Committee for the Hartford-New Britain Judicial District v. Trantolo,* 470 A.2d 228 (Conn. 1984).
10. *Iowa Rules of Professional Conduct,* 3.2:7.2(e).
11. *Trumbull County Bar Association v. Joseph,* 569 N.E. 2d 883 (Ohio 1991).
12. Model Rules of Professional Conduct, Rule 7.3.
13. *In re Primus,* 98 S. Ct. 1893 (1978).
14. *Shapero v. Kentucky Bar Association,* 486 U.S. 466 (1988).
15. *Shapero v. Kentucky Bar Association,* 486 U.S. 466 (1988).
16. *Florida Bar v. Went For It,* 115 S.Ct. 2371 (1995).
17. States that do not permit paralegal names to appear on law firm letterhead include Georgia, New Hampshire, and New Mexico.
18. ABA Informal Opinion 89-1527.
19. ABA Informal Opinion 89-1527.
20. *National Federation of Paralegal Associations Ethics and Disciplinary Opinion No. 95-6* (1995).
21. *State v. Robinson,* 468 S.E. 2d 290 (S.C. 1996).
22. *In re the Matter of the Application for the Discipline of Normal Pearl,* 407 NW2d 678 (Minn. 1987).

Appendix A

State Paralegal Regulation & Definitions of the Terms Paralegal and Legal Assistant

Information compiled, in part, from the NFPA Paralegal Regulation by State Chart.
Last updated February 2007 on www.paralegals.org.

State	Description of Regulation or Paralegal Definition
Alabama	The 1975 Code of Alabama 6-5-572 includes paralegals in its definition of *legal service providers*. 6-5-572: "(2) Legal Service Provider - Anyone licensed to practice law by the State of Alabama or engaged in the practice of law in the State of Alabama. The term legal service provider includes professional corporations, associations, and partnerships and the members of such professional corporations, associations, and partnerships and the persons, firms, or corporations either employed by or performing work or services for the benefit of such professional corporations, associations, and partnerships including, without limitations, law clerks, legal assistants, legal secretaries, investigators, paralegals, and couriers."
Alaska	Alaska Rule of Professional Conduct 5.3 does not define paralegals but considers "paraprofessionals" as nonlawyer assistants. The rule states that lawyers must directly supervise their assistants and are responsible for their assistants' conduct.
Arizona	Certification of Legal Document Preparers: Supreme Court of Arizona adopted § 7-208 of the Arizona Code of Judicial Administration regarding "Legal Document Preparers" effective July 1, 2003. This code requires that anyone preparing legal paperwork without an attorney's supervision must be certified as a legal document preparer. Legal document preparers can provide general legal information but can't give legal advice. Effective July 1,

2005, Legal Document Preparers must complete 10 hours of CLE annually. Effective July 1, 2006, legal document preparers must take an examination.

Definition of "Legal Assistant/Paralegal" 17A A.R.S. Sup.Ct. Rules, Rule 31C. "Legal assistant/paralegal" means a person qualified by education and training who performs substantive legal work requiring a sufficient knowledge of and expertise in legal concepts and procedures, who is supervised by an active member of the State Bar of Arizona, and for whom an active member of the state bar is responsible, unless otherwise authorized by supreme court rule.

Arkansas

Rule 5.3 of the Arkansas Rules of Professional Conduct 5.3 does not define paralegals but considers "paraprofessionals" as nonlawyer assistants. The rule states that lawyers must directly supervise their assistants and are responsible for their assistants' conduct.

California

The California Business and Professions Code provides definitions for both "paralegals" and "legal document assistants." Legal document assistants provide self-help services to the public and do not work under the direct supervision of attorneys. Legal document assistants are subject to registration requirements and other requirements not applicable to paralegals, who work under the supervision of attorneys.

California Business and Professions Code Section 6456-6456: "'Paralegal' means a person who holds himself or herself out to be a paralegal, who is qualified by education, training, or work experience, who either contracts with or is employed by an attorney, law firm, corporation, governmental agency, or other entity, and who performs substantial legal work under the direction and supervision of an active member of the State Bar of California, as defined in Section 6060, or an attorney practicing law in the federal courts of this state, that has been specifically delegated by the attorney to him or her. Tasks performed by a paralegal include, but are not limited to, case planning, development, and management; information; drafting and analyzing legal documents; collecting, compiling, and utilizing technical information to make an independent decision and recommendation to the supervising attorney; and representing clients before a state or federal administrative agency if that representative is permitted by statute, court rule, or administrative rule or regulation."

The definition of Legal Document Assistant does not apply to paralegals provided that the paralegal does not also perform the duties of a legal document assistant. Legal document assistants must be registered in the county in which they provide services. Special requirements for Legal Document Assistants are addressed in several other provisions of the California Business and Professions Code, Sections 6400 – 6415.

Colorado

Rule 5.3 of the Colorado Rules of Professional Conduct 5.3 does not define "paralegals" but considers "paraprofessionals" as nonlawyer assistants. The rule states that lawyers must directly supervise their assistants and are responsible for their assistants' conduct.

Connecticut	Rule of Professional Conduct 5.3 does not define paralegals but considers "paraprofessionals" as nonlawyer assistants. The rule states that lawyers must directly supervise their assistants and are responsible for their assistants' conduct.
Delaware	The Delaware Paralegal Association provides a Delaware Certified Paralegal voluntary certification for its members who meet with qualifications that include a combination of experience and education.
District of Columbia	None
Florida	The state of Florida adopted a new rule effective March 1, 2008, that establishes a two-tier system for regulating paralegals. The first tier encompasses paralegals as currently defined by Bar Rule 10-2.1. That rule holds that a paralegal is someone qualified by education, training, or work experience who, under the supervision of a lawyer, performs delegated, substantive work for which the lawyer is responsible. Tier two paralegals who meet certain experience, education, and continuing education criteria can hold themselves out as "Florida Registered Paralegals."
Georgia	None
Hawaii	Rule of Professional Conduct 5.3 does not define "paralegals" but considers "paraprofessionals" as nonlawyer assistants. The rule states that lawyers must directly supervise their assistants and are responsible for their assistants' conduct.
Idaho	Rule of Professional Conduct 5.3 does not define "paralegals" but considers "paraprofessionals" as nonlawyer assistants. The rule states that lawyers must directly supervise their assistants and are responsible for their assistants' conduct.
Illinois	Illinois Statutes, 5 ILCS 70/1.35 defines "paralegal" as a person who is qualified through education, training or work experience, and is employed by a lawyer, law office, governmental agency or other entity to work under the direction of an attorney in a capacity that involves the performance of substantive legal work that usually requires a sufficient knowledge of legal concepts and would be performed by the attorney in the absence of the paralegal.
Indiana	Iowa Code, I.C. 1-1-4-6, defines paralegal as: As used in this section, "paralegal" means a person who is: (1) qualified through education, training, or work experience; and (2) employed by a lawyer, law office, governmental agency, or other entity; to work under the direction of an attorney in a capacity that involves the performance of substantive legal work that usually requires a sufficient knowledge of legal concepts and would be performed by the attorney in the absence of the paralegal.

	The Indiana Rules of Professional Conduct also include Guidelines for utilization of paralegals in sections 9.1-10.
Iowa	Rule of Professional Conduct 32:5.3 does not define paralegals but considers "paraprofessionals" as nonlawyer assistants. The rule states that lawyers must directly supervise their assistants and are responsible for their assistants' conduct.
Kansas	Rule of Professional Conduct 5.3 does not define paralegals but considers "paraprofessionals" as nonlawyer assistants. The rule states that lawyers must directly supervise their assistants and are responsible for their assistants' conduct. The Kansas Bar Association adopted Official Standards and Guidelines for the Utilization of Legal Assistants/paralegals in Kansas in 2004.
Kentucky	Supreme Court Rule 3.700 defines paralegal as "a person under the supervision and direction of a licensed lawyer, who may apply knowledge of law and legal procedures in rendering direct assistance to lawyers engaged in legal research; design, develop or plan modifications or new procedures, techniques, services, procedures or applications; prepare or interpret legal documents and write detailed procedures for practicing in certain fields of law; select, compile and use technical information from such references as digests, encyclopedias or practice manuals; and analyze and follow procedural problems that involve independent decisions."
Louisiana	In 1996, the Louisiana State Paralegal Association developed a statewide voluntary paralegal certification exam. The two-part certification process includes successful completion of NALA's CLA exam as well as the LCP exam.
Maine	Chapter 18 Sec. 921 of the Maine Statutes defines paralegal as: "Paralegal" and "legal assistant" mean a person, qualified by education, training or work experience, who is employed or retained by an attorney, law office, corporation, governmental agency or other entity and who performs specifically delegated substantive legal work for which an attorney is responsible. (the ABA definition)
Maryland	Rule of Professional Conduct 5.3 does not define paralegals but considers "paraprofessionals" as nonlawyer assistants. The rule states that lawyers must directly supervise their assistants and are responsible for their assistants' conduct.
Massachusetts	Rule of Professional Conduct 5.3 does not define paralegals but considers "paraprofessionals" as nonlawyer assistants. The rule states that lawyers must directly supervise their assistants and are responsible for their assistants' conduct.
Michigan	Rule of Professional Conduct 5.3 does not define paralegals but considers "paraprofessionals" as nonlawyer assistants. The rule states

	that lawyers must directly supervise their assistants and are responsible for their assistants' conduct.
Mississippi	Rule of Professional Conduct 5.3 does not define paralegals but considers "paraprofessionals" as nonlawyer assistants. The rule states that lawyers must directly supervise their assistants and are responsible for their assistants' conduct.
Missouri	Rule of Professional Conduct 5.3 does not define paralegals but considers "paraprofessionals" as nonlawyer assistants. The rule states that lawyers must directly supervise their assistants and are responsible for their assistants' conduct.
Montana	Rule of Professional Conduct 5.3 does not define paralegals but considers "paraprofessionals" as nonlawyer assistants. The rule states that lawyers must directly supervise their assistants and are responsible for their assistants' conduct. MCA 37-60-101. Definitions . . . (12) "Paralegal" or "legal assistant" means a person qualified through education, training, or work experience to perform substantive legal work that requires knowledge of legal concepts and that is customarily but not exclusively performed by a lawyer and who may be retained or employed by one or more lawyers, law offices, governmental agencies, or other entities or who may be authorized by administrative, statutory, or court authority to perform this work.
Nebraska	Rule of Professional Conduct 5.3 does not define paralegals but considers "support person" and "paraprofessionals" as nonlawyer assistants. The rule states that lawyers must directly supervise their assistants and are responsible for their assistants' conduct.
Nevada	The following definition has been adopted by the Legal Assistants Division of the State Bar of Nevada: A legal assistant (also known as a paralegal) is a person, qualified through education, training or work experience, who is employed or retained by a lawyer, law office, governmental agency, or other entity in a capacity or function which involves the performance, under the ultimate direction and supervision of an attorney, of specifically delegated substantive legal work, which work, for the most part, requires a sufficient knowledge of legal concepts that, absent such an assistant, the attorney would perform the task. Rule of Professional Conduct 187 does not define paralegals but considers "paraprofessionals" as nonlawyer assistants. The rule states that lawyers must directly supervise their assistants and are responsible for their assistants' conduct.
New Hampshire	New Hampshire Supreme Court Administrative Rule 25 defines a paralegal as a person not admitted to the practice of law in the state who is under the direct supervision of an active member of the New Hampshire State Bar.

New Jersey	Rule of Professional Conduct 5.3 does not define paralegals but considers "paraprofessionals" as nonlawyer assistants. The rule states that lawyers must directly supervise their assistants and are responsible for their assistants' conduct.
New Mexico	In 2004, the state Supreme Court amended its rules to establish minimum standards for calling oneself a "paralegal" and to discourage disbarred or suspended attorneys along with those not qualified from using the title. Rules governing paralegal services are set forth in New Mexico Statutes, Sections 20-101 through 10-115. Section 20-102 defines "paralegal" as a person who: (1) contracts with or is employed by an attorney, law firm, corporation, governmental agency or other entity; (2) performs substantive legal work under the supervision of a licensed attorney who assumes professional responsibility for the final work product; and (3) meets one or more of the education, training or work experience qualifications set forth in Rule 20-115 NMRA of these rules. "Substantive legal work" is work that requires knowledge of legal concepts and is customarily, but not exclusively, performed by a lawyer. Examples of substantive legal work performed by a paralegal include: case planning, development and management; legal research and analysis; interviewing clients; fact gathering and retrieving information; drafting legal documents; collecting, compiling, and utilizing technical information to make an independent decision and recommendation to the supervising attorney; and representing clients before a state or federal administrative agency if that representation is authorized by law. Substantive legal work performed by a paralegal for a licensed attorney shall not constitute the unauthorized practice of law.
New York	The New York State Bar Association has adopted Guidelines for the Utilization of Paralegals/Legal Assistants which includes the following definition: A legal assistant/paralegal is a person who is qualified through education, training or work experience to be employed or retained by a lawyer, law office, governmental agency, or other entity in a capacity or function that involves the performance, under the ultimate direction and supervision of, and/or accountability to, an attorney, of substantive legal work, that requires a sufficient knowledge of legal concepts such that, absent such legal assistant/paralegal, the attorney would perform the task.
North Carolina	The North Carolina State Bar has adopted a voluntary certification program for paralegals. North Carolina Paralegals must meet a minimum level of education to become a "North Carolina Certified Paralegal" and they must maintain a minimum level of continuing education to maintain the certification. The Plan does not restrict the use of the term "paralegal" nor does it differentiate the services between a certified and a non-certified paralegal.
North Dakota	The North Dakota Rules of Professional Conduct include a definition for "legal assistant" and "paralegal" as follows: a person who assists

lawyers in the delivery of legal services, and who through formal education, training, or experience, has knowledge and expertise regarding the legal system and substantive and procedural law which qualifies the person to do work of a legal nature under the direct supervision of a licensed lawyer.

Ohio	The Ohio State Bar Association (OSBA) has established a credentialing program for paralegals. Paralegals interested in earning a certification good for four years must meet educational standards stipulated by the bar association, have sufficient experience and pass an examination. Applications were available beginning January 1, 2007 at ohiobar.org. The first exam was offered in March 2007.
Oklahoma	The Oklahoma Bar Association has adopted the following definition for paralegals: "Paralegal" and "legal assistant" mean a person, qualified by education, training or work experience, who is employed or retained by an attorney, law office, corporation, governmental agency or other entity and who performs specifically delegated substantive legal work for which an attorney is responsible (the ABA definition).
Oregon	None
Pennsylvania	Pennsylvania Consolidated Statutes Section 2424(a) of Title 42 states paralegals and legal assistants can't deliver legal services without attorney supervision and can't present themselves as people entitled to practice law. The law was passed in 1996 in response to widespread concern that it was misleading to potential clients for people using the terms "paralegal" and "legal assistant" in ads.
Rhode Island	Supreme Court Provisional Order No. 18 was established in 1983 and defines a legal assistant as: "one who under the supervision of a lawyer, shall apply knowledge of the law and legal procedures in rendering direct assistance to lawyers, clients and courts; design, develop and modify procedures, techniques, services and processes; prepare and interpret legal documents, detail procedures for practicing in certain fields of law; research, select, access and compile information from the law library and other references; and analyze and handle procedural problems that involve independent decisions."
South Carolina	Rule 5.3 of the Supreme Court of South Carolina Rules of Conduct does not define paralegals, but considers "paraprofessionals" as nonlawyer assistants. The rule states that lawyers must directly supervise their assistants and are responsible for their assistants' conduct.
South Dakota	South Dakota Supreme Court Rule 97-25 defines legal assistants as a distinguishable group that assists attorneys and has expertise regarding the legal system, substantive and procedural law, the ethical considerations of the legal profession and state rules, which qualify

them to do work of a legal nature under the direct supervision of a licensed attorney. This rule has been changed to replace the term *paralegal* for legal assistant; the rule change was approved by the state bar and submitted to the legislature.

Tennessee	Rule 5.3 effective in 1981, a lawyer should give "nonlawyer assistants" and "paraprofessionals" appropriate instruction and supervision "concerning the ethical aspects of their employment, particularly regarding the obligation not to disclose information relating to representation of the client, and should be responsible for their work product."
Texas	In 2005, the State Bar of Texas Board of Directors, and the Paralegal Division of the State Bar of Texas, adopted a new definition for "Paralegal": A paralegal is a person, qualified through various combinations of education, training, or work experience, who is employed or engaged by a lawyer, law office, governmental agency, or other entity in a capacity or function which involves the performance, under the ultimate direction and supervision of a licensed attorney, of specifically delegated substantive legal work, which work, for the most part, requires a sufficient knowledge of legal principles and procedures that, absent such person, an attorney would be required to perform the task. On April 21, 2006, the State Bar of Texas Board of Directors approved amending this definition by including several standards for paralegals, which are intended to assist the public in obtaining quality legal services, assist attorneys in their utilization of paralegals, and assist judges in determining whether paralegal work is a reimbursable cost when granting attorney fees.
Utah	Supreme Court Rule of Professional Conduct 5.3 states that paralegals work under the ultimate supervision of attorneys, who are responsible for their paralegals' work product and must give appropriate instruction concerning the ethical aspects of their employment, particularly regarding the obligation not to disclose information relating to representation of the client.
Vermont	Vermont Rule of Professional Conduct 5.3 does not define paralegals, but states that lawyers must directly supervise their assistants and are responsible for their assistants' conduct.
Virginia	Virginia Supreme Court Rule 5.3 does not define paralegals but states that lawyers must directly supervise their assistants and are responsible for their assistants' conduct.
Washington	In 2006, the Practice of Law Board established four subcommittees to draft proposed rules for Legal Technicians, who will be educated, tested and certified nonlawyers authorized to provide limited legal services in specific areas. The subcommittees have been established for the areas of family law, immigration law, elder law and housing

	law. Subcommittee and public meetings were held in 2006 and 2007. As of May 2007, no rules had been adopted for legal technicians.
West Virginia	Rule 5.3 states that lawyers must directly supervise their assistants and are responsible for their assistants' conduct.
Wisconsin	None.
Wyoming	Wyoming Rule of Professional Conduct 5.3 does not define paralegals but considers "paraprofessionals" as nonlawyer assistants. The rule states lawyers must directly supervise their assistants and are responsible for their assistants' conduct.

Glossary

Admonition A reprimand given by a judge to a lawyer.

American Bar Association (ABA) The largest voluntary association of lawyers in the country. The ABA provides law school accreditation, continuing legal education for lawyers and paralegals, programs to assist lawyers and judges in their work, and initiatives to improve the legal system. The ABA also adopts model rules of professional conduct to give guidance on ethical conduct to lawyers and to assist state bar associations in adopting their own codes of conduct. Membership in the ABA is available to any lawyer who is in good standing in his or her state. Paralegals may join as associate members.

Attorney-Client Privilege The right of a client and the duty of that client's lawyer to keep confidential the contents of almost all communication between them. More specifically, the attorney-client privilege is a privilege found in evidence law that governs the use of information in a court proceeding. The attorney-client privilege provides that the attorney may not be called on to give testimony concerning confidential information disclosed to the attorney by the client during the course of representation.

Bar Association An organization of members of the bar—at the national, state, or local level—whose primary function is promoting professionalism and enhancing the administration of justice.

Billable Hour Hours that may be billed to the client for legal services performed by each attorney, paralegal, or other timekeeper.

Canon A law, rule, or principle, especially a religious law or an ethical rule of conduct.

Certification The process by which a nongovernmental organization grants recognition to an individual who has met qualifications specified by that organization.

Certified Legal Assistant (CLA) The title bestowed by the National Association of Legal Assistants on a paralegal who has passed the CLA exam and has met other criteria of the NALA. Also referred to as Certified Paralegal.

Chinese Wall Administrative safeguards (and physical separation) that keep individuals (or entire parts of an organization) separate for various reasons, such as to protect client confidences or to avoid legal problems, such as a conflict of interest. A "contaminated" or "tainted" employee who is walled off from any contact with a particular client or case is "quarantined." Also called an "ethical wall."

Code of Ethics The set of rules that establishes the standards and guidelines for ethical behavior and professional responsibility for a certain profession.

Co-defendant A person who is a defendant along with another person in a trial.

Commingling of Funds Act of fiduciary or attorney in combining or mixing together the funds of the beneficiary or client with the funds of the fiduciary or attorney, thereby breaching the fiduciary relationship. Commingling of funds is an act that is subject to disciplinary action under the Model Rules of Professional Conduct.

Competence Properly qualified, adequate, having the right natural or legal qualifications.

Concurrent At the same time. In the practice of law, a concurrent conflict of interest exists if the representation of one client will be directly adverse to the representation of another client or if there is a significant risk that the representation of one client will be materially limited by the attorney's responsibilities to another client, a former client, a third person, or by a personal interest of the attorney.

Confidential Relating to information that is to remain secret and cannot be revealed or disclosed.

Conflict of Interest Being in a position where your own needs and desires could possibly lead you to violate your duty to a person who has a right to depend on you or being in a position where you try to serve two competing masters or clients. A conflict need not even be intentional. For example, a judge who holds XYZ stock may be unconsciously influenced in a case concerning the XYZ Company.

Contempt An act that obstructs a court's work or lessens the dignity of the court.

Contingent Fee Payment to a lawyer of a percentage of the "winnings," if any, from a lawsuit rather than payment of a flat amount of money or payment according to the number of hours worked.

Conversion Any act that deprives an owner of property without that owner's permission and without just cause.

Criminal Prosecution A criminal proceeding instituted in a proper court on behalf of the public to secure the conviction and punishment of one accused of a crime.

Deposition The process of taking a witness's sworn out-of-court testimony. The questioning is usually done by a lawyer, with the lawyer from the other side given a chance to attend and participate. The written document produced from the process is also referred to as a deposition.

Diligence Carefulness, prudence, or doing your duty.

Disbarment The revocation of an attorney's license to practice law.

Disciplinary Board Court-appointed board typically consisting of a mixture of attorneys and nonattorneys formed to receive complaints about attorney misconduct and oversee the disciplinary process.

Disciplinary Counsel Individual appointed to investigate or oversee the investigation of complaints concerning attorney misconduct and either dispense of the matter or bring the facts before the appropriate hearing committee or disciplinary board with a recommendation for disposition of the matter.

Discovery The formal and informal exchange of information between sides in a lawsuit. Two types of discovery are interrogatories and depositions.

Due Process of Law The Fifth and Fourteenth amendments to the U.S. Constitution require that no person be deprived of life, liberty, or property without due process of law. What constitutes due process of law varies from situation to situation, but the core of the idea is that a person should always have notice and a real chance to present his or her side in a legal dispute and that no law or government procedure should be arbitrary or unfair. Some of the specifics of due process include the right to a transcript of court proceedings, the right to question adverse witnesses, etc.

Ethics The study of moral principles and duty that determine what is right and what is wrong and guide human conduct. This includes standards of fair and honest conduct.

Evidence All types of information (observations, recollections, documents, concrete objects, etc.) presented at a trial or other hearing. Statements made by the judge and lawyers, however, are not evidence.

Evidence Law The rules and principles about whether evidence can be admitted (accepted for proof) in a trial and how to evaluate its importance.

Felony A crime of a serious nature often punishable by a prison sentence of one year or more.

Fiduciary Duty The duty owed by a fiduciary (such as an attorney or trustee) to act with good faith, loyalty, and honesty with respect to the interests of the beneficiary while subordinating the fiduciary's personal interests to that of the fiduciary.

Firm A group of lawyers formed for the purpose of practicing law. Includes lawyers in a private firm and lawyers in the legal department of a corporation or other organization or in a legal services organization.

Fraud Intentional misrepresentation or trickery to deceive another, causing that person to act to his or her detriment, cheating that person of money or property. Fraud is usually a tort, but in some cases (especially when conduct is willful), it may be a crime.

Freelance Paralegal A self-employed paralegal who works for attorneys, law firms, or corporations on a contract basis under the supervision of an attorney.

General Retainer Fee paid to an attorney or law firm to retain their services for a specific amount of time rather than for a particular project. During that time period, the attorney and law firm may not accept any conflicting employment.

Health Insurance Portability and Accountability Act (HIPAA) A federal regulation that guarantees patients access to their own medical records and control over the use of their personal health information. HIPAA regulations establish the obligations of healthcare providers to protect health information.

Hearing Committee Committee appointed by the highest court or by the disciplinary board to hear disciplinary matters referred to it by the disciplinary board and reach a decision with regard to the disposition of the matter.

Imputed Disqualification Rule that disqualifies all the members of a firm from representing a particular client when one attorney is disqualified from representing that client due to a conflict of interest.

Independent Paralegal A self-employed paralegal who works directly for the public to provide legal services that are not considered to be the practice of law.

Injunction A judge's order to a person to do or to refrain from doing a particular thing.

Integrated Bar A bar association in which membership is required as a prerequisite to the right to practice law. In states with an integrated bar, the bar has the authority to adopt and enforce the code of ethics that is applicable to all attorneys.

Interest on Lawyers Trust Accounts (IOLTA) Special type of trust account used in some states to pool the funds of several smaller client trust accounts whose funds individually are too small to generate the interest income required to cover the costs of the bank account. Funds from the smaller accounts are pooled into an IOLTA, creating a large enough sum to earn interest. Any interest earned on IOLTAs is donated to nonprofit organizations that provide for the delivery of legal services to low-income individuals.

Interrogatories Written questions sent from one side in a lawsuit to another, attempting to get written answers to factual questions or seeking an explanation of the other side's legal contentions. These are a part of the formal discovery process in a lawsuit and usually take place before the trial.

Irrevocable Trust A trust in which the settlor (the creator of the trust) permanently gives up control of the trust property for the benefit of the trust beneficiary or beneficiaries.

Legal Assistant Same as paralegal. Term traditionally preferred by the National Association of Legal Assistants and its affiliate organizations, although the use of the term "paralegal" is becoming more popular, even with those organizations.

Legal Document Preparers An individual who is not an attorney who prepares or assists in the preparation of legal documents at the direction of an individual who is representing him or herself in a legal matter.

Legal Ethics The moral and professional duties owed by lawyers to their clients, to other lawyers, to the courts, and to the public. This includes the written rules of ethics, such as the Rules of Professional Conduct.

Legal Malpractice Professional misconduct due to an attorney's failure to exercise on behalf of his or her client the knowledge, skill, and ability ordinarily possessed and exercised by members of the legal profession. Legal malpractice is a tort if it results in injury to the client.

License Formal permission to do a particular thing, exercise a certain privilege, carry on a particular business, or pursue a certain occupation.

Litigation A legal action or lawsuit.

Mediation A means of alternative dispute resolution whereby a neutral third party (mediator) helps disputing parties to reach an agreement outside of the court system. The mediator can only recommend solutions and has no power to force a decision on the disputing parties.

Mediator A neutral third party who helps disputing parties reach an agreement outside the court system through the mediation process.

Misappropriation Taking something wrongfully for a purpose other than that for which it is intended.

Misconduct Doing a forbidden act intentionally or willfully.

Misdemeanor Offenses lower than felonies and generally those punishable by fine, penalty, forfeiture, or imprisonment. Under federal law and most state laws, any offense other than a felony is classified as a misdemeanor.

Model Code of Professional Responsibility Model code adopted by the ABA that became effective in 1970. The Model Code of Professional Responsibility (Model Code) is divided into nine canons, which broadly prescribe ethical conduct for lawyers. Within the canons are Disciplinary Rules (DRs) and Ethical Considerations (ECs), which provide more detailed guidance on ethical issues. The Model Code of Professional Responsibility was adopted or followed closely by most jurisdictions soon after its adoption, but the Model Rules of Professional Conduct has recently replaced it.

Model Guidelines for the Utilization of Legal Assistant Services Guidelines drafted by the ABA Standing Committee on Legal Assistants and adopted by the ABA's House of Delegates in 1991 to provide lawyers with useful and authoritative guidance in working with paralegals.

Model Rules of Professional Conduct Model rules adopted by the ABA to replace the Model Code of Professional Responsibility. The Model Rules were adopted in 1983 and have been amended several times. The Model Rules have now been adopted in some form in most jurisdictions in the United States.

National Association of Legal Assistants (NALA) A national organization of legal assistants and paralegals whose purpose is to enhance professionalism and the interests of those in the profession as well as to advance the administration of justice generally. Among its other undertakings, the NALA has established a Code of Professional Responsibility for paralegals and legal assistants and provides professional certifications, continuing education, and assistance in job placement. A person who receives certification through the NALA is entitled to so indicate by the use of CLA (Certified Legal Assistant) after his or her name.

National Federation of Paralegal Associations An association of paralegal and legal assistant organizations nationwide whose purpose is to enhance professionalism and the interests of those in the profession as well as to advance the administration of justice. Among its other undertakings, the NFPA has established the Model Code of Ethics and Professional Responsibility and Guidelines for Enforcement. The NFPA also provides continuing education and assistance in job placement.

Nonintegrated Bar A type of voluntary bar association that exists in some states, to which membership by attorneys practicing in that state is optional. In these states, the judiciary retains the authority to adopt and enforce the code of ethics applicable to all attorneys licensed to practice law in that state.

Paralegal A person who, although not an attorney, performs many of the functions of an attorney under an attorney's supervision. The ABA defines a paralegal as a "person, qualified by education, training, or work experience who is employed or retained by a lawyer, law office, governmental agency or other entity and who performs specifically delegated substantive legal work for which a lawyer is responsible."[1] Another term for paralegal is legal assistant.

Paralegal Advanced Competency Exam (PACE) An exam promoted by the NFPA as a means for experienced paralegals to validate their knowledge to themselves and their employers.

Partnership An unincorporated business organization co-owned by two or more persons. Partnerships are usually owned and managed according to a partnership agreement and each partner usually has full liability for all partnership debts. Partnership income and losses are usually allocated among the partners according to their shares, with taxes paid by the partners individually.

Perjury Lying while under oath, especially in a court proceeding. It is a crime.

Pleadings Written statements of each side in a lawsuit filed to plead their case, including complaints, petitions, answers, counter-complaints, etc.

Precedent A court decision on a question of law (how the law affects the case) that is binding authority on lower courts in the same court system for cases in which those courts must decide a similar question of law involving similar facts. The U.S. court system is based on judges making decisions supported by past precedent rather than by the logic of the judge alone.

Pro Bono For the public good; refers to free legal services done by attorneys and paralegals to help the poor or the community.

Pro Se For him or herself; in his or her own behalf. For example, pro se representation means that a person will handle his or her own case in court without a lawyer.

Probation A trial period during which a person who has failed to perform according to acceptable standards must either conform to those standards or lose their position or license.

Reciprocity Mutuality The term is used to denote the relation existing between two states when each of them gives the subjects of the other certain privileges, on condition that its own subjects shall enjoy similar privileges at the hands of the latter state.

Reprimand A public and formal censure of a severe nature, typically administered to an attorney by a supreme court or bar association for unethical or improper conduct.

Request for the Production of Documents Written request sent from one side in a lawsuit to another as part of the discovery process, asking for that party to provide specified documents or other tangible evidence for inspection and copying.

---

[1] ABA Standing Committee on Legal Assistants, adopted August 1997.

Sanction A penalty or punishment attached to a law to make sure it is obeyed.

Screening A policy within a law firm to screen or shut out a disqualified attorney within the firm from representation of the client presenting the conflict.

Special Retainer Fee paid to an attorney or law firm to retain their services for a specific project or representation.

Specialist Generally, a person with expertise in a particular field; often a person who has been board certified.

Solicitation Asking for; enticing; strongly requesting. This may be a crime if the thing being urged is a crime. A lawyer's drumming up business in too aggressive a way. This is prohibited by the lawyer's Rules of Professional Conduct.

Standing Committee on Ethics and Professional Responsibility Standing committee established by the ABA to issue both formal and informal advisory opinions on ethical questions as guidance to attorneys.

Statute A law passed by a legislature.

Statute of Limitations Statutes setting maximum time periods during which certain actions can be brought or rights enforced. After the statute of limitations time period has run, no legal action can be brought, regardless of whether any cause of action ever existed.

Suspension The temporary withdrawal of a privilege, such as the withdrawal of a license to practice law for a period of time.

Traditional Paralegal An individual who works as a paralegal under the direct supervision of an attorney.

Tribunal A court or other board or commission that sits in judgment.

Unauthorized Practice of Law Engaging in the practice of law by a person who is not a lawyer and does not hold the license required by law.

Whistle-Blower Acts Laws designed to protect employees from retaliation for reporting an employer's misconduct.

Work Product Documents, papers, or other material prepared by counsel in preparing for the trial of a case.

Work Product Rule Under this rule, any notes, working papers, memoranda, or similar materials prepared by an attorney in anticipation of litigation are protected from discovery. Most states have codified the work product rule in some form either by statute or court rule.

Writ of Quo Warranto A judge's order designed to test whether a person exercising a certain power is legally entitled to do so.

Zealous Characterized by great enthusiasm and eagerness.

Index

N

NALA
  Code of Ethics and Professional
    Responsibility, 13, 86–87, 111
  on conflicts of interest for
    paralegals, 137
  definition of paralegal, 47
  Model Standards and Guidelines for
    Utilization of legal assistants, 13–14
  recognition of competence, 43–46
  Web site of, 27
Names of law firms, 167–168
National Association of Legal Assistants
  (NALA). *See* NALA
National Federation of Paralegal
  Associations (NFPA). *See* NFPA
National Reporter, 14
New Jersey, 85
New York
  disciplinary proceeding in, 10
  Lawyer's Code of Professional
    Responsibility, 60
  on sending solicitation letter, 171
  unethical paralegal behavior, 17
NFPA, 13, 27
  on conflicts of interests for
    paralegals, 137–138
  definition of paralegal, 47
  Model Code of Ethics and Professional
    Responsibility, 15–16, 71, 86, 87
  Model Code of Ethics and Professional
    Responsibility and Guidelines for
    Enforcement, 42, 112
  national paralegal associations
    features, 14–15
  paralegals and Model Code of
    Ethics, 64–65
  position in paralegal licensing, 25
Nolo Press, 80
Nonlitigation matters, conflicts in, 128–129

O

Office management, as skill of attorneys, 32
Ohio, 95, 167, 170
Ohio Code of Professional Responsibility,
  violations of, 123
Ohio rules of professional conduct, 60–61
Ohralik v. Ohio State Bar, 162
Online resources, on legal ethics, 27
Organization skills, paralegals and, 38

Outside services, confidential information
  and, 116

P

PACE, 25
  CLA certification *vs.*, 45–46
  as standard for paralegal competency, 42
Paralegal Advanced Competency Exam
  (PACE). *See* PACE
Paralegal associations, 26–27
Paralegal competence and diligence
  communication skills, 38–40
  computer skills, 40, 41
  critical thinking skills, 40
  frequently asked question, 52–53
  interpersonal skills, 41
  legal research and investigation
    skills, 40–41
  maintaining competence, 47
  organization and management skills, 38
  specialties and special concerns, 47–51
  standards, 41–47
Paralegal(s), 1. *See also* Integrity of legal
    profession; Law, unauthorized
    practice of; Paralegal competence
    and diligence; Paralegal specialties
  assisting attorneys, 30–31
  association discipline, in unethical
    behavior, 18
  associations and ethics, 12–13
  certification of, 23
  computer applications used by, 41
  conflicts of interest from
    perspective of, 135–139
  as defined by ABA, 24
  definitions of, 18, 19–23, 46–47
  independent, 85–86
  licensing, 23–24
  registration, 23
  regulation, 18–23
  resources on associations, 26–27
  traditional, 83–84
  unethical behavior consequences, 16–25
Paralegal specialties, 25–26
  corporate paralegal competencies, 49
  criminal law paralegal, 50–51
  family law paralegal, 50
  litigation paralegal, 48
  probate paralegal, 48–49
  real estate paralegal, 49–50

204 Index

Partnership, name of firm and, 168
Patent Office, U.S., 91
*Peel v. Attorney Registration and
    Disciplinary Commission of
    Illinois*, 163
People v. Culpepper, 55
Perjury, 105
Personal injury, paralegals
    specializing in, 117–118
Physical injury, preventing, 104
Pleadings, preparing, 96
Pleas on behalf of clients, 133
Powell, Lewis, 161
Prejudicial conduct to administration of
    justice, 58–59
Prepaid legal service plans, 169
Preparation, as skill of attorneys, 33
Press, confidential information and, 115
Print advertising, 165–166
Privilege, purpose of, 101
Probate court forms, drafting, 97
Probate paralegal competencies, 48–49
Probation, defined, 9
Pro bono
    defined, 63
    for paralegals, 70–72
    service, attorneys and, 63
Procrastination, attorneys and, 36
Professional conduct
    Minnesota Rules of, 11
    State Rules of, 4–6
    violation of rules of, 57
Professional relationship, nature and
    length of, 144–145
Professions, unauthorized practice of law
    and, 79

R

Real estate closings, attending, 97
Real estate paralegals, 49–50, 97–98
Real estate transfer documents, preparing, 97
Reasonable fees, 143–144, 146
Recordkeeping, client trust accounts
    and, 151
Red flags, on bar application, 55
Referral fees, 149–150, 169–170
Registration, paralegal, 23
Regulation(s)
    by definition, 18–23
    of legal ethics, 2–7

Reprimand, defined, 8
Requests for production of documents, 109
Research. *See* Legal research
Resources
    employer's, 26
    online, on legal ethics, 27
    on paralegal associations, 26–27
    on state codes of ethics, 4–6, 26
    on supervising attorney, 26
Respect, unethical paralegal behavior and
    loss of, 17
Rules of ethics. *See also* Integrity of legal
        profession
    addressing advertising, 163
    from Arizona, 123

S

Salary, paralegal certification, 45
Sanctions, 1
Screening, 127
Self-representation
    defined, 79
    factors in increasing, 80
Settlements on behalf of clients, 133
Sexual misconduct with client, 59, 134
Shapero v. Kentucky Bar Association, 170
Skills, attorneys and, 32
Smith, Benjamin Nathanial, 56
Solicitation
    letters, 170–171
    not for profit, 169
    paralegals and, 175–176
    prepaid or group legal services plan, 169
    restrictions on writing, 171
    rules of, 168–169
    by third parties, 170
    third party, referral fees and, 169–170
Special retainer, 147
Specialty(ies)
    advertising and, 167
    client representation and, 34
    paralegal, 47–51
Standards, for paralegal competence, 41–47
Standing Committee on Ethics and
        Professional Responsibility, 7
State agencies, client representation
        and, 92–93
State bar associations, 2–3
State codes of ethics, 26
State ethics committees, 3